CASEBOOK SERIES

OTHER CASEBOOKS ARE IN PREPARATION

Donne

Songs and Sonets

A CASEBOOK

EDITED BY

JULIAN LOVELOCK

MACMILLAN

First published 1973
6th reprint 1989

Published by
MACMILLAN EDUCATION LTD
Houndmills, Basingstoke, Hampshire RG21 2XS
and London
Companies and representatives
throughout the world

Printed in Hong Kong

ISBN 0-333-11660-7

CONTENTS

ACKNOWLEDGEMENTS

The editor and publishers wish to thank the following, who have kindly given permission for the use of copyright material: Clarendon Press for 'Donne and Love Poetry in the Seventeenth Century' by C. S. Lewis and 'The Love Poetry of John Donne: A Reply to Mr C. S. Lewis' by Joan Bennett from *Seventeenth Century Studies Presented to Sir Herbert Grierson*, for 'The Argument about "The Ecstasy" ' by Helen Gardner from *Elizabethan and Jacobean Studies Presented to F. P. Wilson*, ed. Herbert Davis and Helen Gardner, for 'An Elegie upon the death of the Deane of Pauls, Dr John Donne' from *The Poems of Thomas Carew*, ed. Rhodes Dunlap, and for 'The Triple Fool' and extracts from 'Infinitati Sacrum' and 'Introduction' from *The Poems of John Donne*, ed. Herbert J. C. Grierson; J. M. Dent & Sons Ltd and E. P. Dutton & Co. Inc. for 'A Discourse Concerning the Original and Progress of Satire' from *Of Dramatic Poesy and Other Critical Essays* by John Dryden. Intro. by George Watson, 2 vols. Everyman's Library Edition, and for 'Lectures on Comic Writers, III' from *Lectures on the English Comic Writers* by William Hazlitt. Intro. by Arthur Johnston, Everyman's Library Edition; Duke University Press, Durham, North Carolina, for 'Notes of Coleridge on the Poet Donne' in Roberta Florence Brinkley (ed.), *Coleridge on the Seventeenth Century*; Faber & Faber Ltd and Farrar, Straus & Giroux Inc. for 'Lecture on Milton' in T. S. Eliot, *On Poetry and Poets* (1957); Faber & Faber Ltd and Harcourt Brace Jovanovich Inc. for the extract from 'The Metaphysical Poets' in *Selected Essays, New Edition* by T. S. Eliot copyright 1932 by Harcourt Brace Jovanovich Inc. copyright by T. S. Eliot; Harvard University Press, Cambridge, Mass., for T. S. Eliot, 'Donne in Our Time' from Theodore Spencer (ed.), *A Garland for John Donne*, copyright 1931 by the President and Fellows of Harvard College 1959 by Eloise Spencer Wade; Hutchinson

Publishing Group Ltd for 'Logical Structure in the Songs and Sonnets' by J. B. Leishman from *The Monarch of Wit* by J. B. Leishman; Modern Language Association of America for 'Donne's Metrical Practice' by Michael F. Moloney, *P.M.L.A.* LXV (1950); Routledge & Kegan Paul Ltd and Barnes & Noble Inc. for 'Review of the Poems of John Donne' by Rupert Brooke, ed. Herbert Grierson, in *Rupert Brooke: A Reappraisal and Selection* by Timothy Rogers (1971); Rupert Hart-Davis Ltd for 'Lives of the Poets: Abraham Cowley' in *Samuel Johnson*, ed. Mona Wilson; University of Minnesota Press, Minn., for 'The Good Morrow' in Arnold Stein's *John Donne's Lyrics: The Eloquence of Action*, copyright University of Minnesota 1962; University of Notre Dame Press for 'John Donne: Love's Philosophy' in Louis Martz, *The Wit of Love* (1969); M. B. Yeats and Rupert Hart-Davis Ltd for the extract from a letter to Herbert Grierson written by W. B. Yeats from *The Letters of W. B. Yeats*, ed. Allan Wade.

GENERAL EDITOR'S PREFACE

Each of this series of Casebooks concerns either one well-known and influential work of literature or two or three closely linked works. The main section consists of critical readings, mostly modern, brought together from journals and books. A selection of reviews and comments by the author's contemporaries is also included, and sometimes comments from the author himself. The Editor's Introduction charts the reputation of the work from its first appearance until the present time.

The critical forum is a place of vigorous conflict and disagreement, but there is nothing in this to cause dismay. What is attested is the complexity of human experience and the richness of literature, not any chaos or relativity of taste. A critic is better seen, no doubt, as an explorer than as an 'authority', but explorers ought to be, and usually are, well equipped. The effect of good criticism is to convince us of what C. S. Lewis called 'the enormous extension of our being which we owe to authors'. A Casebook will be justified only if it helps to promote the same end.

A single volume can represent no more than a small selection of critical opinions. Some critics have been excluded for reasons of space, and it is hoped that readers will follow up the further suggestions in the Select Bibliography. Other contributions have been severed from their original context, to which some readers may wish to return. Indeed, if they take a hint from the critics represented here, they certainly will.

A. E. DYSON

INTRODUCTION

I

John Donne was born in London in 1572, the son of a prosperous city tradesman who died not long afterwards. The chief influence on his childhood was undoubtedly Roman Catholicism, a religion which had been devalued by the atrocities of Mary Tudor's reign and 'suppressed and afflicted' since Elizabeth's Act of Uniformity : indeed his maternal relations included the famous and persecuted Heywood and Rastell families and, more distantly, the hero-martyr Sir Thomas More himself. Donne's early education was attended to by a private tutor and was continued for three years at Oxford (1584–1587), followed by a slightly shorter spell at Cambridge. In 1591, possibly after journeying to Italy and Spain, he returned to London, entering first Thavies and then Lincoln's Inn, where he remained at least until 1594. During this period at the Inns he led an intense existence, a student not only of law but of theology (his Roman Catholic beliefs were being progressively undermined by an uneasy cynicism), languages, literature, drama, people, love – in short, of life; and it was during this period also that he first became known by his contemporaries as 'a great writer of conceited verses', circulating among them the first two of the *Satyres,* the majority of the *Elegies,* the 'Epithalamion made at Lincolnes Inne' and an indefinite number of the *Songs and Sonets.*

Late in 1597, or in 1598, having served on two naval expeditions which took him to Cadiz and the Azores respectively, and between which he wrote the fourth of the *Satyres* (the date of the third of the *Satyres* is uncertain, though 1596 seems most likely), he was appointed private secretary to Sir Thomas Egerton, the Lord Keeper. He held this post until 1602, both intrigued and disturbed by the life at Court, as we may best gather from the fifth of the *Satyres,* the verse letters to Sir Henry Wotton and the fragment 'The Progresse of the Soule', but all the time widening his circle of influential friends. Then his secret marriage to Ann More put him

from favour and until his ordination in 1615 he was forced to live
mainly on patronage. However he was never idle: he pursued
further his studies of law and theology and wrote prolifically. As
well as publishing the Latin verses on *Volpone* (1607), the prose
Pseudo-Martyr (1610) and *Ignatius his Conclave* (1611), the
first and second 'Anniversaries' (1611 and 1612) and the 'Elegie
upon the untimely death of the incomparable Prince Henry'
(1613), he wrote, most importantly, the prose *Biathanatos*
(1607 or 1608) and *Essays in Divinity* (completed 1614), the
remainder of the *Songs and Sonets* (perhaps with the exception
of 'A nocturnall upon S. Lucies day'), *Elegies* and *Epithala-
mions*, and a number of the *Epicedes and Obsequies* and *Divine
Poems*.

Donne's conversion from Roman Catholicism to Anglicanism
has no single date: rather it was a gradual process, begun at the
Inns and continued up to his ordination and even beyond. Nevertheless his service with the Lord Keeper points to at least a passive
acceptance of Anglican doctrine and between 1606 and 1610 he
may actually have collaborated with Thomas Morton (Dean of
Gloucester and later Bishop of Durham) in the writing of attacks
on the Roman Catholic Church. But in spite of his undoubted
faith, Donne seems to have taken orders for selfish more than
spiritual reasons: he was bent on preferment and James I, who
saw him as a 'learned Divine' and a potentially 'powerful
Preacher', had made it clear that he would only give it to him
within the Church. The king was true to his word and within two
months of his ordination Donne was appointed a royal Chaplain-
in-Ordinary and made a Doctor of Divinity at Cambridge; in 1616
he was chosen Divinity Reader at Lincoln's Inn. After the death
of his wife in 1617 Donne gave himself wholly to the service of the
church and in 1621 he was elected and installed as Dean of St
Paul's, a post which he held until his death in 1631. Between his
ordination and death he wrote the remainder of the *Divine Poems*
and the prose *Devotions upon Emergent Occasions* (1623 and
1624; published 1624) and, of course, the *Sermons* (some published occasionally). Students who wish for fuller details of Donne's
life should consult R. C. Bald's *John Donne: A Life*,[1] which col-
lects together all the available material on its subject, highlighting
the enigmas but making no unwarranted attempts to solve them.

II

I make this biographical emphasis at the outset as a necessary
background to a study of Donne's work and without apology to
those purist critics who divorce art completely from its context,
substituting ingenious explication for real understanding. For to
deny a poem, painting or whatever its essential humanity, is to
scorn and degrade the creative mind. At worst, it can reduce art to
that level of mere verbal ingenuity which implicitly denies its
genesis and its god. And while one must agree with Cleanth Brooks,
in his preface to *The Well Wrought Urn*, that 'there is something
to be said for concentrating on the poem itself as a construct, with
its own organisation and its own logic', one should never forget his
provisos that :

To stress the poet is, of course, a perfectly valid procedure, and it is
interesting and may be useful to consider his ideas, his historical con-
ditioning, his theories of composition, and the background, general
and personal, which underlies his work.

and :

Poems do not grow like cabbages, nor are they put together by com-
puters. They are written by human beings, and this is something that
we are never allowed to forget any more than we are allowed to forget
that poems remain mere potentialities until they are released by some
reader.

In fact Donne criticism is balked not so much by a disregard of
biographical information as by a lack of it. Thus in her analysis of
'Aire and Angels' in *The Business of Criticism*, Helen Gardner was
forced to conclude :

With a great poem, its centre, its unity of moral tone or feeling, should
be self-evident. But there are poems, and I think this is one, where
there is an uncertainty as to the central conception which no amount
of argument can settle with finality. There is a wobble in the line of
thought in the second verse; and the last three lines are grammatically
and metrically isolated in a way which suggests that they are making
a special point. If we read the poem one way, the point seems a cheap
one; if we read it the other, it does not seem sufficiently important

to warrant its position as the poem's final statement. This is the kind
of occasion on which biographical information could be of help. Here
I cry out for some dates. If I could date this poem, and date Donne's
other lyrics, I might be able to support one or other reading by reference to the poems which Donne was writing at about the same time.
Or if I knew how old he was when he wrote it and whether he wrote
it to any particular person, I might use this information to argue that
this or that reading is the more likely in the circumstances in which
the poem is written. Or, if we had Donne's notebooks and could see
from drafts how he had begun and worked at the poem, we might
find a clue. If we saw how the poem began we might feel more certainty about the intention of the poet. For it is the poet's intention
which is not clear in the poem. For that reason I have to decide that
it is not **a** wholly successful poem. The amount of ink that has been
spent on its twenty-eight lines suggests that it has had at any rate
many unsuccessful readers, of whom I am one.

Because of the lack of biographical information, too simple literary
guide-books have tended to stress the general historical and literary
influences on Donne's poetry at the expense of the particular
family and social influences and Donne's own unique make-up as a
man. This error can be traced back to Dr Johnson's 'Life of
Cowley' (1781), or at least to a misreading of it, in which all the
so-called metaphysical poets are apparently (to borrow its famous
phrase) 'yoked by violence together'. For example : 'About the
beginning of the seventeenth century appeared a race of writers
that may be termed the metaphysical poets.'

Obviously Donne did to some extent share a common background with the other metaphysical poets, and indeed was a major
influence on them : like them he was pressured by that harsh, uncomfortable, curious age, which had outgrown its medieval heri-
tage (fascinatingly described by C. S. Lewis in *The Discarded
Image*) and sought to replace it with new philosophies, new
sciences, new worlds, new poetry. But his reactions to that pressure were bound to be individual and different, as indeed Dr
Johnson, by implication, admits :

This kind of writing, which was, I believe, borrowed from Marini and
his followers, had been recommended by the example of Donne, a
man of very extensive and various knowledge; and by Jonson, whose

manner resembled that of Donne more in the ruggedness of his lines
than in the cast of his sentiments.

Therefore when we speak of metaphysical poets or poetry, we
must bear in mind that the term is a blanket one and only useful
in so far as, say, the term 'romantic' can span such unlike poets as
Wordsworth and Keats.

An age of conscious change, such as the metaphysical poets lived
in, is always an age of realism : it sets out, however naïvely, to
shatter myths and replace them with 'truths'. Metaphysical poetry
reflects this realism, breaking free from the elegant but artificial
rhetoric of what is often loosely termed the Petrarchan tradition
(I mean, most immediately, the works of such poets as Spenser,
Sidney, Daniel and the Elizabethan song writers) in favour of a
more colloquial language and tone, a tightness of expression and
the singleminded working out of a theme or argument.

It is in the working out of the theme or argument that we come
up against the most remarkable feature of metaphysical poetry,
its use of the conceit. In her introduction to her edition of *The
Metaphysical Poets* (one of the two best introductions to metaphysical poetry; the other is H. J. C. Grierson's introduction to his
edition of *Metaphysical Lyrics and Poems of the Seventeenth Century*) Helen Gardner explains :

A conceit is a comparison whose ingenuity is more striking than its
justness, or, at least, is more immediately striking. All comparisons
discover likeness in things unlike : a comparison becomes a conceit
when we are made to concede likeness while being strongly conscious
of unlikeness.

She points out that Elizabethan poetry abounds in conceits and
that what differentiates metaphysical conceits is not their 'curious
learning' (something which they by no means all share) but their
rigour. They are on the whole more extended and less ornamental
than other Elizabethan conceits : 'In a metaphysical poem the
conceits are instruments of definition in an argument or instruments to persuade. The poem has something to say which the
conceit explicates or something to urge which the conceit helps
to forward.'

One should no doubt add that in a metaphysical poem the conceits are very frequently linked with an elaborate and often continuing argument, which fuses its own strange quality with the unlikeness, rather than the likeness, of the comparisons used.

Whether metaphysical poetry is ultimately and in a strange way realistic or true, probing, as Eliot would have it in his seminal essay 'The Metaphysical Poets' (1921), 'into the cerebral cortex, the nervous system, and the digestive tracts', or whether, as Dr Johnson puts it, it 'cannot be said to have imitated anything', is still a subject of critical debate. In a sense the debate is an important one, concerning itself, as it must do, with the very nature of poetry, tackling those impossible riddles which that great metaphysical poet Herbert himself posed in the first two stanzas of 'Jordan (I)' where the effectiveness of the riddles as poetry seems to contradict the answers which they imply :

> Who sayes that fictions onely and false hair
> Become a verse? Is there in truth no beautie?
> Is all good structure in a winding stair?
> May no lines passe, except they do their dutie
>   Not to a true, but painted chair?
>
> Is it no verse, except enchanted groves
> And sudden arbours shadow coarse-spunne lines?
> Must purling streams refresh a lovers loves?
> Must all be vail'd, while he that reades, divines,
>   Catching the senses at two removes?

But the debate becomes futile when it seeks simple answers where none exist and even attempts to dictate the nature of poetry (the dogmatism of Johnson and Eliot are both instances). It is precisely here that one has to tear away the metaphysical blanket and consider the individual poets and poems which lie underneath it. And it is here that I return to that individual Donne and the equally individual *Songs and Sonets*.

III

Like the majority of the metaphysical poets, Donne was really an amateur at the craft. For him the writing of poetry was chiefly one of the accomplishments of a society gentleman : he would never

have set out with Milton to 'justifie the wayes of God to men' or
have adopted the bardic stances of Yeats :

> I write it out in a verse –
> MacDonagh and MacBride
> And Connolly and Pearse
> Now and in time to be,
> Wherever green is worn,
> Are changed, changed utterly :
> A terrible beauty is born.

Indeed Donne's attitude to poetry was more one of witty disrespect,
especially during his early life : in the *Songs and Sonets* he calls
it, for example, 'whining Poetry' ('The triple Foole'), 'th'art of
Riming' ('Loves exchange') and 'phantasie' ('The Dreame').

Nevertheless, that Donne only circulated his poetry in manuscript among a small circle of friends and published little of it during his lifetime has been stressed overmuch; even such a consciously
public poet as Sidney ('the Poet is indeed the right Popular Philosopher') published nothing during his lifetime and the fact that
Donne's manuscripts were reproduced by his friends and passed
on meant that his poetry was actually well known at court during
the last years of his life. What should be stressed, rather, is the
influences that Donne's circle of friends had on his work, particularly those whom he knew in his more formative years as a writer,
at the universities and then at the Inns. In *The School of Donne*
(an important book, but one which seems to rely heavily on conjecture and which demands cautious reading), A. Alvarez explains
that Donne was 'a wit writing for wits' :

. . . Donne's first and most formative audience was made up of the
young, literary, middle-class intellectual élite who, like Donne himself, were to become the leading professional men of the time. This,
in Carew's words, was 'The Universall Monarchy of Wit', men of
intellect and wide, varied talents, who, like the subjects in any other
monarchy, had language, customs, conventions and interests in common. Donne was their 'King, that rul'd as hee thought fit'. But that
merely meant that he was more powerful, more authoritative than the
rest. He was not apart from them. Instead he was apart from the
professional poets.

One main influence of Donne's circle of friends was a negative one. Because they were 'apart from the professional poets', Donne could break free from the literary strait-jacket. As Alvarez puts it :

their main interests were not in technical matters. Their literariness was merely one side of their culture. The advantage of this for Donne was not that the group put pressure on him to write in a particular way but that they relieved him of the pressure to use a certain style and certain pieties.

But Donne's poetry was not original in the sense that Donne deliberately set out to revolutionize the language of poetry : it would have taken another professional poet to have done that – a Wordsworth or an Eliot – and with them evolution is surely the more accurate term; neither was it original in the sense that he wrote in ignorance of or ignoring literary conventions. Rather his originality stems from his freedom to draw on a number of different conventions and to adapt them to his own peculiar voice.

In Donne's poetry there are echoes of what one may term the native style – what C. S. Lewis refers to in his essay 'Donne and Love Poetry in the Seventeenth Century' as 'the abrupt, familiar, and consciously manly style in which nearly all Wyatt's lyrics are written'. It is with an echo of the native style that the *Songs and Sonets* begin ('The good-morrow'); fittingly, since it is such echoes, reverberating from the beginning of the sixteenth century and a shadowy beyond, that are dominant in the volume :

> I Wonder by my troth, what thou, and I
> Did, till we lov'd? were we not wean'd till then?
> But suck'd on countrey pleasures, childishly?
> Or snorted we in the seaven sleepers den?
> T'was so; But this, all pleasures fancies bee.
> If ever any beauty I did see,
> Which I desir'd, and got, t'was but a dreame of thee.

There are echoes of what I have referred to as the Petrarchan style– 'the mellifluous, luxurious, "builded rhyme", as in Spenser's "Amoretti" ', as C. S. Lewis puts it. We notice them even though Donne is writing, clearly enough, for the speaking, not for the singing, voice; and even though the dramatic opening, so often noted as a characteristic of his poetry, indicates the degree of debt to Elizabethan dramatic blank verse in general, and notably to Shakespeare. Occasionally, echoes of the earlier styles are used chiefly for their original effect, as in 'Twicknam garden' :

> Blasted with sighs, and surrounded with teares,
> Hither I come to seeke the spring,
> And at mine eyes, and at mine eares,
> Receive such balmes, as else cure every thing;
> But O, selfe traytor, I do bring
> The spider love, which transubstantiates all,
> And can convert Manna to gall,
> And that this place may thoroughly be thought
> True Paradise, I have the serpent brought.

But even here, the infusion of Donne's characteristic wit, in exaggeratedly startling inversions, has led some critics to see the whole poem as comic, and indeed as a conscious parody of the Petrarchan style. More frequently such mellifluous moments are given a sarcastic twist, which mocks the sweetness without altogether devaluing it, changing the ideal to the real; thus these lines from 'Loves growth' (my italics) :

> But if this medicine, love, which cures all sorrow
> *With more* . . .

and

> And though each spring doe adde to love new heate,
> As princes doe in times of action get
> *New taxes* . . .

Then there are echoes of 'the other Petrarchan mode – that characterized by fantastic arguments, emotional extravagance, and peregrine comparisons'. In *John Donne, Petrarchist* Donald L. Guss demonstrates the breadth of the influence of Petrarchism on English renaissance literature, almost to the point of redefining it. He draws some convincing parallels between Donne's lyrics and the lyrics of such poets as Serafino, Tasso and Guarino, but the achievement of his book lies not in providing any specific Petrarchan sources for Donne's poetry but in establishing Donne's place at the centre of English poetic tradition. Indeed, although he admits that 'Donne's manner is clearly different from Spenser's', he argues that the difference is not that one is bound by custom and the other is blind to it, but, with Alvarez, that one is a professional and the other an amateur :

In a Renaissance context, the difference between Spenser and Donne is not that the first, blinded by custom, writes what he has been told, and that the second, clear-eyed and undaunted, writes what he feels. It is that the one writes as a careful, learned artist, and the other as a careless, accomplished wit. Neither, that is, seeks to cleanse his soul from custom : both, in fact, strike for culture. But Spenser's culture, is that of the academy, and Donne's that of the court : Spenser seeks erudition and Donne *sprezzatura,* or brilliant ease.

To be simultaneously original and in the main stream of English poetry is not a contradiction, and for one to see it as such is surely naïvely romantic; but this is what so much of the critical fuss which surrounds Donne's poetry is about. To tamper with his own most famous image, Donne is like 'twin compasses' : one foot is fixed firmly in tradition; the other ranges out, unique, and often with the kick of greatness.

The other main influence of Donne's circle of friends was positive, namely the 'language, customs, conventions and interests' which they shared and which are the stuff of Donne's poetry. One of the most common charges levelled against Donne's poetry is that it is obscure (the cynic might add truthfully that its obscurity is also one of its most common attractions). However, although it is probable that Donne deliberately worked for obscurity and that his friends enjoyed the obscurity as one enjoys a puzzle, one must remember that his learning was largely shared by his friends and the allusions over which modern readers falter would have delighted but rarely have bothered them. And actually, in spite of the numerous studies that have been made into Donne's knowledge of medicine and alchemy, and this and that, average modern readers need falter only as far as the footnotes of H. J. C. Grierson's authoritative edition *The Poems of John Donne,* which offer a more than adequate briefing for most travellers in Donne's 'monarchy'.

More serious than the charge of obscurity is that levelled by C. S.

Lewis (again in 'Donne and Love Poetry in the Seventeenth Century'), which is this:

Paradoxical as it may seem, Donne's poetry is too simple to satisfy. Its complexity is all on the surface – an intellectual and fully conscious complexity that we soon come to the end of. Beneath this we find nothing but a limited series of 'passions' – explicit, mutually exclusive passions which can be instantly and adequately labelled as such – things which can be readily talked about, and indeed, must be talked about because, in silence, they begin to lose their hard outlines and overlap, to betray themselves as partly ficticious. That is why Donne is always arguing. There are puzzles in his work, but we can solve them if we are clever enough; there is none of the depth and ambiguity of real experience in him, such as underlies the apparent simplicity of *How sleep the brave* or *Songs of Innocence*, or even Αἰαῖ Λεψύδριον. The same is true, for the most part, of the specifically 'metaphysical' comparisons. One idea has been put into each and nothing more can come out of it. Hence they tend to die on our hands, where some seemingly banal comparison of a woman to a flower or God's anger to flame can touch us at innumerable levels and renew its virginity at every reading. Of all literary virtues 'originality', in the vulgar sense, has, for this reason, the shortest life. When we have once mastered a poem by Donne there is nothing more to do with it. To use his own simile, he deals in earthquakes, not in that 'trepidation of the spheres' which is so much less violent but 'greater far'.

I do not intend here to enter a lengthy defence of Donne against Lewis's charge: Joan Bennett has done this in her essay 'The Love Poetry of John Donne: a Reply to Mr C. S. Lewis'. But from so generally sensitive a critic, this passage is astonishing. For if Donne can be accused of anything, it is surely of making too much of a comparison, of suggesting areas of likeness of which one would never have otherwise thought, not of letting it 'die on our hands' (consider, for example, the 'tear' images in 'A Valediction: forbidding weeping'). He can be accused of encouraging resonances to the point of chaos – that point in life when joy, sadness, hope, despair, laughter, tears become inextricably mixed and the mind is bewildered, numbed or broken – but not of excluding 'the depth and ambiguity of real experience'. (In 'A nocturnall upon S. Lucies day', for example, the haunting resonances of

'absence, darknesse, death; things which are not' and the poet's
vivid creation of a pre-creational void, 'the first nothing', are plainly more than verbal or philosophical tricks.) If Donne's puzzles are
soluble, then there are usually many valid but conflicting solutions.
We are in the presence of ambivalences, 'paradoxes' as Cleanth
Brooks calls them in *The Well Wrought Urn*, not of mere ambiguities; the mysteries originate in love and religion, in life, not
in art. Thus in his ingenious analysis of 'A Valediction : of weeping' (in *Seven Types of Ambiguity*) William Empson, having
offered several possible interpretations of

> O more then Moone,
> Draw not up seas to drowne me in thy spheare . . .,

is forced to conclude that the total effect of the lines depends as
much on the ever shifting tensions which arise between the possible interpretations as it does on the interpretations themselves :
'It is a question of the proportions in which these meanings are
accepted, and their interactions'.

I have asserted that the obscurity of Donne's poetry was the
inevitable result of Donne's *milieu* – a minor stumbling block, perhaps, to one's appreciation of the poetry, but not in itself an
artistic flaw. I have asserted also that the abundance of learning
in the poetry is a component of its richness and by no means an
easy alternative to it. But what of Dryden's criticism?

[Donne] . . . affects the metaphysics, not only in his satires, but in his
amorous verses, where nature only should reign; and perplexes the
minds of the fair sex with nice speculations of philosophy, when he
should engage their hearts, and entertain them with the softnesses
of love.

The essence of this criticism (and it links with Johnson's) is that
the *Songs and Sonets* are unrealistic. Few lovers intent on engaging
the heart of a mistress would actually address or speak of her as
Donne does. But few lovers would indulge in the extravagances
which are central to the love poetry of, say, Chaucer or the early
Yeats. While Donne analyzes, they idealize; while Donne is sometimes guilty (as in 'The Extasie') of lecturing in 'loves philosophy',
cutting himself off from the depths of passion, they are sometimes

guilty of gross sentimentality, with the same result. Moreover there are ways in which the *Songs and Sonets* are more realistic than other love poetry. They are colloquial in tone. They are rooted in everyday life, as J. B. Broadbent observes in his worthwhile though sketchy chapter on Donne in *Poetic Love* : '[An] . . . element in Donne's naturalness is the pressure of solid objects. All his poems have a locale – bedroom, parlour, horseback, bank of violets – and things in the locale get into the poems – rings, window-panes, fleas, maps, candles, the bric-à-brac of 17th-century life. Above all they introduce one to the fever pitch of love, the welter of confused emotions which are recognizable in one's own most intense relationships. The first stanza of 'A Feaver' is typical :

> Oh doe not die, for I shall hate
> All women so, when thou art gone,
> That thee I shall not celebrate,
> When I remember, thou wast one.

To this extent, and not surprisingly, Dryden's criticism can only be justified with reference to the narrower aspects of those neo-classical canons of taste on which it is based; what is surprising, perhaps, is the continuing currency today of both the criticism and the canons.

But it is precisely here that we encounter the chief failure of the *Songs and Sonets*, which lies in another direction, more human and more tragic – a failure not as great love poems, which I believe many of them are, but as poems of great love. Because the *Songs and Sonets* are so grounded in the turmoil of the real world, they are unable to transcend it to that higher, timeless reality where human love is purified and made spiritual, and human lovers enjoy the assurance, the peace and even the immortality, which are the normal reserve of Christians and other religious believers. It is an irony which would certainly have delighted Donne, tormented though he was as its victim.

I V

The *Songs and Sonets* were first published in a collection of Donne's poetry in 1633. The number of succeeding editions of the volume (1635, 1639, 1649, 1650, 1654, 1669) are a measure of its

popularity in the forty years after Donne's death, but the majority
of early references to the poetry imply that this was largely due to
the *Satyres* and the *Letters to Severall Personages*. Dryden's remarks in 'A Discourse Concerning the Original and Progress of
Satire' (1693), which praised Donne's wit at the expense of his
poetry, marked the beginning of the neo-classical reaction against
the poetry and its subsequent eclipse : with the exception of an
edition in 1719, nothing important was written about it again
until Johnson renewed the attack in 1781. While the neo-classical
rejection of Donne often expresses itself philosophically, it was in
fact an almost instinctual fear. Johnson's preference for Pope's
'true wit' to Donne's 'false wit' is not simply homage to Locke's
epistemology; it is a real fear that Donne's habits of mind are obses-
sive, violent, and verging on the insane.

At the beginning of the nineteenth century the pendulum slowly
began to swing back, in spite of Hazlitt's protestations in 'Lectures
on Comic Writers III' (1818). Predictably such a Romantic period
revalued Donne's spontaneity above his wit, an emphasis which
has since remained. Coleridge made enthusiastic marginal jottings
on the *Songs and Sonets*. In 1823 the first critical essay specifically
on Donne's poetry was published anonymously in the *Retrospective Review;* it, too, concentrates on the *Songs and Sonets* as
Donne's most meritorious work – 'Of Donne's other poems, the
Funeral Elegies, Epistles, Satires, and what he calls his *Divine
Poems,* particularly the last mentioned, we have little to say in
general praise . . .'. But it was not until the very end of the century
that Donne was finally restored to his place among the greatest
English poets. In his introduction to E. K. Chambers's edition of
the poetry (1899), George Saintsbury summed up Donne's attraction for an age which, much influenced by Darwin, saw man as
primarily an emotional rather than a rational being (Freud's *An
Interpretation of Dreams* appeared a year later) :

for those who have experienced, or who at least understand, the ups-
and-downs, the ins-and-outs of human temperament, the alterations
not merely of passion and satiety, but of passion and laughter, of
passion and melancholy reflection, of passion earthly enough and
spiritual rapture almost heavenly, there is no poet and hardly any
writer like Donne.

H. J. C. Grierson published his major edition *The Poetry of Donne* in 1912 and it is still authoritative. A less comprehensive version was published in 1933 with minor alterations to the text : in this Casebook I have standardized all quotations of Donne's poems to this version, except where authors have specified otherwise. Two other editions of the *Songs and Sonets* (as well as individual editions of Donne's other works) have been produced since and are worth consulting. One, edited by Theodore Redpath, is based largely on Grierson's edition and its usefulness lies more in the challenging commentary on the text than on the text itself. The other, edited by Helen Gardner and a work of major and painstaking scholarship, offers several new readings of the poems. In spite of Empson's assertion to the contrary in 'Donne in the New Edition', there is little doubt that Gardner's editing 'machinery' was more sophisticated than Grierson's. But did she rely on it too heavily? The continuing preference of most critics of Grierson's readings is either a matter of conservative bias ('I like what I know') or, more likely, of intuition – somehow Grierson's readings *feel* right. Students interested in the textual problems presented by Donne's poetry would do well to consult Gardner's introduction to her edition in conjunction with Empson's outspoken review and the ensuing correspondence.

Grierson's edition was received with understandable acclaim – Yeats thanked him, 'Your notes tell me exactly what I need to know'; Rupert Brooke thought it enough 'to make even a scholar love poetry, even a poet love scholarship', such is its balance. But it is Brooke's opinion of Donne and not of Grierson which demands the more attention :

He is the most *intellectual* poet in English; and his intellectualism had, even, sometimes, a tendency to the abstract. But to be an intellectual poet does not mean that one writes about intellectual things. The pageant of the outer world of matter and the mid-region world of the passions came to Donne through the brain. The whole composition of the man was made up of brain, soul, and heart in a different proportion from the ordinary prescription. This does not mean that he felt less keenly than others; but when passion shook him, and his being ached for utterance, to relieve the stress, expression came through the intellect.

It was this argument exactly that Eliot popularised in 'The Meta-physical Poets', couching it in a vague historical myth ('the dis-sociation of sensibility') and using it to justify his own Symbolist poetry :

A thought to Donne was an experience; it modified his sensibility. When a poet's mind is perfectly equipped for its work, it is constantly amalgamating disparate experience; the ordinary man's experience is chaotic, irregular, fragmentary. The latter falls in love, or reads Spinoza, and these two experiences have nothing to do with each other, or with the noise of the typewriter or the smell of cooking; in the mind of the poet these experiences are always forming new wholes.

Eliot later recanted, at least partly, in 'Donne in our Time' (1931) and 'Lecture on Milton' (1947), and in a perceptive article 'The Dissociation of Sensibility' (1957) Frank Kermode both explained and exploded the theory :

A period which frankly confessed that it thought and felt by turns did homage to a period when men did these things simultaneously : a double-minded period measured itself by a serenely single-minded one. Intellect deferred to imagination; the slaves of second to the devotees of first causes : men habituated to asking *how* longed for a period when the proper question was *why*? Poets tried once more to be concrete, to banish ratiocination, to be 'physical' rather than 'platonic', to charge their thinking with passion and their passion with thought; to restore to poetry a truth independent of presump-tuous intellect. They looked admiringly toward those early years of the 17th Century when this was normal; and the scholars attended them with explanations of why it was so, and why it ceased to be so. There was an implicit parallel with the Fall; man's soul, since 1650, had been divided against itself, and it would never be the same again, though correct education might achieve something.

and :

what, if you look closely at it, does the phrase 'dissociation of sensi-bility' mean? ... it is only a way of rewriting history to emphasize the importance of poets you happen to like – a very extravagant way; ... it is a way of talking about poems and poets which satisfy certain aesthetic criteria (notably that discourse should be purged from poems so that the poet doesn't appear merely to be thinking about something he felt, or worse still feeling about something he thought; the whole thing has to happen at once.

In defining metaphysical poetry as thought which is experienced and feeling which is reflected on, Eliot was arguably defining great literature *per se*. The oddity is that while the tracing of particular aspects of this fusion in any poetry is a normal critical challenge, Eliot isolates it as a property peculiar to metaphysical poetry. The inevitable crumbling of the theory has left many of its devotees uncomfortably holding its somewhat ridiculous offspring. When F. R. Leavis wrote in 'The Line of Wit' (1936),

> The work has been done, the reorientation affected : the heresies of ten years ago are orthodoxy. Mr Eliot's achievement is matter for academic evaluation, his poetry is accepted, and his early observations on the Metaphysicals and on Marvell provide currency for university lectures and undergraduate exercises. . . .

and went on to imply that all poetry should be judged against a seventeenth-century yardstick, another reorientation was already taking place and the orthodoxies were no longer orthodox at all.

v

During the preparation of this Casebook I have become increasingly aware that the 'early critics' tell as much, if not more, about their own age as they do about Donne's poetry. Dryden and Johnson, standing at the borders of neo-classicism, implicitly accuse Donne of breaking the 'rules' of Art; Coleridge and, to a lesser degree, the author of the *Retrospective Review* essay, writing from a Romantic position, praise Donne's spontaneity; Brooke and Eliot especially drag us into their own cultural dilemmas. But in the later twentieth century no such pattern emerges : in an age which has a violent dislike for dogma of all kinds (except, naturally, the dogma that there should be no dogma), the tendency of literary criticism has been to consider a work on its own terms; to explicate and not to evaluate. Of course there has been a trend away from the Donne 'vogue' of the early century (though Donne is still com-

fortably established in the front rank of English poets) and doubtless students looking back from the future will be able to detect
this more clearly than is presently possible, but the sober reappraisal of Donne's poetry has been effected by individuals and
not by a temporal conspiracy.

For this reason I could see no justification, apart from tradition,
for arranging the essays and extracts in 'Part III' of this volume in
chronological sequence : indeed so small a selection would be as
likely to contradict the trend away from the Donne 'vogue' as to
demonstrate it. Instead I have opened the section with two essays
which represent the two poles of opinions on the *Songs and Sonets* :
C. S. Lewis's 'Donne and Love Poetry in the Seventeenth Century'
and Joan Bennett's 'The Love Poetry of John Donne : a Reply to
Mr C. S. Lewis'. The arguments of both essays are undermined
and flawed by the blindness of prejudice and their conclusions are
too extreme to be tenable; but they are nothing if not thought-
provoking and they raise the central issue of 'whether good love
poetry need be descriptive'. The three pieces which follow lead to
firmer ground than 'these matters of taste and opinion' can afford,
and point, through the study of a poem or poems, to some of the
main themes which run through the *Songs and Sonets* : Arnold
Stein's penetrating analysis of 'The good-morrow' which highlights
Donne's platonism; Louis Martz's study of Donne's concern with
'the problem of the place of human love in a physical world dominated by change and death' in 'John Donne : Love's Philosophy';
and a short piece by A. E. Dyson and myself which investigates
the relationship between human and spiritual love in 'The Sunne
Rising' (all three pieces can usefully be compared with Broadbent's
chapter in *Poetic Love*). From the abstract to the concrete, and to
the treatment of two of the more technical aspects of the poems :
first, J. B. Leishman's 'Logical Structure in the Songs and Sonets'
shows the meticulous construction which underlies, communicates
and creates the confusion of emotions; second, M. F. Moloney's
article 'Donne's Metrical Practice' not only finds the same meti-
culousness beneath Donne's rough, colloquial language, but also
goes on to demonstrate that his 'metrical practice' places him in
the same poetic line as Shakespeare and Milton (for a less specialized account of the metre of the *Songs and Sonets* students should
consult *Donne the Craftsman* by Pierre Legouis).

Keeping the best wine until last is a policy as sound as it is old and Helen Gardner's 'The Argument about "The Ecstasy" ' is vintage stuff. Having given a full account of the critical debate over 'The Extasie', Gardner offers her own thorough analysis of the poem, tracing its source to the Italian philosopher Leone Ebreo's *Dialoghi d'Amore* (1535). (In 'The Metaphysic of Love', written contemporaneously with Gardner's essay, A. J. Smith reaches a similar conclusion.) Perhaps she misses some of the erotic quality of the poem; perhaps by relating it too closely to its source she denies it some of its complexity. But whatever she makes of 'The Extasie' – and I agree with her in regarding it as one of the less successful *Songs and Sonets* – her enthusiasm remains unabated as she endorses Donne's greatness :

In 'The Ecstasy' Donne is too tied to his source. It smells a little of the lamp. In other, more wonderful, poems he was able to tell in his own language and in his own way what he had learned in his experience, as illuminated by the Jewish Platonist, of love's power to 'interinanimate two souls'.

If this Casebook helps students to discover something of the richness of the *Songs and Sonets,* it will achieve its aim.

NOTE

1. With the exception of essays reprinted *in full* in this Casebook and early editions of Donne's poems, full details of all books and essays mentioned in the Introduction are given in the Select Bibliography on page 249.

PART ONE

Earlier Comments

John Donne

I

The triple Foole.

I am two fooles, I know,
For loving, and for saying so
   In whining Poëtry;
But where's that wiseman, that would not be I,
   If she would not deny?
Then as th'earths inward narrow crooked lanes
Do purge sea waters fretfull salt away,
   I thought, if I could draw my paines,
Through Rimes vexation, I should them allay,
Griefe brought to numbers cannot be so fierce,
For, he tames it, that fetters it in verse.

   But when I have done so,
Some man, his art and voice to show,
   Doth Set and sing my paine,
And, by delighting many, frees againe
   Griefe, which verse did restraine.
To Love, and Griefe tribute of Verse belongs,
But not of such as pleases when'tis read,
   Both are increased by such songs :
For both their triumphs so are published,
And I, which was two fooles, do so grow three;
Who are a little wise, the best fooles bee.

SOURCE: *Songs and Sonets* (1633).

*

I I

Others at the Porches and entries of their Buildings set their Armes;
I, my picture; if any colours can deliver a minde so plaine, and flat,
and through light as mine. Naturally at a new Author, I doubt, and
sticke, and doe not say quickly, good. I censure much and taxe; And
this liberty costs mee more then others, by how much my owne things
are worse then others. Yet I would not be so rebellious against my
selfe, as not to doe it, since I love it; nor so unjust to others, to do it
sine talione. As long as I give them as good hold upon mee, they must
pardon mee my bitings. I forbid no reprehender, but him that like
the Trent Councell forbids not bookes, but Authors, damning what
ever such a name hath or shall write. None writes so ill, that he gives
not some thing exemplary, to follow, or flie.

S o u r c e : 'Epistle,' *Infinitati Sacrum* (1601).

Thomas Carew

An Elegie upon the death of the Deane of Pauls, D^r. Iohn Donne.

Can we not force from widdowed Poetry,
Now thou art dead (Great DONNE) one Elegie
To crowne thy Hearse? Why yet dare we not trust
Though with unkneaded dowe-bak't prose thy dust,
Such as the uncisor'd Churchman from the flower
Of fading Rhetorique, short liv'd as his houre,
Dry as the sand that measures it, should lay
Upon thy Ashes, on the funerall day?
Have we no voice, no tune? Did'st thou dispense
Through all our language, both the words and sense?
'Tis a sad truth; The Pulpit may her plaine,
And sober Christian precepts still retaine,
Doctrines it may, and wholesome Uses frame,
Grave Homilies, and Lectures, But the flame
Of thy brave Soule, (that shot such heat and light,
As burnt our earth, and made our darknesse bright,
Committed holy Rapes upon our Will,
Did through the eye the melting heart distill;
And the deepe knowledge of darke truths so teach,
As sense might judge, what phansie could not reach;)
Must be desir'd for ever. So the fire,
That fills with spirit and heat the Delphique quire,
Which kindled first by thy Promethean breath,
Glow'd here a while, lies quench't now in thy death;
The Muses garden with Pedantique weedes
O'rspred, was purg'd by thee; The lazie seeds
Of servile imitation throwne away;
And fresh invention planted, Thou didst pay
The debts of our penurious bankrupt age;
Licentious thefts, that make poëtique rage

A Mimique fury, when our soules must bee
Possest, or with Anacreons Extasie,
Or Pindars, not their owne; The subtle cheat
Of slie Exchanges, and the jugling feat
Of two-edg'd words, or whatsoever wrong
By ours was done the Greeke, or Latine tongue,
Thou hast redeem'd, and open'd Us a Mine
Of rich and pregnant phansie, drawne a line
Of masculine expression, which had good
Old Orpheus seene, Or all the ancient Brood
Our superstitious fooles admire, and hold
Their lead more precious, then thy burnish't Gold,
Thou hadst beene their Exchequer, and no more
They each in others dust, had rak'd for Ore.
Thou shalt yield no precedence, but of time,
And the blinde fate of language, whose tun'd chime
More charmes the outward sense; Yet thou maist claime
From so great disadvantage greater fame,
Since to the awe of thy imperious wit
Our stubborne language bends, made only fit
With her tough-thick-rib'd hoopes to gird about
Thy Giant phansie, which had prov'd too stout
For their soft melting Phrases. As in time
They had the start, so did they cull the prime
Buds of invention many a hundred yeare,
And left the rifled fields, besides the feare
To touch their Harvest, yet from those bare lands
Of what is purely thine, thy only hands
(And that thy smallest worke) have gleaned more
Then all those times, and tongues could reape before;
    But thou art gone, and thy strict lawes will be
Too hard for Libertines in Poetrie.
They will repeale the goodly exil'd traine
Of gods and goddesses, which in thy just raigne
Were banish'd nobler Poems, now, with these
The silenc'd tales o'th' Metamorphoses
Shall stuffe their lines, and swell the windy Page,
Till Verse refin'd by thee, in this last Age

Turne ballad rime, Or those old Idolls bee
Ador'd againe, with new apostasie;
   Oh, pardon mee, that breake with untun'd verse
The reverend silence that attends thy herse,
Whose awfull solemne murmures were to thee
More then these faint lines, A loud Elegie,
That did proclaime in a dumbe eloquence
The death of all the Arts, whose influence
Growne feeble, in these panting numbers lies
Gasping short winded Accents, and so dies :
So doth the swiftly turning wheele not stand
In th'instant we withdraw the moving hand,
But some small time maintaine a faint weake course
By vertue of the first impulsive force :
And so whil'st I cast on thy funerall pile
Thy crowne of Bayes, Oh, let it crack a while,
And spit disdaine, till the devouring flashes
Suck all the moysture up, then turne to ashes.
   I will not draw the envy to engrosse
All thy perfections, or weepe all our losse;
Those are too numerous for an Elegie,
And this too great, to be express'd by mee.
Though every pen should share a distinct part,
Yet art thou Theme enough to tyre all Art;
Let others carve the rest, it shall suffice
I on thy Tombe this Epitaph incise.

Here lies a King, that rul'd as hee thought fit
The universall Monarchy of wit;
Here lie two Flamens, and both those, the best,
Apollo's first, at last, the true Gods Priest.

(1631).

John Dryden

Were he (Donne) translated into numbers, and English, he would yet be wanting in the dignity of expression . . . He affects the metaphysics, not only in his satires, but in his amorous verses, where nature only should reign; and perplexes the minds of the fair sex with nice speculations of philosophy, when he should engage their hearts, and entertain them with the softnesses of love.

SOURCE: 'A Discourse Concerning the Original and Progress of Satire' (1693).

Anonymous (1713)

. . . of all our countrymen, none are more defective in their songs, through a redundancy of wit, than Dr Donne, and Mr Cowley. In them, one point of wit flashes so fast upon another, that the reader's attention is dazzled by the continual sparkling of their imagination; you find a new design started almost in every line, and you come to the end without the satisfaction of seeing any one of them executed.

SOURCE: *Guardian* (1713).

*

Lewis Theobald

. . . Now, the Age, in which Shakespeare liv'd, having, above all others, a wonderful Affection to appear Learned, They declined vulgar Images, such as are immediately fetch'd from Nature, and rang'd thro' the Circle of the Sciences to fetch their Ideas from thence. But as the Resemblances of such Ideas to the Subject must necessarily lie very much out of the common Way, and every Piece of Wit appear a Riddle to the Vulgar; This, that should have taught them the forced, quaint, unnatural Tract they were in, (and induce them to follow a more natural One,) was the very Thing that kept them attach'd to it. The ostentatious Affectation of abstruse Learning, peculiar to that time, the Love that Men naturally have to every Thing that looks like Mystery, fixed them down to this Habit of Obscurity. Thus became the Poetry of D o n n e (tho' the wittiest Man of that Age,) nothing but a continued Heap of Riddles. And our *Shakespeare,* with all his easy Nature about him, for want of Knowledge of the true Rules of Art, falls frequently into this vicious manner.

SOURCE: Preface to Lewis Theobald's edition of *Shakespeare* (1733).

Richard Hurd

The *mutual habitudes and relations* . . ., subsisting between those
innumerable objects of thought and sense, which make up the
entire natural and intellectual world, are indeed infinite; and if the
poet be allowed to associate and bring together all those ideas,
wherein the ingenuity of the mind can perceive any remote sign or
glimpse of *resemblance,* it were truly wonderful, that, in any number of images and allusions, there should be found a close con-
formity of them with those of any other writer. But this is far from
being the case. For . . . the more august poetry disclaims, as un-
suited to its state and dignity, that inquisitive and anxious dili-
gence, which pries into nature's retirements and searches through
all her secret and hidden haunts, to detect a forbidden commerce,
and expose to light some strange unexpected conjunction of ideas.
This quaint combination of remote, unallied imagery, constitutes
a species of entertainment, which, for its *novelty,* may amuse and
divert the mind in other compositions but is wholly inconsistent
with the reserve and solemnity of the *graver* forms. . . . And here,
by the way, it may be worth observing, in honour of a great Poet
of the last century, I mean Dr D o n n e, that, though agreeably
to the turn of his genius, and taste of his age, he was fonder, than
ever poet was, of these *secret and hidden ways* in his lesser poetry;
yet when he had projected his great work 'On the progress of the
Soul' . . . his good sense brought him out into the freer *spaces* of
nature and open *daylight.* . . .

S o u r c e : Richard Hurd, *Horace* (1751).

Joseph Warton

Our English poets may, I think, be disposed in four different classes and degrees. In the first class, I would place, first, our only three sublime and pathetic poets; SPENSER, SHAKESPEARE, MILTON; and then, at proper intervals, OTWAY and LEE. In the second class should be placed, such as possessed the true poetical genius, in a more moderate degree, but had noble talents for moral and ethical poetry. At the head of these are DRYDEN, DONNE, DENHAM, COWLEY, CONGREVE. In the third class may be placed, men of wit, of elegant taste, and some fancy in describing familiar life. Here may be numbered, PRIOR, WALLER, PARNELL, SWIFT, FENTON. In the fourth class, the mere versifiers, however smooth and mellifluous, should be ranked. Such as PITT, SANDYS, FAIRFAX, BROOME, BUCKING-HAM, LANSDOWN.

SOURCE: Joseph Warton, *Essay on the Genius and Writings of Pope* (1756).

Anonymous (1756)

. . . Did any man with a poetical ear, ever yet read ten lines of
Donne without disgust? No. How then comes this Adjuster of
literary rank [Warton] to post him before Denham, Waller, Cow-
c.? In truth, Daniel, Drayton, Randolph, or almost any other
of his contemporary poets, the translator of Du Bartas no
ted, deserve a better place than he. . . .

SOURCE: Monthly Review (1756).

Samuel Johnson

The metaphysical poets were men of learning, and to shew their learning was their whole endeavour; but, unluckily resolving to shew it in rhyme, instead of writing poetry, they only wrote verses, and very often such verses as stood the trial of the finger better than of the ear; for the modulation was so imperfect, that they were only found to be verses by counting the syllables.

If the father of criticism has rightly denominated poetry τέχνη μιμητική, *an imitative art*, these writers will, without great wrong, lose their right to the name of poets: for they cannot be said to have imitated any thing; they neither copied nature nor life; neither painted the forms of matter, nor represented the operations of intellect.

Those however who deny them to be poets, allow them to be wits. Dryden confesses of himself and his contemporaries, that they fall below Donne in wit, but maintains that they surpass him in poetry.

If Wit be well described by Pope, as being 'that which has been often thought, but was never before so well expressed,' they certainly never attained, nor ever sought it; for they endeavoured to be singular in their thoughts, and were careless of their diction. But Pope's account of wit is undoubtedly erroneous : he depresses it below its natural dignity, and reduces it from strength of thought to happiness of language.

If by a more noble and more adequate conception that be considered as Wit, which is at once natural and new, that which, though not obvious, is, upon its first production, acknowledged to be just; if it be that, which he that never found it, wonders how he missed; to wit of this kind the metaphysical poets have seldom risen. Their thoughts are often new, but seldom natural; they are not obvious, but neither are they just; and the reader, far from wondering that he missed them, wonders more frequently by what perverseness of industry they were ever found.

But Wit, abstracted from its effects upon the hearer, may be more rigorously and philosophically considered as a kind of *discordia concors;* a combination of dissimilar images, or discovery of occult resemblances in things apparently unlike. Of wit, thus defined, they have more than enough. The most heterogeneous ideas are yoked by violence together; nature and art are ransacked for illustrations, comparisons, and allusions; their learning instructs, and their subtilty surprises; but the reader commonly thinks his improvement dearly bought, and though he sometimes admires is seldom pleased.

From this account of their compositions it will be readily inferred, that they were not successful in representing or moving the affections. As they were wholly employed on something unexpected and surprising, they had no regard to that uniformity of sentiment which enables us to conceive and to excite the pains and the pleasure of other minds : they never enquired what, on any occasion, they should have said or done; but wrote rather as beholders than partakers of human nature; as Beings looking upon good and evil, impassive and at leisure; as Epicurean deities making remarks on the actions of men, and the vicissitudes of life, without interest and without emotion. Their courtship was void of fondness, and their lamentation of sorrow. Their wish was only to say what they hoped had been never said before.

Nor was the sublime more within their reach than the pathetick; for they never attempted that comprehension and expense of thought which at once fills the whole mind, and of which the first effect is sudden astonishment, and the second rational admiration. Sublimity is produced by aggregation, and littleness by dispersion. Great thoughts are always general, and consist on positions not limited by exceptions, and in descriptions not descending to minuteness. It is with great propriety that Subtlety, which in its original import means exility of particles, is taken in its metaphorical meaning for nicety of distinction. Those writers who lay on the watch for novelty could have little hope of greatness; for great things cannot have escaped former observation. Their attempts were always analytick; they broke every image into fragments; and could no more represent, by their slender conceits and laboured particularities, the prospect of nature, or the scenes of life, than he, who dissects a sun-beam with a prism, can exhibit the wide effulgence of a summer noon.

What they wanted however of the sublime, they endeavoured to supply by hyperbole; their amplification had no limits; they left not only reason but fancy behind them; and produced combinations of confused magnificence, that not only could not be credited, but could not be imagined.

Yet great labour, directed by great abilities, is never wholly lost : if they frequently threw away their wit upon false conceits, they likewise sometimes struck out unexpected truth : if their conceits were far-fetched, they were often worth the carriage. To write on their plan, it was at least necessary to read and think. No man could be born a metaphysical poet, nor assume the dignity of a writer, by descriptions copied from descriptions, by imitations borrowed from imitations, by traditional imagery, and hereditary similies, by readiness of rhyme, and volubility of syllables.

In perusing the works of this race of authors, the mind is exercised either by recollection or inquiry; either something already learned is to be retrieved, or something new is to be examined. If their greatness seldom elevates, their acuteness often surprises; if the imagination is not always gratified, at least the powers of reflection and comparison are employed; and in the mass of materials which ingenious absurdity has thrown together, genuine wit and useful knowledge may be sometimes found, buried perhaps in grossness of expression, but useful to those who know their value; and such as, when they are expanded to perspicuity, and polished to elegance, may give lustre to works which have more propriety, though less copiousness of sentiment.

This kind of writing, which was, I believe, borrowed from Marino and his followers, had been recommended by the example of Donne, a man of very extensive and various knowledge, and by Jonson, whose manner resembled that of Donne more in the ruggedness of his lines than in the cast of his sentiments.

When their reputation was high, they had undoubtedly more imitators, than time has left behind. Their immediate successors, of whom any remembrance can be said to remain, were Suckling, Waller, Denham, Cowley, Cleveland, and Milton. Denham and Waller sought another way to fame, by improving the harmony of our numbers. Milton tried the metaphysick stile only in his lines upon Hobson the Carrier. Cowley adopted it, and excelled his predecessors, having as much sentiment, and more musick. Suckling neither improved versification, nor abounded in conceits. The fashionable stile remained chiefly with Cowley; Suckling could not reach it, and Milton disdained it.

S o u r c e : *Lives of the Poets – Abraham Cowley* (1779).

PART TWO

Selection of Nineteenth-Century and Early Twentieth-Century Criticism

Samuel Coleridge

To read Dryden, Pope, &c., you need only count syllables; but to read Donne you must measure *Time,* and discover the *Time* of each word by the sense of Passion. I would ask no surer test of a Scotchman's *substratum* (for the turf-cover of pretension they all have) than to make him read Donne's satires aloud. If he made manly metre of them and yet strict metre, then, – why, then he wasn't a Scotchman, or his soul was geographically slandered by his body's first appearing there.

Doubtless, all the copies I have even seen of Donne's Poems are grievously misprinted. Wonderful that they are not more so, considering that not one in a thousand of his readers have any notion how his lines are to be read – to the many, five out of six appear anti-metrical. How greatly this aided the compositor's negligence or ignorance, and prevented the corrector's remedy, any man may ascertain by examining the earliest editions of blank verse plays, Massinger, Beaumont and Fletcher, &c. Now, Donne's rhythm was as inexplicable to the many as blank verse, spite of his rhymes – ergo, as blank verse, misprinted. I am convinced that where no mode of rational declamation by pause, hurrying of voice, or apt and sometimes double emphasis, can at once make the verse metrical and bring out the sense of passion more prominently, that there we are entitled to alter the text, when it can be done by simple omission or addition of *that, which, and,* and such 'small deer'; or by mere placing of the same words – I would venture nothing beyond. . . .

*

'A FEAVER'

For I had rather owner bee
Of thee one houre, then all else ever.

Just and affecting, as *dramatic*, i.e., the outburst of a transient feeling, itself the symbol of a deeper feeling, that would have made *one* hour, *known* to be *only* one hour (or even one year), a perfect hell! All the preceding verses are detestable. Shakespeare has nothing of this. He is never positively bad, even in his Sonnets. He may be sometimes worthless (N.B., I don't say he *is*), but nowhere is he *unworthy*. . . .

*

The wit of Donne, the wit of Butler, the wit of Pope, the wit of Congreve, the wit of Sheridan – how disparate things are here expressed by one and the same word, Wit! – Wonder-exciting vigour, intenseness and pecularity of thought, using at will the almost boundless stores of a capacious memory, and exercised on subjects, where we have no right to expect it – this is the wit of Donne! The four others I am just in the mood to describe and inter-distinguish; – what a pity that the marginal space will not let me!

*

My face in thine eye, thine in mine appeares,
And true plain hearts doe in the faces rest,
Where can we finde two better hemispheares
Without sharpe North, without declining West?
                                    'The good-morrow', lines 15–19.

The sense is :—Our mutual loves may in many respects be fitly compared to corresponding hemispheres; but as no simile squares (*nihil simile est idem*), so here the simile fails, for there is nothing in our love that corresponds to the cold north, or the declining west, which in two hemispheres must necessarily be supposed. But an ellipse of such length will scarcely rescue the line from the charge of nonsense or a bull. . . .

S o u r c e : Roberta Florence Brinkley (ed.), *Coleridge on the Seventeenth Century*. The notes were written between 1811 and 1829.

William Hazlitt

... The writers here referred to (such as Donne, Davies, Crashaw, and others) not merely mistook learning for poetry – they thought any thing was poetry that differed from ordinary prose and the natural impression of things, by being intricate, far-fetched, and improbable. Their style was not so properly learned as metaphysical; that is to say, whenever, by any violence done to their ideas, they could make out an abstract likeness or possible ground of comparison, they forced the image, whether learned or vulgar, into the service of the Muses. Any thing would do to 'hitch into rhyme,' no matter whether striking or agreeable, or not, so that it would puzzle the reader to discover the meaning, and if there was the most remote circumstance, however trifling or vague, for the pretended comparison to hinge upon. They brought ideas together not the most, but the least like; and of which the collision produced not light, but obscurity – served not to strengthen, but to confound. Their mystical verses read like riddles or an allegory. They neither belong to the class of lively or severe poetry. They have not the force of the one, nor the gaiety of the other; but are an ill-assorted, unprofitable union of the two together, applying to serious subjects that quaint and partial style of allusion which fits only what is light and ludicrous, and building the most laboured conclusions on the most fantastical and slender premises. The object of the poetry of imagination is to raise or adorn one idea by another more striking or more beautiful : the object of these writers was to match any one idea with any other idea, *for better for worse*, as we say, and whether any thing was gained by the change of condition or not. The object of the poetry of the passions again is to illustrate any strong feeling, by shewing the same feeling as connected with objects or circumstances more palpable and touching; but here the object was to strain and distort the immediate feeling into some barely possible consequence or recondite analogy, in which it required the utmost stretch of misapplied ingenuity to trace the smallest connection with the original impression. In short, the poetry

of this period was strictly the poetry not of ideas, but of *definitions* :
it proceeded in mode and figure, by *genus* and specific difference;
and was the logic of the schools, or an oblique and forced construction of dry, literal matter-of-fact, decked out in a robe of
glittering conceits, and clogged with the halting shackles of verse.
The imagination of the writers, instead of being conversant with
the face of nature, or the secrets of the heart, was lost in the laby-
rinths of intellectual abstraction, or entangled in the technical quib-
bles and impertinent intricacies of language. The complaint so
often made, and here repeated, is not of the want of power in these
men, but of the waste of it; not of the absence of genius, but the
abuse of it. They had (many of them) great talents committed to
their trust, richness of thought, and depth of feeling; but they
chose to hide them (as much as they possibly could) under a false
shew of learning and unmeaning subtlety. From the style which
they had systematically adopted, they thought nothing done till
they had perverted simplicity into affection, and spoiled nature by
art. They seemed to think there was an irreconcileable opposition
between genius, as well as grace, and nature; tried to do without,
or else constantly to thwart her; left nothing to her outward 'im-
press,' on spontaneous impulses, but made a point of twisting and
torturing almost every subject they took in hand, till they had fitted
it to the mould of their self-opinion and the previous fabrications
of their own fancy, like those who pen acrostics in the shape of
pyramids, and cut out trees into the shape of peacocks. Their chief
aim is to make you wonder at the writer, not to interest you in the
subject; and by an incessant craving after admiration, they have
lost what they might have gained with less extravagance and affection. So Cowper, who was of a quite opposite school, speaks feel-
ingly of the misapplication of Cowley's poetical genius.

> And though reclaim'd by modern lights
> From an erroneous taste,
> I cannot but lament thy splendid wit
> Entangled in the cobwebs of the schools.

Donne, who was considerably before Cowley, is without his fancy,
but was more recondite in his logic, and rigid in his descriptions.
He is hence led, particularly in his satires, to tell disagreeable
truths in as disagreeable a way as possible, or to convey a pleasing

and affecting thought (of which there are many to be found in his other writings) by the harshest means, and with the most painful effort. His Muse suffers continual pangs and throes. His thoughts are delivered by the Cæsarean operation. The sentiments, profound and tender as they often are, are stifled in the expression; and 'heaved pantingly forth,' are 'buried quick again' under the ruins and rubbish of analytical distinctions. It is like poetry waking from a trance : with an eye bent idly on the outward world, and half-forgotten feelings crowding about the heart; with vivid impressions, dim notions, and disjointed words. The following may serve as instances of beautiful or impassioned reflections losing themselves in obscure and difficult applications. He has some lines to a Blossom, which begin thus :

> Little think'st thou, poore flower,
> Whom I have watch'd sixe or seaven dayes,
> And seene thy birth, and seene what every houre
> Gave to thy growth, thee to this height to raise,
> And now dost laugh and triumph on this bough,
>   Little think'st thou
> That it will freeze anon, and that I shall
> Tomorrow finde thee falne, or not at all.

This simple and delicate description is only introduced as a foundation for an elaborate metaphysical conceit as a parallel to it, in the next stanza.

> Little think'st thou poore heart
> That labour'st yet to nestle thee,
> And think'st by hovering here to get a part
> In a forbidden or forbidding tree,
> And hop'st her stiffenesse by long siege to bow :
>   Little think'st thou,
> That thou tomorrow, ere that Sunne doth wake,
> Must with this Sunne, and mee a journey take.

This is but a lame and impotent conclusion from so delightful a beginning. – He thus notices the circumstances of his wearing his late wife's hair about his arm, in a little poem which is called 'The Funerall' :

> Who ever comes to shroud me, do not harme
>   Nor question much
> That subtile wreath of haire, which crowns my arme;
> The mystery, the signe you must not touch ...

The scholastic reason he gives quite dissolves the charm of tender and touching grace in the sentiment itself –

> For 'tis my outward Soule,
> Viceroy to that, which then to heaven being gone,
>   Will leave this to controule,
> And keepe these limbes, her Provinces, from dissolution.

Again, the following lines, the title of which is 'Loves Deitie', are highly characteristic of this author's manner, in which the thoughts are inlaid in a costly but imperfect mosaic-work.

> I long to talke with some old lovers ghost,
>   Who dyed before the god of Love was borne;
> I cannot thinke that hee, who then lov'd most,
>   Sunke so low, as to love one which did scorne.
> But since this god produc'd a destinie,
> And that vice-nature, custome, lets it be;
>   I must love her, that loves not mee.

The stanza in the Epithalamion on the Lady Elizabeth, and Count Palatine, has been often quoted against him, and is an almost irresistible illustration of the extravagance to which this kind of writing, which turns upon a pivot of words and possible allusions, is liable.

Speaking of the bride and bridegroom he says, by way of serious compliment –

> Here lyes a shee Sunne, and a hee Moone here,
>   She gives the best light to his Spheare,
>   Or each is both, and all, and so
> They unto one another nothing owe ...

His love-verses and epistles to his friends give the most favourable idea of Donne. His satires are too clerical. He shews, if I may

so speak, too much disgust, and, at the same time, too much contempt for vice. His dogmatical invectives hardly redeem the naus-
eousness of his descriptions, and compromise the imagination of his
readers more than they assist their reason. The satirist does not
write with the same authority as the divine, and should use his
poetical privileges more sparingly. 'To the pure all things are pure,'
is a maxim which a man like Dr Donne may be justified in applying to himself; but he might have recollected that it could not be
construed to extend to the generality of his readers, *without benefit
of clergy.* . . .

S O U R C E : *Lectures on the Comic Writers – On Cowley, Butler,
Suckling, Etherege, &c.* (1818).

Anonymous (1823)

. . . In pieces that can be read with unmingled pleasure, and
admired as perfect wholes, the poetry of Donne is almost entirely
deficient. This may serve, in some degree, to account for the total
neglect which has so long attended him. Almost every beauty we
meet with, goes hand in hand with some striking deformity, of one
kind or another; and the effect of this is, at first, so completely
irritating to the imagination, as well as to the taste, that, after we
have experienced it a few times, we hastily determine to be without
the one, rather than purchase it at the price of the other. But the
reader who is disposed, by these remarks, and the extracts that will
accompany them, to a perusal of the whole of this poet's works,
may be assured that this unpleasant effect will very soon wear off,
and he will soon find great amusement and great exercise for his
thinking faculties, (if nothing else) even in the objectionable parts
of Donne; for he is always, when indulging in his very worst vein,
filled to overflowing with thoughts, and materials for engendering
thought.

The following short pieces are beautiful exceptions to the remark
made just above, as to the mixed character of this poet's writings.
The first is a farewell from a lover to his mistress, on leaving her for
a time. For clearness and smoothness of construction, and a passionate sweetness and softness in the music of the versification, it
might have been written in the present day, and may satisfy the
ear of the most fastidious of modern readers; and for thought,
sentiment, and imagery, it might *not* have been written in the present day; – for, much as we hold in honour our living poets, we
doubt if any one among them is capable of it. In fact, it is one of
those pieces which immediately strike us as being purely and exclusively attributable to the writer of them – which satisfy us, that,
but for him, we never could have become possessed of them –
which bear a mark that we cannot very well expound, even to our-

---

See note, p. 61, on the uncertain authorship of this piece.

selves, but which we know no one could have placed on them but him : and this, by-the-bye, is one of the most unequivocal criterions of a true poet. Perhaps the piece itself will explain better what we mean, than any thing we could say of it.

> As virtuous men passe mildly away,
>   And whisper to their soules, to goe,
> Whilst some of their sad friends doe say,
>   The breath goes now, and some say, no :
>
> So let us melt, and make no noise,
>   No teare-floods, nor sigh-tempests move,
> T'were prophanation of our joyes
>   To tell the layetie our love.
>
> Moving of th' earth brings harmes and feares,
>   Men reckon what it did and meant,
> But trepidation of the spheares,
>   Though greater farre, is innocent.
>
> Dull sublunary lovers love
>   (Whose soule is sense) cannot admit
> Absence, because it doth remove
>   Those things which elemented it.
>
> But we by a love, so much refin'd,
>   That our selves know not what it is,
> Inter-assured of the mind,
>   Care lesse, eyes, lips, and hands to misse.
>
> Our two soules therefore, which are one,
>   Though I must goe, endure not yet
> A breach, but an expansion,
>   Like gold to ayery thinnesse beate.
>
> If they be two, they are two so
>   As stiffe twin compasses are two,
> Thy soule the fixt foot, makes no show
>   To move, but doth, if the' other doe.
>
> And though it in the center sit,
>   Yet when the other far doth rome,
> It leanes, and hearkens after it,
>   And growes erect, as that comes home.

> Such wilt thou be to mee, who must
> Like th' other foot, obliquely runne;
> Thy firmnes makes my circle just,
> And makes me end, where I begunne.

The simile of the compasses, notwithstanding its quaintness, is more perfect in its kind, and more beautiful, than any thing we are acquainted with. Perhaps the above is the only poem we could extract, that is not disfigured by *any* of the characteristic faults of Donne. Several of them have, however, very few. The following is one of these. It has an air of serious gaiety about it, as if it had been composed in the very bosom of bliss. The versification, too, is perfect. It is called, 'The good-morrow'.

> I wonder by my troth, what thou, and I
> Did, till we lov'd? were we not wean'd till then?
> But suck'd on countrey pleasures childishly?
> Or snorted we in the seaven sleepers den?
> T'was so; But this, all pleasures fancies bee.
> If ever any beauty I did see,
> Which I desir'd, and got, t'was but a dreame of thee.
>
> And now good morrow to our waking soules,
> Which watch not one another out of feare;
> For love, all love of other sights controules,
> And makes one little roome, an every where.
> Let sea-discoverers to new worlds have gone,
> Let Maps to other, worlds on worlds have showne,
> Let us possesse one world, each hath one, and is one.
>
> My face in thine eye, thine in mine appeares,
> And true plain hearts doe in the faces rest,
> Where can we finde two better hemispheares,
> Without sharpe North, without declining West?
> What ever dyes was not mixt equally;
> If our two loves be one, or, thou and I
> Love so alike, that none doe slacken, none can die.

. . . The reader will not fail to observe the occasional obscurities which arise out of the extreme condensation of expression in the foregoing pieces, and in most of those which follow. These passages may always be unravelled by a little attention, and they seldom fail to repay the trouble bestowed upon them. But they must be regarded as unequivocal faults nevertheless.

The following is, doubtless, 'high-fantastical', in the last degree; but it is fine notwithstanding, and an evidence of something more than mere ingenuity.

> Let me powre forth
> My teares before thy face, whil'st I stay here,
> For thy face coines them, and thy stampe they bear,
> And by this Mintage they are something worth,
> For thus they bee
> Pregnant of thee;
> Fruits of much griefe they are, emblemes of more,
> When a teare falls, that thou falst which it bore,
> So thou and I are nothing then, when on a divers shore.

> On a round ball
> A workeman that hath copies by, can lay
> An Europe, Afrique, and an Asia,
> And quickly make that, which was nothing, *All,*
> So doth each teare,
> Which thee doth weare,
> A globe, yea world by that impression grow,
> Till thy teares mixt with mine doe overflow
> This world, by waters sent from thee, my heaven dissolved so.

> O more then Moone,
> Draw not up seas to drowne me in thy spheare,
> Weepe me not dead, in thine armes, but forbeare
> To teach the sea, what it may doe too soone;
> Let not the winde
> Example finde,
> To doe me more harme, then it purposeth;
> Since thou and I sigh one another's breath,
> Who e'r sighes most, is cruellest, and hasts the others death.

The feelings which dictated such poetry as this, (for it *is* poetry, and nothing but real feelings *could* dictate it,) must have pierced deeper than the surface of both the heart and the imagination. In fact, they wanted nothing but to have been excited under more favourable circumstances, to have made them well-springs of the richest poetry uttering itself in the rarest words. . . .

The following piece, entitled 'The Funerall', is fantastical and far-fetched to be sure; but it is very fine nevertheless. The comparison of the nerves and the braid of hair, and anticipating similar effects from each, could never have entered the thoughts of any one but Donne; still less could any one have made it *tell* as he has done. The piece is altogether an admirable and most interesting example of his style.

> Who ever comes to shroud me, do not harme
>   Nor question much
> That subtile wreath of haire, which crowns my arme;
> The mystery, the signe you must not touch,
>   For 'tis my outward Soule,
> Viceroy to that, which then to heaven being gone,
>   Will leave this to controule,
> And keepe these limbes, her Provinces, from dissolution.
>
> For if the sinewie thread my braine lets fall
>   Through every part,
> Can tye those parts, and make mee one of all;
> These haires which upward grew, and strength and art
>   Have from a better braine,
> Can better do' it; Except she meant that I
>   By this should know my pain,
> As prisoners then are manacled, when they are condemn'd to die.
>
> What ere shee meant by' it, bury it with me,
>   For since I am
> Loves martyr, it might breed idolatrie,
> If into others hands these Reliques came;
>   As 'twas humility
> To afford to it all that a Soule can doe,
>   So, 'tis some bravery,
> That since you would save none of mee, I bury some of you.

. . . The following (particularly the first stanza) seems to us to express even more than it is intended to express; which is very rarely the case with the productions of this writer. The love expressed by it is a love for the passion excited, rather than the object exciting it; it is a love that lives by '*chewing the cud* of sweet and bitter fancy,' rather than by hungering after fresh food – that broods, like the stock dove, over its own voice, and listens for no other – that is all sufficient to itself, and (like virtue) its own reward. . . .

> I never stoop'd so low, as they
> Which on an eye, cheeke, lip, can prey,
>   Seldome to them, which soare no higher
>   Then vertue or the minde to' admire,
> For sense, and understanding may
>   Know, what gives fuell to their fire :
> My love, though silly, is more brave,
> For may I misse, when ere I crave,
> If I know yet, what I would have.
>
> If that be simply perfectest
> Which can by no way be exprest
>   But *Negatives*, my love is so.
>   To All, which all love, I say no.
> If any who deciphers best,
>   What we know not, our selves, can know,
> Let him teach mee that nothing; This
> As yet my ease, and comfort is,
> Though I speed not, I cannot misse.

The whole of the foregoing extracts are taken from the first department of Donne's poetry – the Love-verses . . .

Of Donne's other poems, the Funeral Elegies, Epistles, Satires, and what he calls his 'Divine Poems,'' particularly the last named, we have little to say in the way of general praise . . .

S O U R C E : *Retrospective Review* (1823).

N O T E

In 'Donne's Poetry in the Nineteenth Century' (see Select Bibliography), Kathleen Tillotson conjectures that the essay from which this extract is taken was written by Thomas Noon Talford; in *Bibliography of John Donne* (1958), Sir Geoffrey Keynes attributes it to J. Spence. As far as I am aware, there is still no substantial evidence in either or any other direction.

George Saintsbury

. . . To my fancy no division of Donne's poems – 'The Second Anniversarie' always excepted – shows him in his quiddity and essence as do the lyrics. Some of these are to a certain extent doubtful. One of the very finest of the whole, 'Absence, hear thou my protestation', with its unapproached fourth stanza, appeared first in Davison's *Poetical Rhapsody* unsigned. But all the best authorities agree (and for my part I would almost go to the stake on it) that the piece is Donne's. In those which are undoubtedly genuine the peculiar quality of Donne flames through and perfumes the dusky air which is his native atmosphere in a way which, though I do not suppose that the French poet had ever heard of Donne, has always seemed to me the true antitype and fulfilment by anticipation of Baudelaire's.

> Encensoir oublié qui fume
> En silence à travers la nuit.

Everybody knows the

> Bracelet of bright haire about the bone

of the late discovered skeleton, identifying the lover : everybody the perfect fancy and phrase of the exordium

> I long to talke with some old lovers ghost,
> Who dyed before the god of Love was borne

But similar touches are almost everywhere. The enshrining once for all in the simplest words of a universal thought

> I wonder by my troth, what thou, and I
> Did, till we lov'd ?

The selection of single adjectives to do the duty of a whole train of surplusage

> Where can we finde two better hemispheares
> Without *sharpe* North, without *declining* West?

meet us, and tell us what we have to expect in all but the earliest.
In comparison with these things, such a poem as 'Goe, and catche
a falling starre', delightful as it is, is perhaps only a delightful
quaintness, and 'The Indifferent' only a pleasant quip consum-
mately turned. In these perversities Donne is but playing *tours de
force*. His natural and genuine work reappears in such poems as
'The Canonization', or as 'The Legacie'. It is the fashion sometimes, and that not always with the worst critics, to dismiss this
kind of heroic rapture as an agreeable but conscious exaggeration,
partly betrayed and partly condoned by flouting-pieces like those
just mentioned. The gloss does not do the critic's knowledge of
human nature or his honesty in acknowledging his knowledge
much credit. Both moods and both expressions are true; but the
rapture is the truer. No one who sees in these mere literary or
fashionable exercises, can ever appreciate such an *aubade* as 'Stay,
O sweet, and do not rise', or such a midnight piece as 'The
Dreame', with its never-to-be-forgotten couplet

> I must confesse, it could not chuse but bee
> Prophane, to thinke thee any thing but thee.

If there is less quintessence in 'The Message', for all its beauty, it
is only because no one can stay long at the point of rapture which
characterizes Donne at his most characteristic, and the relaxation
is natural – as natural as is the pretty face about St Lucy

> Who scarce seaven houres herself unmaskes,

the day under her invocation being in the depths of December. But
the passionate mood, or that of mystical reflection, soon returns,
and in the one Donne shall sing with another of the wondrous
phrases where simplicity and perfection meet

> So to'entergraft our hands, as yet
> Was all the meanes to make us one,
> And pictures in our eyes to get
> Was all our propagation.

Or in the other dwell on the hope of buried lovers

> To make their soules, at the last busie day,
> Meet at this grave, and make a little stay.

I am not without some apprehension that I shall be judged to have fallen a victim to my own distinction, drawn at the beginning of this paper, and shown myself an unreasonable lover of this astonishing poet. Yet I think I could make good my appeal in any competent critical court. For in Donne's case the yea-nay fashion of censorship which is necessary and desirable in the case of others is quite superfluous. His faults are so gross, so open, so palpable, that they hardly require the usual amount of critical comment and condemnation. But this very peculiarity of theirs constantly obscures his beauties even to not unfit readers. They open him; they are shocked, or bored, or irritated, or puzzled by his occasional nastiness (for he is now and then simply and inexcusably nasty), his frequent involution and eccentricity, his not quite rare indulgence in extravagances which go near to silliness; and so they lose the extraordinary beauties which lie beyond or among these faults. It is true that, as was said above, there are those, and many of them, who can never and will never like Donne. No one who thinks *Don Quixote* a merely funny book, no one who sees in Aristophanes a dirty-minded fellow with a knack of Greek versification, no one who thinks it impossible not to wish that Shakespeare had not written the Sonnets, no one who wonders what on earth Giordano Bruno meant by *Gli eroici Furori,* need trouble himself even to attempt to like Donne. 'He will never *have done* with that attempt', as our Dean himself would have unblushingly observed, for he was never weary of punning on his name.

But for those who have experienced, or who at least understand, the ups-and-downs, the ins-and-outs of human temperament, the alternations not merely of passion and satiety, but of passion and laughter, of passion and melancholy reflection, of passion earthly enough and spiritual rapture almost heavenly, there is no poet and hardly any writer like Donne. They may even be tempted to see in the strangely mixed and flawed character of his style, an index and reflection of the variety and the rapid changes of his thought and feeling. To the praise of the highest poetical art he cannot indeed lay claim. He is of course entitled to the benefit of the pleas that it is uncertain whether he ever prepared definitely for the press a single poetical work of his; that it is certain that his age regarded his youth with too much disapproval to bestow any critical care on his youthful poems. But it may be retorted that no one with the finest sense of poetry as an art, could have left things so formless as he has left, that it would have been intolerable pain and grief to any such till he had got them, even in MS., into shape. The retort is valid. But if Donne cannot receive the praise due to the accomplished poetical artist, he has that not perhaps higher but certainly rarer, of the inspired poetical creator. No study could have bettered – I hardly know whether any study could have produced – such touches as the best of those which have been quoted, and as many which perforce have been left out. And no study could have given him the idiosyncrasy which he has. 'Nos passions', says Bossuet, 'ont quelque chose d'infini'. To express infinity no doubt is a contradiction in terms. But no poet has gone nearer to the hinting and adumbration of this infinite quality of passion, and of the relapses and reactions from passion, than the author of 'The second Anniversarie' and 'The Dreame', of 'The Relique' and 'The Extasie'.

S O U R C E : Introduction to E. K. Chambers (ed.), *The Poems of John Donne* (1896).

Anonymous

FROM JOHN DONNE AND HIS CONTEMPORARIES (1900)

... When we try to trace any literary habit to its origin, we generally find that the pedigree is longer than we had supposed. To all appearance, the manner of writing which prevailed at the end of the sixteenth and the beginning of the seventeenth century was a sudden growth. There is nothing like it in the earlier literature of England. If we compare English mediæval romance or poetry with that of France or Provence, we find monotonous imagery, a narrow circle of incident, commonplaces of sentiment, and an almost complete absence of poetic skill. The object of the poetry is to tell again some chivalrous story which has been told already in French, to express the feelings of religious devotion, or to satirise the drones, leeches, and foxes who live at the labourer's cost. Chaucer is a notable exception; but he is almost the only exception to the rule of mediocrity. English literature as a whole was unborn till the sixteenth century, when, in the mental awakening which attends the opening of wider horizons, the nation became aware that it possessed an instrument of music capable of all and perhaps more than all that had been effected by the cultured tongues of the South. The first streams of the 'wide river of speech' were more copious than pure.

Without detailing a catalogue of names, we may say that English reached perfection – we do not say this in disparagement of its later expansion – in Hooker and Spenser, both of whom had too much to say to set their manner above their matter. Both are skilful

---

The article of which this is an extract is primarily a review of *The Life and Letters of John Donne* by Edmund Gosse (1899). The authorship of the article is not certain, but it is possible that J. A. Symonds wrote it.

in the use of words, but both know how to 'disclose a brave neglect'. Hooker's style was fed from Greek and Latin sources, early
and late, for he had no disdain for Christian Greek and Latin;
having at his command a rich treasury of words, he did not scruple
to invent new words when he needed them. He could use long sen-
tences and short with equal skill, could be dry and exact, or rhetorical and flowing, as his subject demanded. Conceits are not un-
known to him, but his style does not depend upon them. His
influence upon the English language takes effect after the Jaco-
bean-Caroline period, and it made little impression upon his own
age. Spenser is modelled upon Ariosto and Tasso for the treatment
of his subject, and to some extent for the copiousness and rapidity
of his style. For language he is much beholden to Chaucer. His
manner is clear, direct, and fluent; he does not despise quaintness
of language and recondite images; but his business is to get on with
his story, and he has no time to spend upon refinements. He had
better metal in his brain than 'a mint of phrases,' and cared more
for a high matter in low words than for a low matter in high
words.[1] He adopted the high romantic Italian manner, not that of
the Italian prose writers, whose affection, somewhat unskilfully
imitated by the Euphuists, poisoned the sources of pure English for
two generations, till Milton, Clarendon, and Barrow turned the
stream back into its proper channel.

The merits of the Jacobean style are nicety of thought, clearness
and conciseness of diction, apt illustration, the just use of conceits,
learned allusions not too far-fetched, whether images or verbal
felicities, 'jewels five words long', lines and short passages which
could not be bettered. The faults of the style are obvious; and the
most serious of them is an affectation which runs into insincerity.
The thought is often subordinate to the manner; and, when too
much attention is given to manner and expression, prettiness takes
the place of solidity.

But the Jacobean writers do not fully enter into the succession
of poets. They lie in a quiet back-water out of the main river, receiving and retaining its water, but not setting the current. We
leave Shakespeare out of this survey. Shakespeare was not a stylist
or a theorist : he accepted all as it came, rejected what was base,
enriched all and glorified all, leaving no rules of art but his own
inimitable example. His influence is too immense and universal to

be brought into a succession of poets. After Shakespeare poetry had a new birth, and poets breathed a different air. We have only to imagine what Milton would have been without Shakespeare, to feel the truth of this.

Mr Gosse, who acknowledges a large debt to Dr Jessopp, has, in his *Life and Letters of John Donne,* thrown much light upon a commanding figure in an interesting age : an age and a subject to which he has given years of study. A 'Life of Donne' was wanted, and Mr Gosse's book does not disappoint us. He has done what he set out to do, 'to present a portrait of Donne as a man and an author'. The portrait cannot but attract attention, even if we fail to recognize some details. We agree with Mr Gosse in looking upon the new influence which for a time changed the direction of English literature as 'malign', whether or not it was pre-eminently due to Donne's influence. It was 'malign' because Euphuism and its Jacobean development brought in the exaggerated pursuit of words, phrases, and conceits beyond their true value, established a new and affected criterion of taste, and in general displayed a preference of matter to manner. 'Great thoughts', says Johnson, 'are always general'. It was the fault of the Euphuistic or, as Johnson styles it, the 'metaphysical' school that it is always occupied with particulars. The poets of this school left the great general thoughts to the Elizabethans. They had had enough of them, and wanted something new – sauces, not meats, they might have said; but human nature goes back with relish to the meats.

Towards the end of the sixteenth century a double influence is observable in European literature. Pedantry was taking the place of learning. The fresh springs of the Renaissance movement had dried up. The soil of ancient Rome had yielded its first crop of statues : Greek manuscripts were no longer to be found in the libraries of East or West. The living world had learnt as much as it wanted to know about the ancients, and left the study of antiquity to the dead world of pedants, those who think knowledge to be the end of knowledge. The scholars now became a class apart from the dilettante circles; from Bembo to Casaubon is as great a social decline as it is an ascent in learning; and where there was one Casaubon there were a hundred professional scholars, doing good and useful work, but work rather scientific than literary – slaves of the lamp of truth, not servants of beauty. The active and speculative intellect of the world took a new line of enquiry, which was marked out by the triumphs of Galileo, Bacon, and Harvey. Speculative philosophy and astronomical and anatomical discovery now held the field, and experimental science impugned authority. The tendency of the age was to investigate rarities and novelties in a scientific spirit; and this habit found its way into literature. Authority, however, had not said its last word, either in theology or in science : the scholastic method was dying, not dead. Real scientific enquiry was strangely mixed up with the study of the Cabbalists, the Schoolmen, Aristotle, Pliny, and Galen – authority and experiment forced into harmony. Occult speculations were confounded with observation of realities : nothing was improbable if it fitted in with a paradox or a parallel. Analogy was now pushed to its extreme; a mystical sense was perceived in natural phenomena; it became the fashion to seek out resemblances and to argue from them. In particular, anatomical facts and theories were adduced as analogies and made the groundwork of argument. The attention of writers was withdrawn from the contemplation of beauty, and diverted to the novelties of science, from large conceptions of nature to minute observations of detail.

This was in itself a declension from the proper objects of poetry; and along with it came in one of the common characteristics of a decadence, an exaggerated attention to form and diction, and the sentimentality which naturally accompanies the search for novelty. The great writers have always been artists in words, and have never thought lightly of the technique of their business; but it is one of the surest signs of a decadence to set the word above the thing signified, and to heighten effect by strangeness. We have heard enough of the *mot propre* and the *mot unique*; and we may see in the confessions of so strong a writer as Stevenson how the pursuit of it hampered his genius, and how its capture sometimes gives his exquisite writing a sense of effort. Imitation – and not of the best authors – was another characteristic of this age. The moderns copied from each other, and the Latin which they all admired and imitated was that of Petronius and Apuleius, not the Ciceronian. There is no fault to be found with Barclay's 'Argenis' and 'Euphormio' in point of Latinity; his popularity is witnessed by edition after edition from the Elzevir press; but what we look for in an author is something from himself, and here is nothing but an echo. Another characteristic was parade of learning. In our own time there is more knowledge abroad in the world, but less learning. The reading public is larger, but less instructed. A writer like Burton or Jeremy Taylor would not get a hearing now. We like literature which represents the current thought of the day, not the literature of museums and libraries and commonplace books. In the reign of James I to be learned was the first thing; to be original without reflection of antiquity was out of taste.

It is impossible to say who set the fashion : it was in the air. It has been attributed to Góngora and the Gongorists, Marini and the Marinists, Ronsard and the Pleiad, Du Bartas, Lyly; but Hallam's characterisation of it as 'an unintelligible refinement, which every nation in Europe seems in succession to have admitted into its poetry',[2] may serve both as a description of the phenomenon and as a note of its date, though not of its cause. The vice which corrupted the literature of this age is, in a word, pedantry, literary, classical, and scientific : the dragging of incongruous qualities and mannerisms into the service of poetry. The pedantry of conceits affected even the great Elizabethan poets, but it was not raised into a principal merit till the latter years of the reign. England was always backward in the race : France, Italy, and Spain were far gone in pedantry before the reign of conceits began in England. Elizabeth's personal influence was not without effect in setting the fashion; her own style – always affected – became later more involved and Euphuistic; and the court language, following the fashion, blossomed into conceits richer and rarer, from the sobriety of Burleigh's times to the exuberance of Speaker Phelips under James I, who was himself one of the most tedious of Euphuists.

Lyly is sober compared with some of his successors. His similes and analogies are out of proportion to their matter, but in themselves they are not usually extravagant or absurd. What makes him distasteful now is that there is little thought or novelty of conception; and the quaintness and copiousness of illustration are fatiguing. Burton keeps up our interest by perpetual novelty and recondite allusions, and Jeremy Taylor by richness of learning and by the powerful thought which it sets off; Lyly is generally tame, and often timid. But it is not difficult to understand how he charmed a society which had tired of flowing numbers, and was beginning to value grace and continuity beyond solidity.

Mr Gosse sets down the 'malign' influence of the new fashion almost entirely to Donne. We should rather have said that Donne followed the fashion already introduced, and gave it the weight of his authority. So great a change is rarely brought about by one writer, especially a writer whose works became known to his contemporaries chiefly as manuscripts passed from hand to hand around a circle of friends. Shakespeare shows how genius can turn the current style to its own uses; Donne, with all his gravity, learning, and passion, imagines nothing beyond the current style. Shakespeare wrote many lines which Donne might have written, and now and then Donne writes like Shakespeare himself. For instance, in the well-known lines –

> her pure and eloquent blood
> Spoke in her cheekes, and so distinctly wrought,
> That one might almost say, her body thought –

he uses the symbolical method in perfection, and enriches a true thought by a beautiful image. Donne's influence no doubt was great; that it was not irresistible we may conclude from the fact that when he set himself to break up smooth versification by new rules of accent, and to depart from the natural iambic of his predecessors, he was not able to effect a revolution; nor was he successful in using the instrument which he had invented.

Other poets of his day, and Shakespeare among them, adopted the suggestion, and Milton's versification owes much to the boldness with which he trusted to balance and weight of syllables rather than to the orderly sequence of accents. But the next generation returned to smoothness, and Donne's experiment was not developed so as to become the character of a school. Donne founded no school; he did not invent conceits; he did not establish a new school of versification. He remains alone; a writer of originality, not the pioneer of poets to be.

If it is true that Donne, as Mr Gosse thinks, felt no admiration or even curiosity in the presence of his great contemporaries, so much the worse for Donne. We will not do his memory the injustice to believe that he had no ears for Spenser and Shakespeare. We can see nothing in his poetry to justify Mr Gosse's theory that Donne, 'as a metrical iconoclast, would have neither part nor lot'

with the old Elizabethan school of Petrarchical poets. The liberties which Donne took with the English language and traditional
prosody occur, for the most part, in the satires, in which he was
imitating the roughness of the Latin satirists; and, as Mr Gosse
allows, this 'experiment' was dropped by Donne after middle life.
It was an experiment; it was not copied by his admirers; perhaps
we should never have heard of it if Milton had not admired something of Donne's principles of rhythm into the structure of his un-
matched blank verse, stateliest of all measures next to Virgil's.

As for Donne's use of metaphors, the realism which made him
(as Mr Gosse says) 'draw his illustrations, not from asphodel or
from the moon', like the Petrarchists, 'but from the humdrum professional employments of his own age, from chemistry, medicine,
law, mechanics, astrology, religious ritual, daily human business of
every sort', in this again Donne was not original. He did not use
the style of his time, a time which liked parade of learning. It is all
in Burton (who was senior to Donne), in ceremonial and Parlia-
mentary speeches, in the diaries of Sir Symonds d'Ewes, and in
pamphlets, letters, and sermons by the dozen. It was neither invented nor brought into currency by Donne or any other single authority. It is the later Euphuism; the Euphuism not of Euphues, but
of the Piercie Shaftons and Armados who buzzed round the king
of pedants, the English Solomon himself.

The 'metaphysical poets' have never been so finely criticised as
by Johnson, who invented the phrase; not a very happy phrase,
perhaps, for their skill lay rather in exciting wonder than in stimu-
lating or expressing thought. Any of our readers who will take the
trouble to turn to the *Lives of the Poets* will find in the biography
of Cowley all that can be said on the subject.

Of wit [says Johnson] thus defined [*i.e. discordia concors,* combination
of dissimilars, or discovery of likeness in unlikeness] they have more
than enough. The most heterogeneous ideas are yoked by violence together; nature and art are ransacked for illustrations, comparisons,
and allusions; their learning instructs and their subtilty surprises;
but the reader commonly thinks his improvement dearly bought, and
though he sometimes admires, is seldom pleased.

The vices of the school are oppressive learning, excessive particu-
larity, and the combination of incongruous ideas by false analogy.

Now and then they flash out a ray of splendid wit. Such lines as those of Donne on the 'twin compasses' cannot be surpassed; it would be hard if the labour of much rocking never brought to light a nugget of pure gold. The workmanship, if always laboured, is often successful; 'limæ labor et mora' deserves and sometimes receives its reward; and no poets have ever filed more industriously than these. It is a literature of art and erudition, not of nature : natural graces may be found there, because nature will out; but the poet values tricks of art more than the thoughts which his art expresses. Jacobean poetry in this resembles Provençal poetry, though, unlike that, it does not care for smoothness and perfection; it should have studied perfection of form, not only neatness of wit. The Jacobean poets might have learnt of Martial, who combined the perfection of wit with elegiac sweetness equal if not superior to the versification of Ovid himself. Martial among the ancients and La Fontaine among the moderns possess the secret beyond all others.

Euphuism, as the term is generally understood, is the result of over-attention to words; an affected, unnatural style, which conceals poverty of invention under a show of learning, and (as Johnson says) wishes rather to surprise than to please. Lyly himself was not a Euphuist in the sense of a seeker after strangeness and affectation; his conceits are of an obvious sort, and his language is that of common life. Sidney introduced a style of which Euphuism is the exaggeration. He did not sacrifice everything to wit. His descriptions, laboured in diction, and tedious from prolixity, are only affected as they are over-learned, self-conscious, and sentimental. They are Italian, not English : if translated into Italian they would be like the writings of the Italian novelists, and they would go very well into Italian; the roughness and manliness of our native English suits them ill, and this alone accuses them of a false taste. They ought to flow in smooth-sliding polysyllables; the imitation of Italian melodies is unsuccessful. Sidney took a wrong direction in literature, and the *Arcadia,* after all, is a curiosity rather than a classic.

Like the Jacobean architecture, Jacobean literature charms by delicacy and originality of detail, but cannot rise to large conceptions. A Jacobean monument, a row of cathedral stalls, such a gem as the Gate of Honour at Cambridge, is delightful in its small way,

but ineffective if compared with a Palladian building or a church
designed by Michael Angelo or Sansovino. A lengthy poem like
Donne's 'Progress of the Soul' is unreadable; but little poems such
as Carew's 'Boldness in Love' are perfection itself. Perhaps Donne
never achieved a higher flight of poetry than in his 'Testament'.
It is as good as that grand poem 'The Lye', which has claimed as
many authors as Homer had birthplaces. It is dignified, bitter,
almost sublime, and yet witty too. When we read this, we understand how Carew could say of him :

> Here lies a King, that rul'd as hee thought fit
> The universall Monarchy of wit.

When we remember that Shakespeare was living at the same time,
how slight appears the account of contemporary fame!

The personality of Donne is quite as interesting as his literary
position. A licentious youth and a politic maturity, in which he
became mixed up with questionable patrons and more than questionable dealings, led to his taking Holy Orders, apparently with no
very holy purpose. His hesitation at this parting of the ways, and
his refusal of a good living offered him by Thomas Morton, the
Dean of Gloucester, are evidences of sincerity. But neither when
he left the Church of Rome nor when he became a priest in the
Church of England is there any record of a conversion, unless Ben
Jonson's 'repenteth highly' and Walton's 'his penitential years' are
to be taken literally. No greater contrast can be than that between
Donne's adoption of the clerical profession and George Herbert's
devotion of himself to the ministry. Donne apparently took Orders
because James I desired it, and not without a view to Church preferment. Herbert, when he put on his 'canonical coat', destroyed
his early poems, and dedicated himself to a saintly life, deliberately rejecting brilliant court prospects and the certainty of rising
to the highest places.

> Whereas my birth and spirit rather took
> The way that takes the town,
> Thou didst betray me to a lingering book,
> And wrap me in a gown.

There is no looking back, no hankering after court flesh-pots : the
sacrifice is complete and without regret.

The parallel suggested by Izaak Walton between Donne and Herbert must be given up. It goes no further than the resemblance between their fortunes as courtiers and scholars turned Churchmen. There is no fervour in Donne's conversion to the Anglican communion, and no self-immolation in his dedication to the ministry. Donne's nature was above all intellectual : the question between Rome and England interested him more as a problem of theology and politics than as a vital question of life and practice. His letters written about the time of his change in 1609 (some of the most interesting in Mr Gosse's book) throw light on his motives, and in our judgment remove him from suspicion of time-service. A man may change his religion upon considerations of reasonable truth, or of authority perceived, or of security, or of fitness and convenience, if he thinks little of externals. Donne had seen enough of English Catholics to be aware that it was not easy to be a good subject of James I in their company. This was a sufficient motive for a change, if it could be justified *in foro conscientiæ*; and in matters of conscience Donne's turn of mind was more allied to the cynicism with which all public men of those days were tainted than to the scruples of a soul faint from wrestling with itself.

A statesman like Wotton, who knew the workings of Continental catholicism, would have drawn a broad line between Rome and the Protestant bodies, considering the latter as engaged together in one cause; so too would nine out of ten Englishmen; only the High Anglicans of Little Gidding and Peterhouse would have been shy of Lutherans and Calvinists. Donne's sympathies were those of a philosopher, and embraced all creeds. In one of his letters he weighs the consideration whether the Pope has not as good a right to claim spiritual supremacy as the King temporal, each being the only judge of his prerogative. In another letter, which is that of an honest man, a clear thinker, and a politician, he says :

You know I never fettered nor imprisoned the word Religion, not straightening it friarly, *ad religiones factitias* (as the Romans call well their Orders of Religion), nor immuring it in a Rome, a Wittemberg, or a Geneva [he might have added 'a Lambeth']; they are all virtual beams of one Sun, and wheresoever they find clay hearts, they harden them and moulder them into dust; and they entender and mollify waxen. They are not so contrary as the North and South Poles, and . . . they are co-natural pieces of one circle. Religion is Christianity, which being too spiritual to be seen by us, doth therefore take an apparent body of good life and works; so salvation requires an honest Christian.[3]

Not so Crashaw :

> What heaven-entreated heart is this
> Stands trembling at the gate of bliss? ...
> Whose definition is a doubt
> 'Twixt life and death, 'twixt in and out? ...
>
> Disband dull fears; give Faith the day;
> To save your life, kill your delay....
> Yield then, O yield, that Love may win
> The fort at last, and let Life in.

Not so Newman :

It is, indeed, a dreadful responsibility to act as I am doing; and I feel His hand heavy on me without intermission, Who is all wisdom and love, so that my mind and heart are tired out, just as the limbs might be from a load on one's back; that sort of dull aching pain is mine.[4]

Such thoughts as these may have been in Donne's mind; but they do not appear in his writings, and we may doubt whether his nature was so transfused with religious feeling as to be capable of them. Donne was a great wit, but neither a great poet nor a great saint, for all Izaak Walton's praises. Mr Gosse is an iconoclast. He shows us how untrustworthy Walton's portrait painting is; how he smoothed over incongruities and heightened beauties, producing by his magical art harmonies which existed only in his imagination, playing freely with dates and names, and making all serve the purpose of ideal portraiture. Mr Gosse's picture is more accurate; but we have lost our Donne, and have to imagine a new Donne, a more interesting but less attractive personage, a problem in morality, not a model of Anglican Churchmanship. Mr Gosse shows us no combination of sage and saint, but a full-blooded, secularly-minded man, a seeker after honour and money, not over-scrupulous in suing for the favour of the great; a bold adventurer, too eager for advancement to boggle at trifles; a friend of

Essex so long as he lasted, but leaving him when his companion-
ship and patronage became dangerous; courting the vile Somerset when his star was in the ascendant, and all but implicated
in some of the darkest episodes of his career; needy and covetous,
burdened with an increasing family, and suggesting that funerals
would bring him relief if he could find money to pay for them; then
under pressure from the King taking upon him the vows of priest-
hood, and becoming a court divine. There is nothing venerable or
even respectable in all this. But the reputation in which the Dean
of Paul's lived and died, the names and credit of his friends, and
above all the witness of his own pen make us believe that he was
no hypocrite. We must take Walton's evidence, at the lowest esti-
mate, for no less than what it is worth; and Walton chose his
subjects because he believed in them. We may surmise that Donne
never ceased to have worldly interests without concluding that
he had no heavenly aspirations.

It is a difficult problem to harmonize what repels and what
attracts in so complex a character. One is tempted to wonder
whether Donne did not leave his own character as one of the riddles
which he wished posterity to solve. At any rate, the ghost of Donne
would take pleasure in the thought that the moderns do not know
whether to set him, with Walton, at the side of George Herbert, or,
with Mr Gosse, in the questionable society of Bacon and Somerset.
The child's question, 'Was he a good man or a bad man?' cannot
in this case be easily and simply answered.

Donne's undoubted pre-eminence among the wits of his time
was probably in some measure due to his credit at court, at a time
when the court was more than it ever was before or since; and in
some measure to a mysteriousness which Donne affected. His fasti-
diousness shrouded itself in enigma. He was not a simple-minded
man, and he did not wish to be thought so. We can conceive that
Donne may have thought Wotton superficial, Herbert misplaced,
Jonson a pedant, Shakespeare a mad wag, Herrick a rustic, Drummond a Scotchman, Hales – he must have liked Hales better than
the rest, as being also an enigma. One would like to know what was
the society which his wit and learning illuminated. The Dean of
Paul's could not attend such a Session of the Poets as was held a
generation earlier at the 'Mermaid'. His choicest company must
have met at the Deanery, where his table was doubtless furnished

with good talk, like Wotton's at Eton. He was known to his friends as a delightful host, to the wits as a poet and epigrammatist of high pretensions, to the world in general as a preacher.

Those were the days of the sermon. The theatre, the club, the Tusculan villa, the Academy of Athens or Florence, the Porch, the *salon,* have in their different methods and degrees supplied a focus in which human speech may be concentrated and sifted of its commonplaces. In our time the power of the spoken word is at its lowest. Our public speakers address themselves to the newspapers, and it is only now and then that an orator has the opportunity of stirring a great assemblage of presence, language, voice, and action as Gladstone and Bright could do. The drum ecclesiastic has ceased to sound war's alarms, and no one takes the trouble to tune the pulpits. Our preachers hold forth to Laodicean congregations; the article and the fugitive note put into an attractive and digestible form what might be our thoughts if we had time to think; and, as Plato says, the art which finds favour now is that of the cook or the maker of sauces and sweetmeats.

In Donne's time the sermon was a grave reality. Old men were living who could remember the Smithfield fires, and Alva's hecatombs were fresh in memory. The Gunpowder Plot and the assassinations of William the Silent and Henry of Navarre were recent or contemporary events. The danger from Spain and Rome was no chimera. The clergy had not lost their right of speaking with authority. The Members of Parliament came into St Margaret's with 'their little pocket-Bibles with gilt edges' (as Selden said), prepared to judge the preacher, but also to listen to him as their teacher. The weekly sermon, an hour or more long, was an intellectual exercise supplying food for thought, a purging of conscience, a study of rhetoric, a parade-ground of erudition, and a political fact. It corresponded, on a public stage, to the private prayer-meetings, lectures, discussions, searchings of conscience, and Scriptural exercises which made up so much of the serious life of the times – times in which secular business, and pre-eminently politics, were based upon religion, or at least were conceived in terms of religion. The monarchy of Charles I and the usurpation of Cromwell were upset by sermons, achieving results at which they did not aim. Hugh Peters and the Blackfriars conventicles were powers to be reckoned with, and addressed themselves directly to a larger body of public opinion than Pym and Hampden, whose speeches were not reported and are better known to us than to their contemporaries. The pamphlet was the only intellectual power which could compare with the pulpit.

To be the chief preacher of his day, as Donne was, was a great position and a great responsibility, and Donne must have known that the pulpit of St Paul's raised him higher in the eyes of the world than a chair at a tavern or a seat at the Lord Keeper's dinner-table. His sermons were not political, but to those who listened to them they were a training in sound thinking, as well as an excursion into regions of profound learning and high literature. They cannot be read now except by students. To us they are abstract essays, full indeed of masculine thought, but full also of recondite allusion and wearisome subtlety. But there was a time when they were alive, not lucubrations of the study, but direct addresses to a congregation; political and ethical realities, not the dreamy disquisitions of a pedant.

However set off [says Donne's successor, Dean Milman[5]], as by all accounts they were, by a most graceful and impressive delivery, it is astonishing to us that he should hold a London congregation enthralled, unwearied, unsatiated. Yet there can be no doubt that this was the case. And this congregation consisted both of the people down to the lowest, and the most noble, wise, accomplished of that highly intellectual age. They sate, even stood, undisturbed, except by their own murmurs of admiration, sometimes by hardly suppressed tears. One of Donne's poetical panegyrists writes :

> And never were we wearied till we saw
> The hour, and but an hour, to end did draw.

We must understand, then, in appreciating the measure of Donne's ascendency, that he must not be judged only as a man of letters by the value of his poems, but as a man speaking with authority, who knew his place and his power, and never undervalued it. This consideration will give him a higher position in our judgment than if we think of him merely as a factor in literature.

By his position, his character, and his peculiar genius Donne whilst living occupied a larger place among men of letters than later times have given him. Mr Gosse labours to restore this place to him : but the verdict is given and will hardly be reversed on appeal. Dryden wished that he could be 'translated into numbers and English, and complained that even so he would want 'dignity of expression'. Ben Jonson 'esteemed him the first poet in the world in some things', and set him 'first, and far from all second', among the 'Anacreontic lyrics' and epigrammatists, but said withal that 'for not keeping accent, he deserved hanging'. Donne will be studied by a few, and remain an interesting figure to many who do not study him; but for our pleasure we shall read Herrick. . . .

SOURCE: *Quarterly Review* (1900).

NOTES

1. Armado in *Love's Labour Lost*, I, i.
2. *Literature of Europe*, part II, chap. V, vol. II, p. 117.
3. Gosse, vol. I, p. 226.
4. *Letters*, vol. II, p. 465.
5. *Annals of St Paul's*, p. 328.

Herbert Grierson

... Objections to admit the poetic worth and interest of Donne's love-poetry come from two sides – from those who are indisposed to admit that passion, and especially the passion of love, can ever speak so ingeniously (this was the eighteenth-century criticism); and from those, and these are his more modern critics, who deny that Donne is a great poet because with rare exceptions, exceptions rather of occasional lines and phrases than of whole poems, his songs and elegies lack beauty. Can poetry be at once passionate and ingenious, sincere in feeling and witty – packed with thought, and that subtle and abstract thought, scholastic dialectic? Can love-poetry speak a language which is impassioned and expressive but lacks beauty, is quite different from the language of Dante and Petrarch, the loveliest language that lovers ever spoke, or the picturesque hyperboles of *Romeo and Juliet*? Must not the imagery and the cadences of love poetry reflect 'l'infinita, ineffabile bellezza' which is its inspiration?

The first criticism is put very clearly by Steele, who goes so far as to exemplify what the style of love-poetry should be; and certainly it is something entirely different from that of 'The Extasie' or the 'Nocturnall upon S. Lucies Day'. Nothing could illustrate better the 'return to nature' of our Augustan literature than Steele's words:

I will suppose an author to be really possessed with the passion which he writes upon and then we shall see how he would acquit himself. This I take to be the safest way to form a judgement upon him : since if he be not truly moved, he must at least work up his imagination as near as possible to resemble reality. I choose to instance in love, which is observed to have produced the most finished performances in this kind. A lover will be full of sincerity, that he may be believed by his mistress; he will therefore think simply; he will express himself perspicuously, that he may not perplex her; he will therefore write unaffectedly. Deep reflections are made by a head undisturbed; and points of wit and fancy are the work of a heart at ease; these two dangers then into which poets are apt to run, are effectually removed out of the lover's way. The selecting proper circumstances, and placing them in agreeable lights, are the finest secrets of all poetry; but the recollection of little circumstances is the lover's sole meditation, and relating them pleasantly, the business of his life. Accordingly we find that the most celebrated authors of this rank excel in love-verses. Out of ten thousand instances I shall name one which I think the most delicate and tender I ever saw.

> To myself I sigh often, without knowing why;
> And when absent from Phyllis methinks I could die.

A man who hath ever been in love will be touched by the reading of these lines; and everyone who now feels that passion, actually feels that they are true.

It is not possible to find so distinct a statement of the other view to which I have referred, but I could imagine it coming from Mr Robert Bridges, or (since I have no authority to quote Mr Bridges in this connexion) from an admirer of his beautiful poetry. Mr Bridges' love-poetry is far indeed from the vapid naturalness which Steele commended in *The Guardian*. It is as instinct with thought, and subtle thought, as Donne's own poetry; but the final effect of his poetry is beauty, emotion recollected in tranquillity, and recollected especially in order to fix its delicate beauty in appropriate and musical words:

> Awake, my heart, to be loved, awake, awake!
> The darkness silvers away, the morn doth break,
> It leaps in the sky : unrisen lustres slake
> The o'ertaken moon. Awake, O heart, awake!
>
> She too that loveth awaketh and hopes for thee;
> Her eyes already have sped the shades that flee,
> Already they watch the path thy feet shall take :
> Awake, O heart, to be loved, awake, awake!
>
> And if thou tarry from her, – if this could be, –
> She cometh herself, O heart, to be loved, to thee;
> For thee would unashamed herself forsake :
> Awake to be loved, my heart, awake, awake!

Awake, the land is scattered with light, and see,
Uncanopied sleep is flying from field and tree :
And blossoming boughs of April in laughter shake;
Awake, O heart, to be loved, awake, awake !

Lo all things wake and tarry and look for thee :
She looketh and saith, 'O sun, now bring him to me.
Come more adored, O adored, for his coming's sake,
And awake my heart to be loved : awake, awake !'

Donne has written nothing at once so subtle and so pure and lovely as this, nothing the end and aim of which is so entirely to leave an untroubled impression of beauty.

But it is not true either that the thought and imagery of love-poetry must be of the simple, obvious kind which Steele supposes, that any display of dialectical subtlety, any scintillation of wit, must be fatal to the impression of sincerity and feeling, or on the other hand that love is always a beautiful emotion naturally expressing itself in delicate and beautiful language. To some natures love comes as above all things a force quickening the mind, intensifying its purely intellectual energy, opening new vistas of thought abstract and subtle, making the soul 'intensely, wondrously alive'. Of such were Donne and Browning. A love-poem like 'Come into the garden, Maud' suspends thought and fills the mind with a succession of picturesque and voluptuous images in harmony with the dominant mood. A poem such as 'The Anniversarie' or 'The Extasie', 'The Last Ride Together' or 'Too Late', is a record of intense, rapid thinking, expressed in the simplest, most appropriate language – and it is a no whit less natural utterance of passion. Even the abstractness of the thought, on which Mr Courthope lays so much stress in speaking of Donne and the 'metaphysicals' generally, is no necessary implication of want of feeling. It has been said of St Augustine 'that his most profound thoughts regarding the first and last things arose out of prayer . . . concentration of his whole being in prayer led to the most abstract observation'. So it may be with love-poetry – so it was with Dante in the *Vita Nuova,* and so, on a lower scale, and allowing for the time that the passion is a more earthly and sensual one, the thought more capricious and unruly, with Donne. 'A nocturnall upon S. Lucies day' is not less passionate because that passion finds expression in abstract and subtle thought. Nor is it true that all love-poetry is beautiful. Of none of the four poems I have mentioned in the last paragraph is pure beauty, beauty such as is the note of Mr Bridges' song, the distinctive quality. It is rather vivid realism :

> And alive I shall keep and long, you will see !
> I knew a man, was kicked like a dog
> From gutter to cesspool; what cared he
> So long as he picked from the filth his prog?
> He saw youth, beauty and genius die,
> And jollily lived to his hundredth year.
> But I will live otherwise : none of such life !
> At once I begin as I mean to end.

But this sacrifice of beauty to dramatic vividness is a characteristic of passionate poetry. Beauty is not precisely the quality we should predict of the burning lines of Sappho translated by Catullus :

> lingua sed torpet, tenuis sub artus
> flamma demanat, sonitu suopte
> tintinant aures geminae, teguntur
> lumina nocte.

Beauty is the quality of poetry which records an ideal passion recollected in tranquillity, rather than of poetry either dramatic or lyric which utters the very movement and moment of passion itself.

Donne's love-poetry is a very complex phenomenon, but the two dominant strains in it are just these : the strain of dialectic, subtle play of argument and wit, erudite and fantastic; and the strain of vivid realism, the record of a passion which is not ideal nor conventional, neither recollected in tranquillity nor a pure product of literary fashion, but love as an actual, immediate experience in all its moods, gay and angry, scornful and rapturous with joy, touched with tenderness and darkened with sorrow – though these last two moods, the commonest in love-poetry, are with Donne the rarest. The first of these strains comes to Donne from the Middle Ages, the dialectic of the Schools, which passed into mediaeval love-poetry almost from its inception; the second is the expression of the new temper of the Renaissance as Donne had assimilated it in Latin countries. Donne uses the method, the dialectic of the mediaeval love poets, the poets of the *dolce stil nuovo,* Guinicelli, Cavalcanti, Dante, and their successors, the intellectual, argumentative evolution of their *canzoni,* but he uses it to express a temper of mind and a conception of love which are at the opposite pole from their lofty idealism. The result, however, is not so entirely disintegrating as Mr Courthope seems to think : 'This fine Platonic edifice is ruthlessly demolished in the poetry of Donne. To him love, in its infinite variety and inconsistency, represented the principle of perpetual flux in nature.'[1] The truth is rather that, owing to the fullness of Donne's experience as a lover, the accident that made of the earlier libertine a devoted lover and husband, and from the play of his restless and subtle mind on the phenomenon of love conceived and realized in this less ideal fashion, there emerged in his poetry the suggestion of a new philosophy of love which, if less transcendental than that of Dante, rests on a juster, because a less dualistic and ascetic, conception of the nature of the love of man and woman.

The fundamental weakness of the mediaeval doctrine of love, despite its refining influence and its exaltation of woman, was that it proved unable to justify love ethically against the claims of the counter-ideal of asceticism. Taking its rise in a relationship which excluded the thought of marriage as the end and justification of love, which presumed in theory that the relation of the 'servant' to his lady must always be one of reverent and unrewarded service, this poetry found itself involved from the beginning in a dualism from which there was no escape. On the one hand the love of woman is the great ennobler of the human heart, the influence which elicits its latent virtue as the sun converts clay to gold and precious stones. On the other hand, love is a passion which in the end is to be repented of in sackcloth and ashes. Lancelot is the knight whom love has made perfect in all the virtues of manhood and chivalry; but the vision of the Holy Grail is not for him, but for the virgin and stainless Sir Galahad.

In the high philosophy of the Tuscan poets of the 'sweet new style' that dualism was apparently transcended, but it was by making love identical with religion, by emptying it of earthly passion, making woman an Angel, a pure Intelligence, love of whom is the first awakening of the love of God. 'For Dante and the poets of the learned school love and virtue were one and the same thing; love *was* religion, the lady beloved the way to heaven, symbol of philosophy and finally of theology.'[2] The culminating moment in Dante's love for Beatrice arrives when he has overcome even the desire that she should return his salutation and he finds his full beatitude in 'those words that do praise my lady'. The love that begins in the *Vita Nuova* is completed in the *Paradiso.*

The dualism thus in appearance transcended by Dante re-appears sharply and distinctly in Petrarch. 'Petrarch,' says Gaspary, 'adores not the idea but the person of his lady; he feels that in his affections there is an earthly element, he cannot separate it from the desire of the senses; this is the earthly tegument which draws us down. If not as, according to the ascetic doctrine, sin, if he could not be ashamed of his passion, yet he could repent of it as a vain and frivolous thing, regret his wasted hopes and griefs.'[3] Laura is for Petrarch the flower of all perfection herself and the source of every virtue in her lover. Yet his love for Laura is a long and weary aberration of the soul from her true goal, which is the love of God. This is the contradiction from which flow some of the most lyrical strains in Petrarch's poetry, as the fine canzone 'I'vo pensando', where he cries :

> E sento ad ora ad or venirmi in core
> Un leggiadro disdegno, aspro e severo,
> Ch'ogni occulto pensero
> Tira in mezzo la fronte, ov' altri 'l vede;
> Che mortal cosa amar con tanta fede,
> Quanta a Dio sol per debito convensi,
> Più si disdice a chi più pregio brama.

Elizabethan love-poetry is descended from Petrarch by way of Cardinal Bembo and the French poets of the *Pléiade,* notably Ronsard and Desportes. Of all the Elizabethan sonneteers the most finely Petrarchian are Sidney and Spenser, especially the former. For Sidney, Stella is the school of virtue and nobility. He too writes at times in the impatient strain of Petrarch :

> But ah ! Desire still cries, give me some food.

And in the end both Sidney and Spenser turn from earthly to heavenly love :

> Leave me, O love, which reachest but to dust
> And thou, my mind, aspire to higher things :
> Grow rich in that which never taketh rust,
> Whatever fades but fading pleasure brings.

And so Spenser :

> Many lewd lays (Ah ! woe is me the more)
> In praise of that mad fit, which fools call love,
> I have in the heat of youth made heretofore ;
> That in light wits affection loose did move,
> But all these follies now I do reprove.

But two things had come over this idealist and courtly love-poetry by the end of the sixteenth century. It had become a literary artifice, a refining upon outworn and extravagant conceits, losing itself at times in the fantastic and absurd. A more important fact was that this poetry had begun to absorb a new warmth and spirit, not from Petrarch and mediaeval chivalry, but from classical love-poetry with its simpler, less metaphysical strain, its equally intense but more realistic description of passion, its radically different conception of the relation between the lovers and of the influence of love in a man's life. The courtly, idealistic strain was crossed by an Epicurean and sensuous one that tends to treat with scorn the worship of woman, and echoes again and again the Pagan cry, never heard in Dante or Petrarch, of the fleetingness of beauty and love :

> Vivamus, mea Lesbia, atque amemus !
> Soles occidere et redire possunt :
> Nobis quum semel occidit brevis lux
> Nox est perpetua una dormienda.

> Vivez si m'en croyez, n'attendez à demain ;
> Cueillez dès aujourd'hui les roses de la vie.

> Since brass, nor stone, nor earth, nor boundless sea,
> But sad mortality o'er-sways their power,
> How with this rage shall beauty hold a plea
> Whose action is no stronger than a flower?

Now if we turn from Elizabethan love-poetry to the *Songs and Sonets* and the *Elegies* of Donne, we find at once two distinguish-

ing features. In the first place his poetry is in one respect less classical than theirs. There is far less in it of the superficial evidence of
classical learning with which the poetry of the 'University Wits'
abounds, pastoral and mythological imagery. The texture of his
poetry is more mediaeval than theirs in as far as it is more dialectical, though a dialectical evolution is not infrequent in the Elizabethan sonnet, and the imagery is less picturesque, more scientific,
philosophic, realistic, and homely. The place of the

> goodly exiled train
> Of gods and goddesses

is taken by images drawn from all the sciences of the day, from
the definitions and distinctions of the Schoolmen, from the travels
and speculations of the new age, and (as in Shakespeare's tragedies
or Browning's poems) from the experiences of everyday life. Maps
and sea discoveries, latitude and longitude, the phoenix and the
mandrake's root, the Scholastic theories of Angelic bodies and
Angelic knowledge, Alchemy and Astrology, legal contracts and
non obstantes, 'late schoolboys and sour prentices', 'the king's real
and his stamped face' – these are the kind of images, erudite, fanciful, and homely, which give to Donne's poems a texture so different
at a first glance from the florid and diffuse Elizabethan poetry,
whether romantic epic, mythological idyll, sonnet, or song; while
by their presence and their abundance they distinguish it equally
(as Mr Gosse has justly insisted) from the studiously moderate and
plain style of 'well-languaged Daniel'.

But if the imagery of Donne's poetry be less classical than that
of Marlowe or the younger Shakespeare, there is no poet the spirit
of whose love-poetry is so classical, so penetrated with the sensual,
realistic, scornful tone of the Latin lyric and elegiac poets. If one
reads rapidly through the three books of Ovid's *Amores,* and then
in the same continuous rapid fashion the *Songs* and the *Elegies* of
Donne, one will note striking differences of style and treatment.
Ovid develops his theme simply and concretely, Donne dialectically and abstractly. There is little of the ease and grace of Ovid's
verses in the rough and vehement lines of Donne's *Elegies.* Compare the song

> Busie old foole, unruly Sunne,

with the famous thirteenth Elegy of the first book

Iam super oceanum venit a seniore marito,
Flava pruinoso quae vehit axe diem.

Ovid passes from one natural and simple thought to another, from one aspect of dawn to another equally objective. Donne just touches one or two of the same features, borrowing them doubtless from Ovid, but the greater part of the song is devoted to the subtle and extravagant, if you like, but not the less passionate development of the thought that for him the woman he loves is the whole world.

But if the difference between Donne's metaphysical conceits and Ovid's naturalness and simplicity is palpable it is not less clear that the emotions which they express, with some important exceptions to which I shall recur, are identical. The love which is the main burden of their song is something very different from the ideal passion of Dante or of Petrarch, of Sidney or Spenser. It is a more sensual passion. The same tone of witty depravity runs through the work of the two poets. There is in Donne a purer strain which, we shall see directly, is of the greatest importance, but such a rapid reader as I am contemplating might be forgiven if for the moment he overlooked it, and declared that the modern poet was as sensual and depraved as the ancient, that there was little to choose between the social morality reflected in the Elizabethan and in the Augustan poet.

And yet even in these more cynical and sensual poems a careful reader will soon detect a difference between Donne and Ovid. He will begin to suspect that the English poet is imitating the Roman, and that the depravity is in part a reflected depravity. In revolt from one convention the young poet is cultivating another, a cynicism and sensuality which is just as little to be taken *au pied de la lettre* as the idealizing worship, the anguish and adoration of the sonneteers. There is, as has been said already, a gaiety in the poems elaborating the thesis that love is a perpetual flux, fickleness the law of its being, which warns us against taking them too seriously; and even those *Elegies* which seem to our taste most reprehensible are aerated by a wit which makes us almost forget their indecency. In the last resort there is all the difference in the world

between the untroubled, heartless sensuality of the Roman poet
and the gay wit, the paradoxical and passionate audacities and
sensualities of the young Elizabethan law-student impatient of an
unreal convention, and eager to startle and delight his fellow
students by the fertility and audacity of his wit.

It is not of course my intention to represent Donne's love-poetry
as purely an 'evaporation' of wit, to suggest that there is in it no
reflection either of his own life as a young man or the moral atmosphere of Elizabethan London. It would be a much less interesting
poetry if this were so. Donne has pleaded guilty to a careless and
passionate youth :

> In mine Idolatry what showres of raine
> Mine eyes did waste? what griefs my heart did rent?
> That sufferance was my sinne; now I repent;
> Cause I did suffer I must suffer pain.

From what we know of the lives of Essex, Raleigh, Southampton,
Pembroke, and others it is probable that Donne's *Elegies* come
quite as close to the truth of life as Sidney's Petrarchianism or
Spenser's Platonism. The later cantos of *The Faerie Queene* reflect
vividly the unchaste loves and troubled friendships of Elizabeth's
Court. Whether we can accept in its entirety the history of Donne's
early amours which Mr Gosse has gathered from the poems or
not, there can be no doubt that actual experiences do lie behind
these poems as behind Shakespeare's sonnets. In the one case as in
the other, to recognize a literary model is not to exclude the probability of a source in actual experience.

But however we may explain or palliate the tone of these poems
it is impossible to deny their power, the vivid and packed force with
which they portray a variously mooded passion working through
a swift and subtle brain. If there is little of the elegant and accomplished art which Milton admired in the Latin Elegiasts while
he 'deplored' their immorality, there is more strength and sincerity
both of thought and imagination. The brutal cynicism of

> Fond woman, which would'st have thy husband die,

the witty anger of 'The Apparition', the mordant and paradoxical

wit of 'The Perfume' and 'The Bracelet', the passionate dignity
and strength of 'His Picture',

> My body' a sack of bones broken, within,
> And powders blew staines scatter'd on my skinne,

the passion that rises superior to sensuality and wit, and takes wing
into a more spiritual and ideal atmosphere, of 'His parting from
her',

> I will not look upon the quickning Sun,
> But straight her beauty to my sense shall run;
> The ayre shall note her soft, the fire most pure;
> Water suggest her clear, and the earth sure—

compare these with Ovid and the difference is apparent between
an artistic, witty voluptuary and a poet whose passionate force
redeems many errors of taste and art. Compare them with the
sonnets and mythological idylls and *Heroicall Epistles* of the Elizabethans and it is they, not Donne, who are revealed as witty and
'fantastic' poets content to adorn a conventional sentiment with
mythological fancies and verbal conceits. Donne's interest is his
theme, love and woman, and he uses words not for their own sake
but to communicate his consciousness of these surprising phenomena in all their varying and conflicting aspects. The only contemporary poems that have the same dramatic quality are Shakespeare's sonnets and some of Drayton's later sonnets. In Shakespeare this dramatic intensity and variety is of course united with
a rarer poetic charm. Charm is a quality which Donne's poetry
possesses in a few single lines. But to the passion which animates
these sensual, witty, troubled poems the closest parallel is to be
sought in Shakespeare's sonnets to a dark lady and in some of the
verses written by Catullus to or of Lesbia :

> The expense of spirit in a waste of shame.

But neither sensual passion, nor gay and cynical wit, nor scorn
and anger, is the dominant note in Donne's love-poetry. Of the
last quality there is, despite the sardonic emphasis of some of the
poems, less than in either Shakespeare or Catullus. There is nothing
in his poetry which speaks so poignantly of an outraged heart, a

love lavished upon one who was worthless, as some of Shake-speare's sonnets and of Catullus's poems. The finest note in Donne's love-poetry is the note of joy, the joy of mutual and contented passion. His heart might be subtle to plague itself; its capacity for joy is even more obvious. Other poets have done many things which Donne could not do. They have invested their feelings with a garb of richer and sweeter poetry. They have felt more deeply and finely the reverence which is in the heart of love. But it is only in the fragments of Sappho, the lyrics of Catullus, and the songs of Burns that one will find the sheer joy of loving and being loved expressed in the same direct and simple language as in some of Donne's songs, only in Browning that one will find the same simplicity of feeling combined with a like swift and subtle dialectic.

> I wonder by my troth, what thou, and I
> Did, till we lov'd?

> For Godsake hold your tongue, and let me love.

> If yet I have not all thy love,
> Deare, I shall never have it all.

Lines like these have the same direct, passionate quality as

> φαίνεταί μοι κῆνος ἴσος θένισιν
> ἔμμεν ὤνηρ

or

> O my love's like a red, red rose
> That's newly sprung in June.

The joy is as intense though it is of a more spiritual and intellectual quality. And in the other notes of this simple passionate love-poetry, sorrow which is the shadow of joy, and tenderness, Donne does not fall far short of Burns in intensity of feeling and direct-ness of expression. These notes are not so often heard in Donne, but

> So, so breake off this last lamenting kisse

is of the same quality as

> Had we never lov'd sae kindly

or

> Take, O take those lips away.

And strangest of all perhaps is the tenderness which came into Donne's poetry when a sincere passion quickened in his heart, for tenderness, the note of

> O wert thou in the cauld blast,

is the last quality one would look for in the poetry of a nature at once so intellectual and with such a capacity for caustic satire. But the beautiful if not flawless 'Elegy XVI',

> By our first strange and fatall interview,

and the 'Valedictions' which he wrote on different occasions of parting from his wife, combine with the peculiar *élan* of all Donne's passionate poetry and its intellectual content a tenderness as perfect as anything in Burns or in Browning :

> O more then Moone,
> Draw not up seas to drowne me in thy spheare,
> Weepe me not dead, in thine armes, but forbeare
> To teach the sea, what it may doe too soone.

> Let not thy divining heart
> Forethinke me any ill,
> Destiny may take thy part,
> And may thy feares fulfill;
> But thinke that wee
> Are but turn'd aside to sleepe;
> They who one another keepe
> Alive, ne'r parted bee.

> Such wilt thou be to mee, who must
> Like th' other foot, obliquely runne;
> Thy firmnes makes my circle just,
> And makes me end, where I begunne.

The poet who wrote such verses as these did not believe any longer that 'love . . . represents the principle of perpetual flux in nature'.

But Donne's poetry is not so simple a thing of the heart and of
the senses as that of Burns and Catullus. Even his purer poetry has
more complex moods – consider 'The Prohibition' – and it is metaphysical, not only in the sense of being erudite and witty, but in the
proper sense of being reflective and philosophical. Donne is always
conscious of the import of his moods; and so it is that there emerges
from his poems a philosophy or a suggested philosophy of love
to take the place of the idealism which he rejects. Set a song of
the joy of love by Burns or by Catullus such as I have cited beside
Donne's 'The Anniversarie',

> All Kings, and all their favorites,
> All glory of honors, beauties, wits,
> The Sun it selfe, which makes times, as they passe,
> Is elder by a yeare, now, then it was
> When thou and I first one another saw,

and the difference is at once apparent. Burns gets no further than
the experience, Catullus than the obvious and hedonistic reflection
that time is flying, the moment of pleasure short. In Donne's poem
one feels the quickening of the brain, the vision extending its range,
the passion gathering sweep with the expanding rhythms, and
from the mind thus heated and inspired emerges, not a cry that
time might stay its course,

> Lente, lente currite noctis equi,

but a clearer consciousness of the eternal significance of love, not
the love that aspires after the unattainable, but the love that unites
contented hearts. The method of the poet is, I suppose, too dialectical to be popular, for the poem is in few anthologies. It may be
that the Pagan and Christian strains which the poet unites are not
perfectly blended – if it is possible to do so – but to me it seems that
the joy of love has never been expressed at once with such intensity
and such elevation.

And it is with sorrow as with joy. There is the same difference of
manner in the expression between Donne and these poets, and the
deepest thought is the same. 'A nocturnall upon S. Lucies day' is
at the opposite pole of Donne's thought from 'The Anniversarie',
and compared with

Had we never loved sae kindly

or

Take, O take those lips away,

both the feeling and its expression are metaphysical. But the passion is felt through the subtle and fantastic web of dialectic; and the thought from which the whole springs is the emptiness of life without love.

What, then, is the philosophy which disengages itself from Donne's love-poetry studied in its whole compass? It seems to me that it is more than a purely negative one, that consciously or unconsciously he sets over against the abstract idealism, the sharp dualism of the Middle Ages, a justification of love as a natural passion in the human heart the meaning and end of which is marriage. The sensuality and exaggerated cynicism of so much of the poetry of the Renaissance was a reaction from courtly idealism and mediaeval asceticism. But a mere reaction could lead nowhither. There are no steps which lead only backward in the history of human thought and feeling. Poems like Donne's *Elegies,* like Shakespeare's *Venus and Adonis,* like Marlowe's *Hero and Leander* could only end in penitent outcries like those of Sidney and Spenser and of Donne himself. The true escape from courtly or ascetic idealism was a poetry which should do justice to love as a passion in which body and soul alike have their part, and of which there is no reason to repent.

And this with all its imperfections Donne's love-poetry is. It was not for nothing that Sir Thomas Egerton's secretary made a runaway match for love. For Dante the poet, his wife did not exist. In love of his wife Donne found the meaning and the infinite value of love. In later days he might bewail his 'idolatry of profane mistresses'; he never repented of having loved. Between his most sensual and his most spiritual love-songs there is no cleavage such as separates natural love from Dante's love of Beatrice, who is in the end Theology. The passion that burns in Donne's most outspoken elegies, and wantons in the *Epithalamia,* is not cast out in 'The Anniversarie' or 'The Canonization', but absorbed. It is purified and enriched by being brought into harmony with his whole

nature, spiritual as well as physical. It has lost the exclusive consciousness of itself which is lust, and become merged in an entire
affection, as a turbid and discoloured stream is lost in the sea.

This justification of natural love as fullness of joy and life is the
deepest thought in Donne's love-poems, far deeper and sincerer
than the Platonic conceptions of the affinity and identity of souls
with which he plays in some of the verses addressed to Mrs Herbert. The nearest approach that he makes to anything like a reasoned statement of the thought latent rather than expressed in 'The
Anniversarie' is in 'The Extasie', a poem which, like the 'Nocturnall', only Donne could have written. Here with the same intensity
of feeling, and in the same abstract, dialectical, erudite strain he
emphasizes the interdependence of soul and body :

> As our blood labours to beget
> Spirits, as like soules as it can,
> Because such fingers need to knit
> That subtile knot, which makes us man :
> So must pure lovers soules descend
> T'affections, and to faculties,
> Which sense may reach and apprehend,
> *Else a great Prince in prison lies.*

It may be that Donne has not entirely succeeded in what he
here attempts. There hangs about the poem just a suspicion of the
conventional and unreal Platonism of the seventeenth century. In
attempting to state and vindicate the relation of soul and body he
falls perhaps inevitably into the appearance, at any rate, of the
dualism which he is trying to transcend. He places them over
against each other as separate entities and the lower bulks unduly.
In love, says Pascal, the body disappears from sight in the intellectual and spiritual passion which it has kindled. That is what hap-
pens in 'The Anniversarie', not altogether in 'The Extasie'. Yet no
poem makes one realize more fully what Jonson meant by calling
Donne 'the first poet in the world for some things'. 'I should never
find any fault with metaphysical poems', is Coleridge's judgement,
'if they were all like this or but half as excellent.'

It was only the force of Donne's personality that could achieve
even an approximate harmony of elements so divergent as are
united in his love-verses, that could master the lower-natured steed

that drew the chariot of his troubled and passionate soul and make it subservient to his yoke-fellow of purer strain who is a lover of honour, and modesty, and temperance, and the follower of true glory. In the work of his followers, who were many, though they owed allegiance to Jonson also, the lower elements predominated. The strain of metaphysical love-poetry in the seventeenth century with its splendid *élan* and sonorous cadence is in general Epicurean and witty. It is only now and again – in Marvell, perhaps in Herrick's

> Bid me to live, and I will live,
> Thy Protestant to be,

certainly in Rochester's songs, in

> An age in her embraces past
> Would seem a winter's day,

or the unequalled :

> When wearied with a world of woe
> To thy safe bosom I retire,
> Where love, and peace, and truth does flow,
> May I contented there expire,

that the accents of the *heart* are clearly audible, that passion prevails over Epicurean fancy or cynical wit. On the other hand, the idealism of seventeenth-century poetry and romances, the Platonism of the Hôtel de Rambouillet that one finds in Habington's *Castara,* in Kenelm Digby's *Private Memoirs,* in the French romances of chivalry and their imitations in English is the silliest, because the emptiest, that ever masqueraded as such in any literature, at any period. A sensual and cynical flippancy on the one hand, a passionless, mannered idealism on the other, led directly to that thinly veiled contempt of women which is so obvious in the satirical essays of Addison and Pope's *Rape of the Lock.*

But there was one poet who meditated on the same problem as Donne, who felt like him the power and greatness of love, and like him could not accept a doctrine of love which seemed to exclude or depreciate marriage. In 1640, just before his marriage, as rash in its way as Donne's but less happy in the issue, Milton, defending his character against accusations of immorality, traced the development of his thought about love. The passage, in *An Apology against a Pamphlet called 'A Modest Confutation'*, &c., has been taken as having a reference to the *Paradise Lost*. But Milton rather seems at the time to have been meditating a work like the *Vita Nuova* or a romance like that of Tasso in which love was to be a motive as well as religion, for the whole theme of his thought is love, true love and its mysterious link with chastity, of which, however, 'marriage is no defilement.' In the arrogance of his youthful purity Milton would doubtless have looked with scorn or loathing on the *Elegies* and the more careless of Donne's songs. But perhaps pride is a greater enemy of love than such faults of sense as Donne in his passionate youth was guilty of, and from which Dante by his own evidence was not exempt. Whatever be the cause – pride, and the disappointment of his marriage, and political polemic – Milton never wrote any English love-poetry, except it be the one sonnet on the death of the wife who might have opened the sealed wells of his heart; and some want of the experience which love brought to Dante has dimmed the splendour of the great poem in which he undertook to justify the ways of God to men. Donne is not a Milton, but he sounded some notes which touch the soul and quicken the intellect in a way that Milton's magnificent and intense but somewhat hard and objective art fails to achieve.

S O U R C E : *The Poems of John Donne – Introduction and Commentary* (1912).

NOTES

1. *History of English Poetry*, II 154. Mr Courthope qualifies this statement somewhat on the next page : 'From this spirit of cynical lawlessness he was perhaps reclaimed by genuine love,' etc. But he has, I think, insufficiently analysed the diverse strains in Donne's love-poetry.

2. Gaspary, *History of Italian Literature* (Oelsner's translation) (1904). Consult also Karl Vossler, *Die philosophischen Grundlagen des 'süssen neuen Stils'* (Heidelberg, 1904), and *La Poesia giovanile &c di Guido Cavalcanti: Studi di Giulio Salvadori* (Roma, 1895).

3. Gaspary, op. cit.

W. B. Yeats

Nov. 14 (1912)   *Coole Park*
Dear Prof Grierson : I write to thank you for your edition of
Donne. It was very generous of you to send it to me. I have been
using it constantly and find that at last I can understand Donne.
Your notes tell me exactly what I want to know. Poems that I could
not understand or could but understand are now clear and I notice
that the more precise and learned the thought the greater the
beauty, the passion; the intricacy and subtleties of his imagination
are the length and depths of the furrow made by his passion. His
pedantry and his obscenity – the rock and the loam of his Eden –
but make me the more certain that one who is but a man like us
all has seen God. . . .

SOURCE : *Letter to Herbert Grierson* (1912).

Rupert Brooke

Praise is the prerogative of the good. And those who are wise as well as good spend all their waking hours, it is well known, in laudation. In general they praise beauty, the sun, colour, virtue, and the rest of the doxology; in the intervals more particular things: Charing Cross Bridge by night, the dancing of Miss Ethel Levey, the Lucretian hexameter, the beer at an inn in Royston I will not advertise, the sausages at another inn above Princes Risborough, and the Clarendon Press editions of the English poets. But the beer and the sausages will change, and Miss Levey one day will die, and Charing Cross Bridge will fall; so the Clarendon Press books will be the only thing our evil generation may show to the cursory eyes of posterity, to prove it was not wholly bad. They are lovely things, these books; beautiful in arrangement, size, and type; filled with good stuff to read; and prepared with the exact amount of scholarship that shall escape pedantry and yet rise far above dilettantism. These two volumes of Donne crown the series. To open them is to make even a scholar love poetry, even a poet adore scholarship. Mr Grierson's services to the text cannot be over-praised. Any fool can write criticism, but it takes a man who understands poetry really to restore a faulty text to perfection. Other editors of Donne will come, who will perhaps be able to show more clearly the two or more different original versions of some of the poems. That is all they will find to do. The commentary is a little less complete than the work on the text, but almost equally rich a gift. Donne is the one poet who demands a commentary, not for allusions, but, sometimes, for his entire train of thought. And in the same way he is the one poet who requires a perfect text, for (it is a minor merit) all his lines always *mean* something. Both text and commentary are prepared for us by Mr Grierson, with a result which must have demanded an extraordinary amount of work, and a rarely patient and unlapsing judgement. Mr Grierson is very good in the one point where nearly all modern English literary scholarship is mad and bad enough to shock the most imbecile lawyer : in knowledge of the laws of evidence. Mr Grierson has both our praise and our gratitude. Donne was labelled, by Johnson, a 'metaphysical' poet; and the term has been repeated ever since, to the great confusion of critics. Mr Grierson attempts to believe that it means erudite, and that erudition is one of the remarkable and eponymous characteristics of Donne's poetry. It rested on erudition, no doubt, as Mr Grierson has valuably shown; but it was not so especially erudite – not so erudite as the writings of Ben Jonson, a far less 'metaphysical' poet. But the continual use of this phrase may have aimed vaguely at a most important feature there is in Donne's poetry. He is the most *intellectual* poet in English; and his intellectualism had, even, sometimes, a tendency to the abstract. But to be an intellectual poet does not mean that one writes about intellectual things. The pageant of the outer world of matter and the mid-region world of the passions came to Donne through the brain. The whole composition of the man was made up of brain, soul, and heart in a different proportion from the ordinary prescription. This does not mean that he felt less keenly than others; but when passion shook him, and his being ached for utterance, to relieve the stress, expression came through the intellect. Under the storm of emotion, it is common to seek for relief by twisting some strong stuff. Donne, as Coleridge said, turns intellectual pokers into love-knots. An ordinary poet, whose feelings find far stronger expression than a common man's, but an expression according to the same prescription, praises his mistress with some common idea, intensely felt :

> Oh, thou art fairer than the evening air,
> Clad in the beauty of a thousand stars!

Donne, equally moved and equally sincere, would compare her to a perfectly equilateral triangle, or to the solar system. His intellect must find satisfaction. If a normal poet – it is not very probable – in thinking of his mistress being ill with a fever, had had suggested to him the simile of these fevers soon passing and dying away in her, just as shooting stars consume and vanish in the vastness and purity of the sky, he would have tried to bring the force of his thought home by sharpening and beautifying the imagined vision. He might have approached it on the lines of :

Through the serene wide dark of you
They trail their transient gold, and die.

Donne feels only the idea. He does not try to visualize it. He never
visualizes, or suggests that he has any pleasure in looking at things.
His poems might all have been written by a blind man in a world
of blind men. In 'A Feaver' he gives you the thought thus :

These burning fits but meteors bee,
Whose matter in thee is soone spent.
Thy beauty,' and all parts, which are thee,
Are unchangeable firmament.

The mediation of the senses is spurned. Brain does all.

And as Donne saw everything through his intellect, it follows, in
some degree, that he could see everything humorously. He could
see it the other way, too. But humour was always at his command.
It was part of his realism; especially in the bulk of his work, his
poems dealing with love. There is no true lover but has sometimes
laughed at his mistress, and often at himself. But you would not
guess that from the love-songs of many poets. Their poems run the
risk of looking a little flat. They are unreal by the side of Donne.
For while his passion enabled him to see the face of love, his
humour allowed him to look at it from the other side. So we behold
his affairs in the round.

But it must not appear that his humour, or his wit, and his passion, alternated. The other two are his passion's handmaids. It
should not be forgotten that Donne was one of the first great
English satirists, and the most typical and prominent figure of a
satirical age. Satire comes with the Bible of truth in one hand and
the sword of laughter in the other. Donne was true to the reality of
his own heart. Sometimes you hear the confident laughter of lovers
who have found their love :

I wonder by my troth, what thou, and I
Did, till we lov'd? were we not wean'd till then?
But suck'd on countrey pleasures, childishly?
Or snorted we in the seaven sleepers den?

and there is the bitterer mirth of the famous –

> For Godsake hold your tongue, and let me love . . .

He could combine either the light or the grave aspects of love with this lack of solemnity that does but heighten the sharpness of the seriousness. His colloquialism helped him. It has been the repeated endeavour of half the great English poets to bring the language of poetry, and the accent and rhythm of poetry, nearer to those of the intensest moments of common speech. To attempt this was especially the mark of many of the greatest of the Elizabethans. Shakespeare's 'Prithee, undo this button!' finds its lyrical counterpart in several of Donne's poems. Yet he did not confine his effects to laughter and slang. He could curiously wed fantastic imagination with the most grave and lofty music of poetry; as in the great poem where he compares his wife to the stationary leg of a compass, himself to the voyaging one:

> And though it in the center sit,
>   Yet when the other far doth rome,
> It leanes, and hearkens after it,
>   And growes erect, as that comes home.
>
> Such wilt thou be to mee, who must
>   Like th'other foot, obliquely run;
> Thy firmnes makes my circle just,
>   And makes me end, where I begunne.

For indeed, while the quality of his imagination was unique and astonishing, he expressed it most normally as a great poet, with all the significance and beauty that English metre and poetry can give:

> O more then Moone,
> Draw not up seas to drowne me in thy spheare!

and –

> Thou art not soft, and clear, and straight, and fair,
> As down, as stars, cedars, and lilies are;
> But thy right hand, and cheek, and eyes, only
> Are like thy other hand, and cheek, and eye –

contain as much inexplicable loveliness and strangeness as any of the writings of the Romantics. The mere technique of his poetry has been imitated and followed by many of all the poets who followed him and loved him, from Dryden to Swinburne. It is a good thing that he is slowly spreading from the select band of readers to a wider public. This edition has opportunely appeared at the time of the spreading of his fame. It is fitting he should be read in an age when poetry is beginning to go back from nature, romance, the great world, and the other fine hunting-places of the Romantics, by devious ways and long *ambages,* to that wider home which Donne knew better than any of the great English poets, the human heart. 'The heart's a wonder'.

SOURCE: *Poetry and Drama* (June 1913).

T. S. Eliot

... Donne, and often Cowley, employ a device which is sometimes considered characteristically 'metaphysical'; the elaboration (contrasted with the condensation) of a figure of speech to the furthest stage to which ingenuity can carry it. Thus Cowley develops the commonplace comparison of the world to a chess-board through long stanzas ('To Destiny'), and Donne, with more grace, in 'A Valediction', the comparison of two lovers to a pair of compasses. But elsewhere we find, instead of the mere explication of the content of a comparison, a development by rapid association of thought which requires considerable agility on the part of the reader.

> On a round ball
> A workeman that hath copies by, can lay
> An Europe, Afrique, and an Asia,
> And quickly make that, which was nothing, *All*,
> So doth each teare,
> Which thee doth weare,
> A globe, yea world by that impression grow,
> Till thy teares mixt with mine doe overflow
> This world, by waters sent from thee, my heaven dissolved so.

Here we find at least two connexions which are not implicit in the first figure, but are forced upon it by the poet : from the geographer's globe to the tear, and the tear to the deluge. On the other hand, some of Donne's most successful and characteristic effects are secured by brief words and sudden contrasts :

> A bracelet of bright hair about the bone,

where the most powerful effect is produced by the sudden contrast of associations of 'bright hair' and of 'bone'. This telescoping of images and multiplied associations is characteristic of the phrase of some of the dramatists of the period which Donne knew : not to

mention Shakespeare, it is frequent in Middleton, Webster, and
Tourneur, and is one of the sources of the vitality of their
language. . . .

It is certain that the dramatic verse of the later Elizabethan and
early Jacobean poets expresses a degree of development of sensibility which is not found in any of the prose, good as it often is. If
we except Marlowe, a man of prodigious intelligence, these dramatists were directly or indirectly (it is at least a tenable theory) affected by Montaigne. Even if we except also Jonson and Chapman,
these two were notably erudite, and were notably men who incorporated their erudition into their sensibility : their mode of feeling
was directly and freshly altered by their reading and thought. In
Chapman especially there is a direct sensuous apprehension of
thought, or a recreation of thought into feeling, which is exactly
what we find in Donne :

> in this one thing, all the discipline
> Of manners and of manhood is contained;
> A man to join himself with th' Universe
> In his main sway, and make in all things fit
> On with that All, and go on, round as it;
> Not plucking from the whole his wretched part,
> And into straits, or into nought revert,
> Wishing the complete Universe might be
> Subject to such a rag of it as he;
> But to consider great Necessity.

We compare this with some modern passage :

> No, when the fight begins within himself,
> A man's worth something. God stoops o'er his head,
> Satan looks up between his feet – both tug –
> He's left, himself, i' the middle; the soul wakes
> And grows. Prolong that battle through his life !

It is perhaps somewhat less fair, though very tempting (as both
poets are concerned with the perpetuation of love by offspring),
to compare with the stanzas already quoted from Lord Herbert's
Ode the following from Tennyson :

One walked between his wife and child,
With measured footfall firm and mild,
And now and then he gravely smiled.
  The prudent partner of his blood
  Leaned on him, faithful, gentle, good,
  Wearing the rose of womanhood.
And in their double love secure,
The little maiden walked demure,
Pacing with downward eyelids pure.
  These three made unity so sweet,
  My frozen heart began to beat,
  Remembering its ancient heat.

The difference is not a simple difference of degree between poets. It is something which had happened to the mind of England between the time of Donne or Lord Herbert of Cherbury and the time of Tennyson and Browning; it is the difference between the intellectual poet and the reflective poet. Tennyson and Browning are poets, and they think; but they do not feel their thought as immediately as the odour of a rose. A thought to Donne was an experience; it modified his sensibility. When a poet's mind is perfectly equipped for its work, it is constantly amalgamating disparate experience; the ordinary man's experience is chaotic, irregular; fragmentary. The latter falls in love, or reads Spinoza, and these two experiences have nothing to do with each other, or with the noise of the typewriter or the smell of cooking; in the mind of the poet these experiences are always forming new wholes.

We may express the difference by the following theory: The poets of the seventeenth century, the successors of the dramatists of the sixteenth, possessed a mechanism of sensibility which could devour any kind of experience. They are simple, artificial, difficult, or fantastic, as their predecessors were; no less nor more than Dante, Guido Cavalcanti, Guinicelli, or Cino. In the seventeenth century a dissociation of sensibility set in, from which we have never recovered; and this dissociation, as is natural, was aggravated by the influence of the two most powerful poets of the century, Milton and Dryden.

SOURCE: 'The Metaphysical Poets' (1921).

II

. . . Donne was, I insist, no sceptic : it is only that he is interested
in and amused by ideas in themselves, and interested in the way
in which he *feels* an idea; almost as if it were something that he
could touch and stroke. To turn the attention to the mind in this
way is a kind of creation, because the objects alter by being
observed so curiously. To contemplate an idea, because it is
present for the moment in my own mind, to observe my emotion
colour it, and to observe it colour my emotions, to play with it,
instead of using it as a plain and simple meaning, brings often
odd or beautiful objects to light, as a deep sea diver inspects the
darting and crawling life of the depths; though it may lend itself,
this petting and teasing of one's mental objects, to extremities of
torturing of language. With Donne it is not, as it is with the
Elizabethans in their worst excesses, the word, the vocabulary
that is tormented – it is the thought itself. In the poem

I wonder by my troth, what thou, and I . . .

the *idea* is thoroughly teased and touseled. The choice and arrange-
ments of words is simple and direct and felicitous. There is a startling directness (as often at the beginning of Donne's poems) about
the idea, which must have occurred to many lovers, of the abrupt
break and alteration of the new life. These *trouvailles* themselves
are enough to set Donne apart from some of his imitators : Cowley
never found anything so good. But the usual course for Donne is
not to pursue the meaning of the idea, but to arrest it, to play cat-
like with it, to develop it dialectically, to extract every minim of the
emotion suspended in it. And as to the poetic justification of this
method of dialectic I have no doubts.

SOURCE : 'Donne in our Time' (1931).

*

III

. . . I believe that the general affirmation represented by the phrase 'dissociation of sensibility' (one of the two or three phrases of my coinage – like 'objective correlative' – which have had a success in the world astonishing to their author) retains some validity; but . . . to lay the burden on the shoulders of Milton and Dryden was a mistake. If such a dissociation did take place, I suspect that the causes are too complex and too profound to justify our accounting for the change in terms of literary criticism. All we can say is, that something like this did happen; that it had something to do with the Civil War; that it would even be unwise to say it was caused by the Civil War, but that it is a consequence of the same causes which brought about the Civil War; that we must seek the causes in Europe, not in England alone; and for what these causes were, we may dig and dig until we get to a depth at which words and concepts fail us.

S o u r c e : 'Lecture on Milton' (1947).

PART THREE

Recent Studies

C. S. Lewis

DONNE AND LOVE POETRY IN THE SEVENTEETH CENTURY (1938)

'Little of Manfred (but not very much of him)' – W. S. GILBERT

I have seen an old history of literature in which the respective claims of Shelley and Mrs Hemans to be the greatest lyrist of the nineteenth century were seriously weighed; and Donne, who was so inconsiderable fifty years ago, seems at the moment to rank among our greatest poets.

If there were no middle state between absolute certainty and what Mr Kellett calls the whirligig of taste, these fluctuations would make us throw up criticism in despair. But where it is impossible to go quite straight we may yet resolve to reel as little as we can. Such phenomena as the present popularity of Donne or the growing unpopularity of Milton are not to be deplored; they are rather to be explained. It is not impossible to see why Donne's poetry should be overrated in the twentieth and underrated in the eighteenth century; and in so far as we detect these temporary disturbing factors and explain the varying appearances of the object by the varying positions of the observers, we shall come appreciably nearer to a glimpse of Donne *simpliciter*. I shall concern myself in what follows chiefly with his love poetry.

In style this poetry is primarily a development of one of the two styles which we find in the work of Donne's immediate predecessors. One of these is the mellifluous, luxurious, 'builded rhyme', as in Spenser's *Amoretti*: the other is the abrupt, familiar and consciously 'manly' style in which nearly all Wyatt's lyrics are written. Most of the better poets make use of both, and in *Astrophel and Stella* much of Sidney's success depends on deliberate contrast between such poetry as

That golden sea whose waves in curls are broken

and such poetry as

> He cannot love : no, no, let him alone.

But Wyatt remains, if not the finest, yet much the purest example of the plainer manner, and in reading his songs, with their conversational openings, their surly (not to say sulky) defiances, and their lack of obviously poetic ornaments, I find myself again and again reminded of Donne. But of course he is a Donne with most of the genius left out. Indeed, the first and most obvious achievement of the younger poet is to have raised this kind of thing to a much higher power; to have kept the vividness of conversation where Wyatt too often had only the flatness; to sting like a lash where Wyatt merely grumbled. The difference in degree between the two poets thus obscures the similarity in kind. Donne has so far surpassed not only Wyatt but all the Elizabethans in what may be called their Wyatt moments, and has so generally abstained from attempting to rival them in their other vein, that we hardly think of him as continuing one side of their complex tradition; he appears rather as the innovator who substituted a realistic for a decorated kind of love poetry.

Now this error is not in itself important. In an age which was at all well placed for judging the comparative merits of the two styles, it would not matter though we thought that Donne had invented what in fact he only brought to perfection. But our own age is not so placed. The mellifluous style, which we may agree to call Petrarchan though no English poet is very like Petrarch, has really no chance of a fair hearing. It is based on a conception of poetry wholly different from that of the twentieth century. It descends from old Provençal and Italian sources and presupposes a poetic like that of Dante. Dante, we may remember, thinks of poetry as something to be made, to be 'adorned as much as possible', to have its 'true sense' hidden beneath a rich vesture of 'rhetorical colouring'. The 'Petrarchan' sonneteers are not trying to make their work sound like the speaking voice. They are not trying to communicate faithfully the raw, the merely natural, impact of actual passion. The passion for them is not a specimen of 'nature' to be followed so much as a lump of ore to be refined : they ask themselves not 'How can I record it with the least sophistication?'

but 'Of its bones what coral can I make?', and to accuse them of insincerity is like calling an oyster insincere because it makes its disease into a pearl. The aim of the other style is quite different. It wishes to be convincing, intimate, naturalistic. It would be very foolish to set up these two kinds of poetry as rivals, for obviously they are different and both are good. It is a fine thing to hear the living voice, the voice of a man like ourselves, whispering or shouting to us from the printed page with all the heat of life; and it is a fine thing, too, to see such life – so pitiably like our own, I doubt not, in the living – caught up and transfigured, sung by the voice of a god into an ecstasy no less real though in another dimension.[1] There is no necessary quarrel between the two. But there are many reasons why one of them should start with overwhelming odds in its favour at the present moment. For many years our poetics have been becoming more and more expressionistic. First came Wordsworth with his theory, and we have never quite worked it out of our system; even in the crude form that 'you should write as you talk', it works at the back of much contemporary criticism. Then came the final break-up of aristocracy and the consequent, and still increasing, distaste for arduous disciplines of sentiment – the wholesale acceptance of the merely and unredeemedly natural. Finally, the psychological school of criticism overthrew what was left of the old conception of a poem as a construction and set up instead the poem as 'document'. In so far as we admire Donne for being our first great practitioner in one of the many possible kinds of lyric, we are on firm ground; but the conception of him as liberator, as one who substituted 'real' or 'live' or 'sincere' for 'artificial' or 'conventional' love lyric, begs all the questions and is simply a prejudice *de siècle*.

But of course when we have identified the Wyatt element in Donne, we have still a very imperfect notion of his manner. We have described 'Busie old foole' and 'I wonder by my troth' and 'For Godsake hold your tongue, and let me love'; but we have left out the cleaving remora, the triple soul, the still twin compasses, and a hundred other things that were not in Wyatt. There were indeed a great many things not in Wyatt, and his manly plainness can easily be over-praised – 'pauper videri Cinna vult et est pauper'. If Donne had not reinforced the style with new attractions it would soon have died of very simplicity. An account of these reinforcements will give us a rough notion of the unhappily named 'metaphysical' manner.

The first of them is the multiplication of conceits – not conceits of any special 'metaphysical' type but conceits such as we find in all the Elizabethans. When Donne speaks of the morning coming from his mistress's eyes, or tells how they wake him like the light of a taper, these fanciful hyperboles are not, in themselves, a novelty. But, side by side with these, we find, as his second characteristic, what may be called the difficult conceit. This is clearly a class which no two readers will fill up in quite the same way. An example of what I mean comes at the end of 'The Sunne Rising' where the sun is congratulated on the fact that the two lovers have shortened his task for him. Even the quickest reader will be checked, if only for an infinitesimal time, before he sees how and why the lovers have done this, and will experience a kind of astonished relief at the unexpected answer. The pleasure of the thing, which can be paralleled in other artistic devices, perhaps in rhyme itself, would seem to depend on recurrent tension and relaxation. In the third place, we have Donne's characteristic choice of imagery. The Petrarchans (I will call them so for convenience) had relied for their images mainly on mythology and on natural objects. Donne uses both of these sparingly – though his sea that 'Leaves embroider'd works upon the sand' is as fine an image from nature as I know – and taps new sources such as law, science, philosophy, and the commonplaces of urban life. It it this that has given the Metaphysicals their name and been much misunderstood. When Johnson said that they were resolved to show their learning he said truth in fact, for there is an element of pedantry, of dandyism, an *odi profanos* air, about Donne – the old printer's address not to the *readers* but to the *understanders* is illuminating. But Johnson was none the less misleading. He encouraged the idea that the abstruse nature of some of Donne's similes was poetically relevant for good or ill. In fact, of course, when we have once found out what Donne is talking about – that is, when Sir Herbert Grierson has told us – the learning of the poet becomes unimportant. The image will stand or fall like any other by its intrinsic merit – its power of conveying a meaning 'more luminously and with a sensation of delight'. The matter is worth mentioning only because Donne's reputation in this respect repels some humble readers and attracts some prigs. What is important for criticism in his avoidance of the obviously poetical image; whether the intractable which he is determined to poetize is fetched from Thomas Aquinas or from the London underworld, the method is essentially the same. Indeed it would be easy to exaggerate the amount of learned imagery in his poems and even the amount of his learning. He knows much, but he seems to know even more because his knowledge so seldom overlaps with our own; and some scraps of his learning, such as that of angelic consciousness or of the three souls in man, come rather too often – like the soldiers in a stage army, and with the same result. The choice of imagery is closely connected with the surprising and ingenious nature of the connexions which Donne makes between the image and the matter in hand, thus getting a double surprise. No one, in the first place, expects lovers to be compared to compasses; and no one, even granted the comparison, would guess in what respect they are going to be compared.

But all these characteristics, in their mere enumeration, are what Donne would have called a 'ruinous anatomie'. They might all be used – indeed they all are used by Herbert – to produce a result very unlike Donne's. What gives their peculiar character to most of the *Songs and Sonets* is that they are dramatic in the sense of being addresses to an imagined hearer in the heart of an imagined conversation, and usually addresses of a violently argumentative character. The majority of lyrics, even where nominally addressed to a god, a woman, or a friend, are meditations or introspective narratives. Thus Herbert's 'Throw away thy rod' is formally an apostrophe; in fact, it is a picture of Herbert's own state of mind. But the majority of the *Songs and Sonets,* including some that are addressed to abstractions like Love, present the poet's state of mind only indirectly and are ostensibly concerned with badgering, wheedling, convincing, or upbraiding an imagined hearer. No poet, not even Browning, buttonholes us or, as we say, 'goes for' us like Donne. There are, of course, exceptions. 'Goe, and catche a falling starre', though it is in the form of an address, has not this effect; and 'Twicknam garden' or the 'Nocturnall' are in fact, as well as in pretension, soliloquies. These exceptions include some of Donne's best work; and indeed, one of the errors of contemporary criticism, to my mind, is an insufficient distinction between Donne's best and Donne's most characteristic. But I do not at present wish

to emphasize this. For the moment it is enough to notice that the
majority of his love lyrics, and of the *Elegies,* are of the type I have
described. And since they are, nearly always, in the form of arguments, since they attempt to extort something from us, they are
poetry of an extremely exacting kind. This exacting quality, this
urgency and pressure of the poet upon the reader in every line,
seems to me to be the root both of Donne's weakness and his
strength. When the thing fails it exercises the same dreadful fas-
cination that we feel in the grip of the worst kind of bore – the
hot-eyed, unescapable kind. When it succeeds it produces a rare
intensity in our enjoyment – which is what a modern critic meant
(I fancy) when he claimed that Donne made all other poetry sound
less 'serious'. The point is worth investigation.

For, of course, in one sense these poems are not serious at all.
Poem after poem consists of extravagant conceits woven into the
preposterous semblance of an argument. The preposterousness is
the point. Donne intends to take your breath away by the combined subtlety and impudence of the steps that lead to his conclusion. Any attempt to overlook Donne's 'wit' in this sense, or to
pretend that his rare excursions into the direct expression of passion are typical, is false criticism. The paradox, the surprise, are
essential; if you are not enjoying these you are not enjoying what
Donne intended. Thus 'Womans constancy' is of no interest as a
document of Donne's 'cynicism' – any fool can be promiscuously
unchaste and any fool can say so. The merit of the poem consists
in the skill with which it leads us to expect a certain conclusion and
then gives us precisely the opposite conclusion, and that, too, with
an appearance of reasonableness. Thus, again, the art of 'The Will'
consists in keeping us guessing through each stanza what universal
in the concluding triplet will bind together the odd particulars in
the preceding six lines. The test case is 'The Flea'. If you think this
very different from Donne's other poems you may be sure that you
have no taste for the real Donne. But for the accident that modern
cleanliness by rendering this insect disgusting has also rendered it
comic, the conceit is exactly on the same level as that of the tears
in 'A Valediction : of weeping'.

And yet the modern critic was right. The effect of all these
poems is somehow serious. 'Serious' indeed is the only word. Seldom profound in thought, not always passionate in feeling, they

are none the less the very opposite of gay. It is as though Donne performed in deepest depression those gymnastics which are usually a sign of intellectual high spirits. He himself speaks of his '*concupiscence* of wit'. The hot, dark word is well chosen. We are all familiar – at least if we have lived in Ireland – with the type of mind which combines furious anger with a revelling delight in eloquence, nay grows more rhetorical as anger increases. In the same way, wit and the delight in wit are, for Donne, not only compatible with, but actually provoked by, the most uneasy passions – by contempt and self-contempt and unconvinced sensuality. His wit is not so much the play as the irritability of intellect. But none the less, like the angry Irishman's *clausulae,* it is still enjoyed and still intends to produce admiration; and if we do not hold our breaths as we read, wondering in the middle of each complication how he will resolve it, and exclaiming at the end 'How ever did you think of *that*?' (Carew speaks of his 'fresh invention'), we are not enjoying Donne.

Now this kind of thing can produce a very strong and a very peculiar pleasure. Our age has nothing to repent of in having learned to relish it. If the Augustans, in their love for the obviously poetical and harmonious, were blind to its merits, so much the worse for them. At the same time it is desirable not to overlook the special congeniality of such poetry to the twentieth century, and to beware of giving to this highly specialized and, in truth, very limited kind of excellence, a place in our scheme of literary values which it does not deserve. Donne's rejection of the obviously poetical image was a good method – for Donne; but if we think that there is some intrinsic superiority in this method, so that all poetry about pylons and *non obstantes* must needs be of a higher order than poetry about lawns and lips and breasts and orient skies, we are deceived – deceived by the fact that we, like Donne, happen to live at the end of a great period of rich and nobly obvious poetry. It is natural to want your savoury after your sweets; but you must not base a philosophy of cookery on that momentary preference. Again, Donne's obscurity and occasional abstruseness have sometimes (not always) produced magnificent results, and we do well to praise them. But, as I have hinted, an element of dandyism was present in Donne himself – he 'would have no such readers as he could teach' – and we must be very cautious here lest shallow call to shallow. There is a great deal of dandyism (largely Franco-American importation) in the modern literary world. And finally, what shall we say of Donne's 'seriousness', of that persistency, that nimiety, that astringent quality (as Boehme would have said) which makes him, if not the saddest, at least the most uncomfortable, of our poets? Here, surely, we find the clearest and most disturbing congeniality of all. It would be foolish not to recognize the growth in our criticism of something that I can only describe as literary Manichaeism – a dislike of peace and pleasure and heartsease simply as such. To be bilious is, in some circles, almost the first qualification for a place in the Temple of Fame.[2] We distrust the pleasures of imagination, however hotly and unmerrily we preach the pleasures of the body. This seriousness must not be confused with profundity. We do not like poetry that essays to be wise, and Chaucer would think we had rejected 'doctryne' and 'solas' about equally. We want, in fact, just what Donne can give us – something stern and tough, though not necessarily virtuous, something that does not conciliate. Born under Saturn, we do well to confess the liking complexionally forced upon us; but not to attempt that wisdom which dominates the stars is pusillanimous, and to set up our limitation as a norm – to believe, against all experience, in a Saturnocentric universe – is folly.

Before leaving the discussion of Donne's manner I must touch, however reluctantly, on a charge that has been brought against him from the time of Ben Jonson till now. Should he, or should he not, be hanged for not keeping the accent? There is more than one reason why I do not wish to treat this subject. In the first place, the whole nature of Donne's stanza, and of what he does within the stanza, cannot be profitably discussed except by one who knows much more than I do about the musical history of the time. 'Confined Love', for example, is metrically meaningless without the tune. But I could make shift with that difficulty : my real trouble is of quite a different kind. In discussing Donne's present popularity, the question of metre forces me to a statement which I do not make without embarrassment. Some one must say it, but I do not care for the office, for what I have to say will hardly be believed among scholars and hardly listened to by any one else. It is simply this – that the opinions of the modern world on the metre of any poet are, in general, of no value at all, because most modern readers of poetry do not know how to scan. My evidence for this amazing charge is twofold. In the first place I find that very many of my own pupils – some of them from excellent schools, most of them great readers of poetry, not a few of them talented and (for their years) well-informed persons – are quite unable, when they first come to me, to find out from the verse how Marlowe pronounced Barabas or Mahomet. To be sure, if challenged, they will say that they do not believe in syllable-counting or that the old methods of scansion have been exploded, but this is only a smoke screen. It is easy to find out that they have not got beyond the traditional legal fiction of longs and shorts and have never even got so far : they are in virgin ignorance. And my experience as an examiner shows me that this is not peculiar to my own pupils. My second piece of evidence is more remarkable. I have heard a celebrated belle-lettrist – a printed critic and poet – repeatedly, in the same lecture, so mispronounce the name of a familiar English poem as to show that he did not know a decasyllabic line when he met it. The conclusion is unavoidable. Donne may be metrically good or bad, in fact; but it is obvious that he might be bad to any degree without offending the great body of his modern admirers. On that side, his present vogue is worth precisely nothing. No doubt this widespread metrical ignorance is itself a symptom of some deeper change; and I am far from suggesting that the appearance of *vers libre* is simply a result of the ignorance. More probably the ignorance, and the deliberate abandonment, of accentual metres are correlative phenomena, and both the results of some revolution in our whole sense of rhythm – a revolution of great importance reaching deep down into the unconscious and even perhaps into the blood. But that is not our business at the moment.

The sentiment of Donne's love poems is easier to describe than their manner, and its charm for modern readers easier to explain. No one will deny that the twentieth century, so far, has shown an extraordinary interest in the sexual appetite and has been generally marked by a reaction from the romantic idealization of that appetite. We have agreed with the romantics in regarding sexual love as a subject of overwhelming importance, but hardly in anything else. On the purely literary side we are wearied with the floods of uxorious bathos which the romantic conception undoubtedly liberated. As psychologists we are interested in the new discovery of the secreter and less reputable operations of the instinct. As practical philosophers we are living in an age of sexual experiment. The whole subject offers us an admirable field for the kind of seriousness I have just described. It seems odd, at first sight, that a sixteenth-century poet should give us so exactly what we want; but it can be explained.

The great central movement of love poetry, and of fiction about love, in Donne's time is that represented by Shakespeare and Spenser. This movement consisted in the final transmutation of the medieval courtly love or romance of adultery into an equally romantic love that looked to marriage as its natural conclusion. The process, of course, had begun far earlier – as early, indeed, as the *Kingis Quhair* – but its triumph belongs to the sixteenth century. It is most powerfully expressed by Spenser, but more clearly and philosophically by Chapman in that under-estimated poem, his *Hero and Leander*. These poets were engaged, as Professor Vinaver would say, in reconciling Carbonek and Camelot, virtue and courtesy, divine and human love; and incidentally in laying down the lines which love poetry was to follow till the nineteenth century. We who live at the end of the dispensation which they inaugurated and in reaction against it are not well placed for evaluating their work. Precisely what is revolutionary and creative in it seems to us platitudinous, orthodox, and stale. If there were a poet, and a strong poet, alive in their time who was failing to move with them, he would inevitably appear to us more 'modern' than they.

But was Donne such a poet? A great critic has assigned him an almost opposite role, and it behoves us to proceed with caution. It may be admitted at once that Donne's work is not, in this respect, all of a piece; no poet fits perfectly into such a scheme as I have outlined – it can be true only by round and by large. There are poems in which Donne attempts to sing a love perfectly in harmony with the moral law, but they are not very numerous and I do not think they are usually his best pieces. Donne never for long gets rid of a medieval sense of the sinfulness of sexuality; indeed, just because the old conventional division between Carbonek and Camelot is breaking up, he feels this more continuously and restively than any poet of the Middle Ages.

Donne was bred a Roman Catholic. The significance of this in relation to his learned and scholastic imagery can be exaggerated; scraps of Calvin, or, for that matter, of Euclid or Bacon, might have much the same poetical effect as his scraps of Aquinas. But it is all-important for his treatment of love. This is not easily understood by the modern reader, for laterday conceptions of the Puritan and the Roman Catholic stand in the way. We have come to use the word 'Puritan' to mean what should rather be called 'rigorist' or 'ascetic', and we tend to assume that the sixteenth-century Puritans were 'puritanical' in this sense. Calvin's rigorist theocracy at Geneva lends colour to the error. But there is no understanding the period of the Reformation in England until we have grasped the fact that the quarrel between the Puritans and the Papists was not primarily a quarrel between rigorism and indulgence, and that, in so far as it was, the rigorism was on the Roman side. On many questions, and specially in their view of the marriage bed, the Puritans were the indulgent party; if we may without disrespect so use the name of a great Roman Catholic, a great writer, and a great man, they were much more Chestertonian than their adversaries. The idea that a Puritan was a repressed and repressive person would have astonished Sir Thomas More and Luther about equally. On the contrary, More thought of a Puritan as one who 'loved no lenten fast nor lightly no fast else, saving breakfast and eat fast and drink fast and luske fast in their lechery' – a person only too likely to end up in the 'abominable heresies' of the Anabaptists about communism of goods and wives. And Puritan theology, so far from being grim and gloomy, seemed to More to err in the direction of fantastic optimism, 'I could for my part', he writes, 'be very well content that sin and pain and all were as shortly gone as Tindall telleth us : but I were loth that he deceived us if it be not so'. More would not have understood the idea, sometimes found in the modern writers, that he and his friends were defending a 'merry' Catholic England against sour precisions; they were rather defending necessary severity and sternly realistic theology against wanton labefaction – penance and 'works' and vows of celibacy and mortification and Purgatory against the easy doctrine, the mere wish-fulfilment dream, of salvation by faith. Hence when we turn from the religious works of More to Luther's *Table-talk* we are at once struck by the geniality of the latter. If Luther is right, we have waked from nightmare into sunshine : if he is wrong, we have entered a fools' paradise. The burden of his charge against the Catholics is that they have needlessly tormented us with scruples; and, in particular, that 'Antichrist will regard neither God nor the love of women'. 'On what pretence have they forbidden us marriage? 'Tis as though we were forbidden to eat, to drink, to sleep'. 'Where women are not honoured, temporal and domestic government are despised.' He praises women repeatedly : More, it will be remembered, though apparently an excellent husband and father, hardly ever mentions a woman save to ridicule her. It is easy to see why Luther's marriage (as he called it) or Luther's 'abominable bichery' (if you prefer) became almost a symbol. More can never keep off the subject for more than a few pages.

This antithesis, if once understood, explains many things in the history of sentiment, and many differences, noticeable to the present day, between the Protestant and the Catholic parts of Europe. It explains why the conversion of courtly love into romantic monogamous love was so largely the work of English, and even of Puritan, poets; and it goes far to explain why Donne contributes so little to that movement.

I trace in his poetry three levels of sentiment. On the lowest level (lowest, that is, in order of complexity), we have the celebration of simple appetite, as in Elegy XIX. If I call this a pornographic poem, I must be understood to use that ugly word as a descriptive, not a dyslogistic, term. I mean by it that this poem, in my opinion, is intended to arouse the appetite it describes, to affect not only the imagination but the nervous system of the reader.[3] And I may as well say at once – but who would willingly claim to be a judge in such matters? – that it seems to me to be very nearly perfect in its kind. Nor would I call it an immoral poem. Under what conditions the reading of it could be an innocent act is a real moral question; but the poem itself contains nothing intrinsically evil.

On the highest, or what Donne supposed to be the highest, level we have the poems of ostentatiously virtuous love, 'The undertaking', 'A Valediction : forbidding mourning', and 'The Extasie'. It is here that the contrast between Donne and his happier contemporaries is most marked. He is trying to follow them into the new age, to be at once passionate and innocent; and if any reader will make the experiment of imagining Beatrice or Juliet or Perdita, or again, Amoret or Britomart, or even Philoclea or Pamela, as the auditress throughout these poems, he will quickly feel that something is wrong. You may deny, as perhaps some do, that the romantic conception of 'pure' passion has any meaning; but certainly, if there is such a thing, it is not like this. It does not prove itself pure by talking about purity. It does not keep on drawing distinctions between spirit and flesh to the detriment of the latter and then explaining why the flesh is, after all, to be used. This is what Donne does, and the result is singularly unpleasant. The more he labours the deeper 'Dun is in the mire', and it is quite arguable that 'The Extasie' is a much nastier poem than the nineteenth Elegy. What any sensible woman would make of such a wooing it is difficult to imagine – or would be difficult if we forgot the amazing protective faculty which each sex possesses of not listening to the other.

Between these two extremes falls the great body of Donne's love poetry. In certain obvious, but superficial, respects, it continues the medieval tradition. Love is still a god and lovers his 'clergie'; oaths may be made in 'reverentiall feare' of his 'wrath'; and the man who resists him is 'rebell and atheist'. Donne can even doubt, like Soredamors, whether those who admit Love after a struggle have not forfeited his grace by their resistance, like

> Small townes which stand stiffe, til great shot
> Enforce them.

He can personify the attributes of his mistress, the 'enormous gyant' her Disdain and the 'enchantress *Honor*', quite in the manner of *The Romance of the Rose*. He writes *Albas* for both sexes, and in the *Holy Sonnets* repents of his love poetry, writing his palinode, in true medieval fashion. A reader may wonder, at first, why the total effect is so foreign to the Middle Ages : but Donne himself has explained this when he says, speaking of the god of Love,

> If he wroung from mee a teare, I brin'd it so
> With scorne or shame, that him it nourish'd not.

This admirable couplet not only tells us, in brief, what Donne has effected but shows us that he knew what he was doing. It does not, of course, cover every single poem. A few pieces admittedly express delighted love and they are among Donne's most popular works; such are 'The good-morrow' and 'The Anniversarie' – poems that again remind us of the difference between his best and his typical. But the majority of the poems ring the changes on five themes, all of them grim ones – on the sorrow of parting (including death), the miseries of secrecy, the falseness of the mistress, the fickleness of Donne, and finally on contempt for love itself. The poems of parting stand next to the poems of happy love in general popularity and are often extremely affecting. We may hear little of the delights of Donne's loves, and dislike what we hear of their 'purity'; the pains ring true. The song 'Sweetest love, I do not goe' is remarkable for its broken, but haunting, melody, and nowhere else has Donne fused argument, conceit, and classical imitation into a more perfect unity. 'The Feaver' is equally remarkable, and that for a merit very rare in Donne – its inevitability. It is a single jet of music and feeling, a straight flight without appearance of effort. The remaining four of our five themes are all various articulations of the 'scorne or shame' with which Donne 'brines' his reluctantly extorted tributes to the god of Love; monuments, unparalleled outside Catullus, to the close kinship between certain kinds of love and certain kinds of hate. The faithlessness of women is sometimes treated, in a sense, playfully; but there is always something – the clever surprise in 'Womans constancy' or the grotesque in 'Goe, and catche a falling starre' – which stops these poems short of a true anacreontic gaiety. The theme of faithlessness rouses Donne to a more characteristic, and also a better, poetry in such a hymn of hate as 'The Apparition', or in the sad mingling of fear, contempt, and self-contempt in 'A Lecture upon the Shadow'. The pains of secrecy give opportunity for equally fierce and turbulent writing. I may be deceived when I find in the sixteenth Elegy, along with many other nauseas and indignations, a sickened male contempt for the whole female world of nurses and 'midnight startings' and hysterics; but 'The Curse' is unambiguous. The ending here is particularly delicious just because the main theme – an attack on *Jalosie* or the 'lozengiers' – is so medieval and so associated with the 'honour of love'. Of the poet's own fickleness one might expect, at last, a merry treatment; and perhaps in 'The Indifferent' we get it. But I am not sure. Even this seems to have a sting in it. And of 'Loves Usury' what shall I say? The struggle between lust and reason, the struggle between love and reason, these we know; but Donne is perhaps the first poet who has ever painted lust holding love at arm's length, in the hope 'that there's no need to trouble himself with any such thoughts yet' – and all this only as an introduction to the crowning paradox that in old age even a reciprocated love must be endured. The poem is, in its way, a masterpiece, and a powerful indirect expression of Donne's habitual 'shame and scorne'. For, in the long run, it must be admitted that 'the love of hatred and the hate of love' is the main, though not the only, theme of the *Songs and Sonets*. A man is a fool for loving and a double fool for saying so in 'whining poetry'; the only excuse is that the sheer difficulty of drawing one's pains through rhyme's vexation 'allays' them. A woman's love at best will be only the 'spheare' of a man's – inferior to it as the heavenly spheres are to their intelligences or air to angels. Love is a spider that can transubstantiate all sweets into bitter : a devil who differs from his fellow devils at court by taking the soul and giving nothing in exchange. The mystery which the Petrarchans or their medieval predecessors made of it is 'imposture all', like the claims of alchemists. It is a very simple matter (*foeda et brevis voluptas*), and all it comes to in the end is

> that my man
> Can be as happy as I can.

Unsuccessful love is a plague and tyranny; but there is a plague even worse – Love might try

> A deeper plague, to make her love mee too !

Love enjoyed is like gingerbread with the gilt off. What pleased the whole man now pleases one sense only –

> And that so lamely, as it leaves behinde
> A kinde of sorrowing dulnesse to the minde.

The doctors say it shortens life.

It may be urged that this is an unfair selection of quotations, or even that I have arrived at my picture of Donne by leaving out all his best poems, for one reason or another, as 'exceptions', and then describing what remains. There is one sense in which I admit this. Any account of Donne which concentrates on his love poetry must be unfair to the poet, for it leaves out much of his best work. By hypothesis, it must neglect the dazzling sublimity of his best religious poems, the grotesque charm of *The Progresse of the Soule,* and those scattered, but exquisite, patches of poetry that appear from time to time amidst the insanity of the first and second 'Anniversaries'. Even in the *Epistles* there are good passages. But as far as concerns his love poetry, I believe I am just. I have no wish to rule out the exceptions, provided that they are admitted to be exceptions. I am attempting to describe the prevailing tone of his work, and in my description no judgement is yet implied.

To judgement let us now proceed. Here is a collection of verse describing with unusual and disturbing energy the torments of a mind which has been baffled in its relation to sexual love by certain temporary and highly special conditions. What is its value? To admit the 'unusual and disturbing energy' is, of course, to admit that Donne is a poet; he has, in the modern phrase, 'put his stuff across'. Those who believe that criticism can separate inquiry into the success of communication from that into the value of the thing communicated will demand that we should now proceed to evaluate the 'stuff'; and if we do so, it would not be hard to point out how transitory and limited and, as it were, accidental the appeal of such 'stuff' must be. But something of the real problem escapes under this treatment. It would not be impossible to imagine a poet dealing with this same stuff, marginal and precarious as it is, in a way that would permanently engage our attention. Donne's real limitation is not that he writes *about,* but that he writes *in,* a chaos of violent and transitory passions. He is perpetually excited and therefore perpetually cut off from the deeper and more permanent springs of his own excitement. But how is this to be separated from his technique – the nagging, nudging, quibbling stridency of his manner? If a man writes thus, what can he communicate but excitement? Or again, if he finds nothing but excitement to communicate, how else should he write? It is impossible here to distinguish cause from effect. Our concern, in the long run, must be with the actual poetry (the 'stuff' *thus* communicated, this communication of *such* 'stuff') and with the question how far that total phenomenon is calculated to interest human imagination. And to this question I can see only one answer : that its interest, save for a mind specially predisposed in its favour, must be short-lived and superficial, though intense. Paradoxical as it may seem, Donne's poetry is too simple to satisfy. Its complexity is all on the surface – an intellectual and fully conscious complexity that we soon come to the end of. Beneath this we find nothing but a limited series of 'passions' – explicit, mutually exclusive passions which can be instantly and adequately labelled as such – things which can be readily talked about, and indeed, must be talked about because, in silence, they begin to lose their hard outlines and overlap, to betray themselves as partly fictitious. That is why Donne is always arguing. There are puzzles in his work, but we can solve them all if we are clever enough; there is none of the depth and ambiguity of real experience in him, such as underlies the apparent simplicity of *How sleep the brave* or *Songs of Innocence*, or even Αἰαῖ Λευλύδριον.[4] The same is true, for the most part, of the specifically 'metaphysical' comparisons. One idea has been put into each and nothing more can come out of it. Hence they tend to die on our hands, where some seemingly banal comparison of a woman to a flower or God's anger to flame can touch us at innumerable levels and renew its virginity at every reading. Of all literary virtues 'originality', in the vulgar sense, has, for this reason, the shortest life. When we have once mastered a poem by Donne there is nothing more to do with it. To use his own simile, he deals in earthquakes, not in that 'trepidation of the spheres' which is so much less violent but 'greater far'.

Some, of course, will contend that his love poems should interest me permanently because of their 'truth'. They will say that he has shown me passion with the mask off, and catch at my word 'uncomfortable' to prove that I am running away from him because he tells me more truth than I can bear. But this is the mere frenzy of anti-romanticism. Of course, Donne is true in the sense that passions such as he presents do occur in human experience. So do a great many other things. He makes his own selection, like Dickens, or Gower, or Herrick, and his world is neither more nor less 'real' than theirs; while it is obviously less real than the world of Homer, or Virgil, or Tolstoy. In one way, indeed, Donne's love poetry is less true than that of the Petrarchans, in so far as it largely omits the very thing that all the pother is about. Donne shows us a variety

of sorrows, scorns, angers, disgusts, and the like which arise out
of love. But if any one asked 'What is all this *about*? What is the
attraction which makes these partings so sorrowful? What is the
peculiarity about this physical pleasure which he speaks of so con-
temptuously, and how has it got tangled up with such a storm of
emotions?', I do not know how we could reply except by pointing
to some ordinary love poetry. The feeblest sonnet, almost, of the
other school would give us an answer with coral lips and Cupid's
golden wings and the opening rose, with perfumes and instruments of music, with some attempt, however trite, to paint that
iridescence which explains why people write poems about love at
all. In this sense Donne's love poetry is parasitic. I do not use this
word as a term of reproach; there are so many good poets, by now,
in the world that one particular poet is entitled to take for granted
the depth of passion and deal with its froth. But as a purely descriptive term, 'parasitic' seems to me true. Donne's love poems could
not exist unless love poems of a more genial character existed first.
He shows us amazing shadows cast by love upon the intellect, the
passions, and the appetite; to learn of the substance which casts
them we must go to other poets, more balanced, more magnani-
mous, and more humane. There are, I well remember, poems
(some two or three) in which Donne himself presents the substance; and the fact that he does so without much luxury of language and symbol endears them to our temporarily austere taste.
But in the main, his love poetry is *Hamlet* without the prince.

   Donne's influence on the poets of the seventeenth century is a
commonplace of criticism. Of that influence at its best, as it is seen
in the great devotional poetry of the period, I have not now to
speak. In love poetry he was not, perhaps, so dominant. His
nequitae probably encouraged the cynical and licentious songs of
his successors, but, if so, the imitation is very different from the
model. Suckling's impudence, at its best, is light-hearted and very
unlike the ferocity of Donne; and Suckling's chief fault in this vein
– a stolid fleshliness which sometimes leads him to speak of his
mistress's body more like a butcher than a lecher – is entirely his
own. The more strictly metaphysical elements in Donne are, of
course, lavishly reproduced; but I doubt if the reproduction succeeds best when it is most faithful. Thus Carew's stanzas 'When
thou, poor Excommunicate' or Lovelace's 'To Lucasta, going be-

yond the Seas' are built up on Donne's favourite plan, but both, as
it seems to me, fail in that startling and energetic quality which
this kind of thing demands. They have no edge. When these poets
succeed it is by adding something else to what they have learned
from Donne – in fact by reuniting Donne's manner with something
much more like ordinary poetry. Beauty (like cheerfulness) is always breaking in. Thus the conceit of asking where various
evanescent, beautiful phenomena go when they vanish and reply-
ing that they are all to be found in one's mistress is the sort of conceit that Donne might have used; and, starting from that end, we
could easily work it up into something tolerably like bad Donne.
As thus :

> Oh fooles that aske whether of odours burn'd
> The seminall forme live, and from that death
> Conjure the same with chymique arte – 'tis turn'd
> To that quintessence call'd her Breath !

But if we use the same idea as Carew uses it we get a wholly
different effect :

> Aske me no more where *Jove* bestowes,
> When *June* is past, the fading rose :
> For in your beautyies orient deepe,
> These flowers, as in their causes, sleepe.

The idea is the same. But the choice of the obvious and obviously
beautiful rose, instead of the recondite seminal form of vegetables,
the great regal name of Jove, the alliteration, the stately volup-
tuousness of a quatrain where all the accented syllables are also
long in quantity (a secret little known) – all this smothers the sharpness of thought in sweetness. Compared with Donne, it is almost
soporific; compared with it, Donne is shrill. But the conceit is
there; and 'as in their causes, sleep' which looks at first like a
blunder, is in fact a paradox that Donne might have envied. So
again, the conceit that the lady's hair outshines the sun, though
not much more than an Elizabethan conceit, might well have
appeared in the *Songs and Sonets*; but Donne would neither have
wished, nor been able, to attain the radiance of Lovelace's.

> But shake your head and scatter day !

This process of enchanting, or, in Shakespeare's sense, 'translating' Donne was carried to its furthest point by Marvell. Almost every element of Donne – except his metrical roughness – appears in the 'Coy Mistress'. Nothing could be more like Donne, both in the grimness of its content and in its impudently argumentative function, than the conceit that

> Worms shall try
> That long preserved Virginity . . .

All the more admirable is the art by which this, and everything else in that poem, however abstruse, dismaying, or sophistical, is subordinated to a sort of golden tranquillity. What was death to Donne is mere play to Marvell. 'Out of the strong', we are tempted to say, 'has come sweetness', but in reality the strength is all on Marvell's side. He is an Olympian, ruling at ease for his own good purposes, all that intellectual and passionate mobility of which Donne was the slave, and leading Donne himself, bound, behind his chariot.

From all this we may conclude that Donne was a 'good influence' – a better influence than many greater poets. It would hardly be too much to say that the final cause of Donne's poetry is the poetry of Herbert, Crashaw, and Marvell; for the very qualities which make Donne's kind of poetry unsatisfying poetic food make it a valuable ingredient.

S o u r c e : *Seventeenth Century Studies Presented to Sir Herbert Grierson* (1938).

NOTES

1. Those who object to 'emotive terms' in criticism may prefer to read 'used by an accomplished poet to produce an attitude relevant not directly to outer experience but to the central nucleus of the total attitude-and-belief-feeling system'. It must not be supposed, however, that the present writer's theory of either knowledge or value would permit him, in the long run, to accept the restatement.

2. In this we have been anticipated. See *Emma*, chap. 25 : 'I know what worthy people they are. Perry tells me that Mr Cole never touches malt liquor. You would not think it to look at him, but he is bilious – Mr Cole is very bilious'.

3. The restatement of this in terms acceptable to the Richardian school (for whom all poetry equally is addressed to the nervous system) should present no difficulty. For them it will be a distinction between parts, or functions, of the system.

4. The superficial simplicity here is obvious; the deeper ambiguity becomes evident if we ask whether Lipsydrion is an object of detestation or of nostalgic affection.

Joan Bennett

THE LOVE POETRY OF
JOHN DONNE – A REPLY TO
MR C. S. LEWIS (1938)

In that brilliant and learned book *The Allegory of Love* Mr Lewis
writes, 'cynicism and idealism about women are twin fruits on the
same branch – are the positive and negative poles of a single
thing'. Few poets provide a better illustration of this than John
Donne. These *Songs and Sonets* and *Elegies* which, Mr Lewis
would have us believe, never explain 'why people write poems
about love at all', are the work of one who has tasted every fruit
in love's orchard, from that which pleased only while he ate it –

> And when hee hath the kernell eate
> Who doth not fling away the shell? –

to that which raised a thirst for even fuller spiritual satisfaction,
so that he wrote :

> Here the admyring her my mind did whett
> To seeke thee God.

How is it then that distinguished critics wonder what it is all about;
that Dryden declares 'Donne perplexes the minds of the fair sex
with nice speculations of philosophy, when he should engage their
hearts and entertain them with the softness of love'; and that Mr
Lewis wonders 'what any sensible woman can make of such love-
making'? A part of the trouble is, I believe, that they are accustomed to, or that they prefer, another kind of love poetry, in which
the poet endeavours to paint the charms of his mistress :

> Some asked me where Rubies grew
> And nothing I did say :
> But with my finger pointed to
> The lips of Julia.

> Some asked how Pearls did grow and where?
> Then spoke I to my Girle,
> To part her lips and show them there
> The Quarelets of Pearl.

Donne tells us very little about that beauty of 'colour and skin' which he describes in 'The Undertaking' as 'but their oldest clothes'. He writes almost exclusively about the emotion, and not about its cause; he describes and analyses the experience of being in love, if I may use that word for the moment to cover his many kinds of experience which range from the mere sensual delight presupposed in Elegy XIX to the 'marriage of true minds' celebrated in 'The good-morrow', or in 'The Valediction : forbidding mourning'. In Elegy XIX, for instance, Donne is writing of the same kind of experience as that of which Carew writes in 'The Rapture'. But Carew expends his poetic gifts in description of the exquisite body of the woman, so that the reader can vicariously share his joys. Donne, on the other hand, gives two lines to description, and even so they are not really about what he sees; he is content to suggest by analogy the delight of the eye when the woman undresses :

> Your gown going off, such beautious state reveals,
> As when from flowry meads th'hills shadow steales.

The poem is not about her exquisite body, but about what he feels like when he stands there waiting for her to undress. Now it may be that 'any sensible woman' would rather be told of

> Thy bared snow and thy unbraided gold,

but I am not sure. She can see that in her looking-glass, or she may believe she sees these things reflected in the work of some painter, for the painter's art can show such things better than any words. It may interest her more to know what it feels like to be a man in love. In any case, it is of that that Donne chooses to write. He is not incapable of describing physical charms; his description of a blush in 'The second Anniversarie' :

> her pure, and eloquent blood
> Spoke in her cheekes, and so distinctly wrought,
> That one might almost say, her body thought;

is better, in my judgement, than Spenser's

> And troubled bloud through his pale face was seene
> To come and goe with tydings from the hart.[1]

Or again, Mr Lewis speaks of the radiance of Lovelace's line,

> But shake your head and scatter day,

which was anticipated, and perhaps suggested, by Donne's

> Ev'ry thy haire for love to worke upon
> Is much too much, some fitter must be sought;
> For, nor in nothing, nor in things
> Extreme, and scatt'ring bright, can love inhere.

But the fact remains that such touches of description are very rare in Donne's poetry. His interest lay elsewhere, namely in dramatizing, and analysing, and illustrating by a wealth of analogy the state, or rather states, of being in love.

But what does he mean by love? We have the whole mass of Donne's poems before us, thrown together higgledy-piggledy with no external evidence as to when or to whom any one of them was written. And in some of them love is 'imposture all', or 'a winter-seeming summers night'; in others physical union is all in all so that two lovers in bed are a whole world; and elsewhere we are told that

> Difference of sex no more wee knew
> Than our Guardian Angells doe.

And elsewhere again :

> Our bodies why doe wee forbeare?
> They'are ours, though they'are not wee, Wee are
> The intelligences, they the spheare.
> We owe them thankes, because they thus,
> Did us, to us, at first convay,
> Yeelded their forces, sense, to us,
> Nor are drosse to us, but allay.

The temptation to assign each poem to a particular period and to associate each with a particular woman is very strong. It has been yielded to again and again, not only in Sir Edmund Gosse's biography, but much more recently. Yet it must be resisted for two reasons : first because we have no evidence as to when any one of the *Songs and Sonets* was written, and secondly because we cannot know how far the experience of which any one of them treats was real or imaginary. Mr Lewis is very well aware of these things. But it is no less misleading to go to the other extreme and read them as though they were all written at one time, or all with equal seriousness and sincerity. We have some important facts to guide us. Between the years 1597 and 1601 Donne fell in love with Anne More. He married her in 1601, as Walton puts it, 'without the allowance of those friends whose approbation always was, and ever will be necessary, to make even a virtuous love become lawful'. He had nine children by her, and watched over them with her when they were sick, and suffered with her when some of them died. He had been married seven years when he wrote a letter headed 'From mine hospital at Mitcham', in which he says :

I write from the fire-side in my parlour, and in the noise of three gamesome children, and by the side of her whom, because I have transplanted to such a wretched fortune, I must labour to disguise that from her by all such honest devices, as giving her my company and discourse.

Three years later, in 1611, Donne is reluctant to leave home and travel with his patron Sir Robert Drury, because his wife, who was then with child, 'professed an unwillingness to allow him any absence from her saying her divining soul boded her some ill in his absence'. The wording of that sentence, quoted by Walton, is heard again in one of Donne's loveliest songs, but the sense is reversed. Experience tells us that when we are afraid to let a loved one go it is not, as a rule, because *we* may come to harm in his absence. It is much more probable that Anne Donne was afraid for her husband on those dangerous seas to which his poetry so often refers, and that he then wrote the lyric for her, which pleads :

> Let not thy divining heart
> Forethinke me any ill,
> Destiny may take thy part,
> And may thy feares fulfill;
> But thinke that wee
> Are but turn'd aside to sleepe;
> They who one another keepe
> Alive, ne'r parted bee.

This is of course conjecture, and I claim no more than a strong probability. It was on this journey with Sir Robert, which Donne finally and reluctantly undertook, that he saw that 'vision of his wife with a dead child in her arms' that Walton so convincingly describes. I am not concerned with the authenticity or otherwise of the vision, but with the direction of Donne's thoughts. In 1614, thirteen years after his marriage, we have further evidence of the constancy and of the quality of Donne's love for his wife. In a letter to Sir Robert More, on 10 August of that year, he again explains why he cannot and will not leave Anne in solitude :

When I begin to apprehend that, even to myself, who can relieve myself upon books, solitariness was a little burdensome, I believe it would be much more so to my wife if she were left alone. So much company therefore, as I am, she shall not want; and we had not one another at so cheap a rate as that we should ever be weary of one another.

Such words need no comment. But if any more evidence is required as to the nature and endurance of Donne's love for his wife, we have Holy Sonnet XVII, written after her death in 1617 :

> Since she whom I lov'd hath payd her last debt
> To Nature, and to hers, and my good is dead,
> And her Soule early into heaven ravished,
> Wholly on heavenly things my mind is sett.
> Here the admyring her my mind did whett
> To seek thee God; so streames do shew their head.

Without claiming any knowledge as to the dates of particular poems, we are bound to recognize that seventeen years of married love will have taught Donne something he did not know when he wrote, for instance, Elegy VII. And we do, in fact, find that the poems express views of love which could scarcely all have been held at the same time.

Mr Lewis, of course, recognizes that Donne's love poetry is 'not all of a piece'. 'There are poems', he admits, 'in which Donne attempts to sing of a love perfectly in harmony with the moral law, but they are not very numerous and I do not think they are usually among his best pieces.' That judgement seems to me very cold, but it is impossible to discuss it without first deciding of what 'moral law' we are thinking. The moral law governing sexual relations has been very differently conceived of in different periods of the world's history. No one has expounded the medieval view more clearly than Mr Lewis himself in *The Allegory of Love* where he explains[2] that, for the medieval Church,

love itself was wicked and did not cease to be wicked if the object of it were your own wife. . . . The views of the medieval churchman on the sexual act within marriage are limited by two complementary agreements. On the one hand nobody ever asserted that the act was intrinsically sinful. On the other hand all were agreed that some evil element was present in every concrete instance of it since the Fall.

Mr Lewis believes that Donne never for long freed himself from his 'medieval sense of the sinfulness of sexuality'. Born a Roman Catholic, and deeply read in the Fathers of the Church, he must of course have considered it. But does his poetry support the belief that he continued to accept it? The value of Donne's love poetry largely depends upon the answer. 'The great central movement of love poetry in Donne's time', Mr Lewis reminds us, was at variance with the medieval view. It was now believed that marriage sanctified sexual love; and for Spenser, once the marriage ceremony is over, the sexual act is its proper consummation and the chaste moon bears witness to it in the 'Epithalamion':

> Who is the same, which at my window peepes?
> Or whose is that faire face that shines so bright?
> Is it not Cinthia, she that never sleepes,
> But walkes about high heaven al the night?
> O fayrest goddesse, do thou not envy
> My love with me to spy:

For thou likewise didst love, though now unthought,
And for a fleece of wooll, which privily
The Latmian shepherd once unto thee brought,
His pleasure with the wrought.
Therefore to us be favorable now;
And sith of women's labours thou hast charge,
And generation goodly dost enlarge,
Encline thy will t'effect our wishful vow,
And the chaste wombe informe with timely seed,
That may our comfort breed :
Till which we cease our hopeful hap to sing,
Ne let the woods us answere, nor our Eccho ring.

On the other hand, in Chapman's *Hero and Leander*, to which Mr
Lewis especially invites our attention, we have the reverse aspect
of this view of the morality of love. The sexual act before marriage, albeit the expression of true love, is not in harmony with
the moral law :

By this the Sovereign of Heavens golden fires,
And young *Leander,* Lord of his desires,
Together from their lovers armes arose :
Leander into Hellespontus throwes
His Hero-handled bodie, whose delight
Made him disdaine each other Epithete,
And as amidst the enamoured waves he swims,
The God of gold of purpose guilt his lims,
That this word guilt, including double sence,
The double guilt of his *Incontinence,*
Might be exprest, that had no stay t'employ
The treasure which the Love-God let him joy
In his deare Hero, with such sacred thrift,
As had beseemed so sanctified a gift :
But like a greedie vulgar Prodigall
Would on the stock dispend, and rudely fall
Before his time, to that unblessed blessing,
Which for lusts plague doth perish with possessing.

Where does Donne stand in relation either to this belief that marriage, and marriage alone, sanctifies the sexual act, or to the
medieval view that it is alike sinful within or without the marriage

bond? If I read the poetry aright, he accepts neither view, or rather he totally rejects the second and does not consider the first. The purity or otherwise of the act depends for him on the quality of the relation between the lovers. We have in 'The Sunne Rising' a celebration of the same event as in the stanza quoted from 'Epithalamion'; but the difference in treatment is noteworthy. Donne is joyously impudent to the sun, whereas Spenser is ceremoniously respectful to the moon, and (which is the point here relevant), in Donne's poem we neither know nor care whether the marriage ceremony has taken place. For Donne, if delight in one another is mutual, physical union is its proper consummation; but, if the lovers are not 'interassuréd of the mind', then 'the sport' is 'but a winter-seeming summers night', and

> at their best
> Sweetnesse and wit they are but *mummy* possest.

There are a number of poems in which Donne is writing about love which has not reached physical consummation, but there is only one, 'The undertaking', in which he writes as though this state of affairs were satisfactory. Elsewhere he makes it plain that he has merely acquiesced, not without protest, in the human laws that forbade what he holds to be the natural expression of human loves. This reluctant obedience to the rules is most clearly stated in 'The Relique', where he explains precisely how he and the woman behaved, and makes known in a parenthesis what he thinks of the law that inhibited them :

> Comming and going, wee
> Perchance might kisse, but not between those meales;
> Our hands ne'r toucht the seales,
> Which nature, injur'd by late law, sets free.

Donne's poetry is not about the difference between marriage and adultery, but about the difference between love and lust. He does not establish the contrast between them in any one poem, but we arrive at his views by submitting ourselves to the cumulative evidence of all his poetry, and, in so far as they are relevant, of his prose and of his life as well. The most important part of this evi-

dence is the violent contrast between his cynical poems and those
in which he celebrates.

> our waking souls
> Which watch not one another out of feare.

In order to establish that contrast I must, unfortunately, refer
to the vexed question of Donne's rhythm. Mr Lewis assures us that
'most modern readers do not know how to scan'. However that
may be, unless they can hear the difference between quick and slow
movements, or between smooth and staccato, and unless they can
submit to the rhythm sufficiently to throw the emphasis precisely
where Donne has arranged for it to fall, they cannot understand
his poetry. If they can hear these things they will be aware of the
difference between the bored, flippant tone of

> Will no other vice content you?
> Will it not serve your turn to do, as did your mothers?
> Or have you all old vices spent, and now would find out others?
> Or doth a feare, that men are true, torment you?
> Oh we are not, be not you so,
> Let mee, and doe you, twenty know;

and the tone of angry scorn in

> Must I alas
> Frame and enamell Plate, and drinke in Glasse?
> Chase waxe for others seales? breake a colts force
> And leave him then, beeing made a ready horse;

and, so utterly remote from either, the controlled emotion in

> I scarce beleeve my love to be so pure
> As I had thought it was,
> Because it doth endure
> Vicissitude, and season, as the grasse;
> Me thinkes I lyed all winter, when I swore,
> My love was infinite, if spring make'it more.

The greatness of Donne's love poetry is largely due to the fact
that his experience of the passion ranged from its lowest depths to
its highest reaches. No one, not even Shakespeare, knew better than
he that

> The expense of spirit in a waste of shame
> Is lust in action; and till action, lust
> Is perjured, murderous, bloody, full of blame,
> Savage, extreme, rude, cruel, not to trust;
> Enjoy'd no sooner but despised straight;
> Past reason hunted; and no sooner had,
> Past reason hated.

Many of the *Songs and Sonets* and the *Elegies* dramatize the experience which Shakespeare here describes. But Donne came to know also the 'marriage of true minds', and many of his poems are about that experience. Nor does he repent of this love poetry in the *Holy Sonnets;* on the contrary, he expressly states that love for his wife led directly to the love of God. He does not even overlook his grosser experiences, but is prepared to use 'prophane love' to illustrate his faith in Christ's pity :

> No, no, but as in my idolatrie
> I said to all my profane mistresses
> Beauty, of pitty, foulnesse only is
> A signe of rigour : so I say to thee,
> To wicked spirits are horrid shapes assign'd
> This beauteous forme assures a piteous minde.

There is no note of shame here, neither wallowing self-abasement nor a hiding or forgetting of the past. He is simply using, characteristically, just what is relevant for his present purpose. Physical beauty, which his poetry so seldom describes, he nevertheless accepts as a type of the soul's beauty :

> For though mind be the heaven where love doth sit
> Beauty a convenient type may be to figure it.

Donne never despised the flesh. Even in a Lenten sermon he asks his hearers 'what Christian is denied a care of his health and a good habitude of body, or the use of those things which may give a cheerfulness to his heart and a cheerfulness to his countenance', and in his 'The Litanie' he prays

> From thinking us all soule, neglecting thus
> Our mutuall duties, Lord deliver us.

Mr Lewis's objections to 'The Extasie' depend upon Donne's treatment of the relation between soul and body, and it is therefore important to discover what in fact Donne thought about this. 'Love does not', writes Mr Lewis, 'prove itself pure by talking about purity. It does not keep on drawing distinctions between spirit and flesh to the detriment of the latter and then explaining that the flesh is after all to be used.' I must admit that I find this rather perplexing. Perhaps nothing can be proved by talking about it, neither the purity of love nor the purity of Donne's poetry. But language is the poet's only means of communication, and if Chapman is allowed to express his conception of the immorality of premarital relations by talking about it, why may not Donne, by the same means, express his belief that

> As our blood labours to beget
>   Spirits, as like soules as it can,
> Because such fingers need to knit
>   That subtile knot, which makes us man :
> So must pure lovers soules descend
>   T'affections, and to faculties,
> Which sense may reach and apprehend,
>   Else a great Prince in prison lies.

On what grounds does Mr Lewis object to Donne 'drawing distinctions between spirit and flesh to the detriment of the latter'? What else could he do? Could a man of his time and of his religion have thought of the flesh either as equal to or as indistinguishable from the spirit? Donne, like any man of his time, and, I suppose, any Christian of any time, thinks of the body as inferior to the soul, although it can be the 'temple of the Holy Ghost'. He is not singular in supposing that, in this life, the soul can and must express itself through the body. Milton goes so far as to assert that even the Angels need some equivalent for this means of expression :

> Whatever pure thou in the body enjoy'st
> (And pure thou wert created,) we enjoy
> In eminence; and obstacle find none
> Of membrane, joint, or limb, exclusive bars;
> Easier than air with air, if Spirits embrace,
> Total they mix, union of pure with pure
> Desiring, nor restrain'd conveyance need,
> As flesh to mix with flesh, or soul with soul.[3]

Donne, in 'The Extasie', is attempting (by this usual means of
employing a series of analogies) to explain that the union of spirit
with spirit expresses itself in the flesh, just as the soul lives in the
body and, in this world, cannot exist without it. The passage quoted
above includes one of these analogies, an obscure one for modern
readers because it depends on contemporary physiology. Sir Herbert Grierson supplies a quotation from Burton's *Anatomy of
Melancholy* which gives the explanation :

The spirits in a man which are the thin and active part of the blood,
and so are of a kind of middle nature, between soul and body, those
spirits are able to doe, and they doe the office, to unite and apply the
faculties of the soul to the organs of the body, and so there is a man.

Sir Herbert also refers us to Donne's twenty-sixth sermon which
throws yet more light on the notion to which the poem refers :

As the body is not the man [writes Donne], nor the soul is not the
man, but the union of the soul and the body, by those spirits through
which the soul exercises her faculties in the organs of the body, makes
up the man; so the union of the Father and the Son to one another,
and of both to us, by the Holy Ghost, makes up the body of the
Christian religion.

There are, I suppose, three possible views of the relation between
soul and body : the Manichaean view that the body is the work of
the Devil; the materialist view that 'explains all psychical processes
by physical and chemical changes in the nervous system', and so
makes the soul non-existent; and the orthodox Christian view that
the body and the soul are both from God and therefore both good.
We seem to have wandered far from Donne's 'Extasie', and if Mr
Lewis is right in thinking it a 'nasty poem', these philosophical considerations are irrelevant, and these theological considerations even
worse. But is he right? The point Donne wishes to make in 'The
Extasie', as in so many of his serious love poems, is that a man and
a woman united by love may approach perfection more nearly
than either could do alone :

> A single violet transplant
>   The strength, the colour, and the size,
>   (All which before was poore, and scant,)
>   Redoubles still, and multiplies.

> When love, with one another so
> Interinanimates two soules,
> That abler soule, which thence doth flow,
> Defects of lonelinesse controules.

I have tried to show that Donne was very far from retaining 'the medieval view of the sinfulness of sex'; but Mr Lewis has yet another accusation to bring, equally incompatible with my own belief that Donne is one of the greatest love poets in the English language. Contempt for women seems to him to permeate the poetry. Once again I shall be forced to assume that readers are more sensitive to rhythm than Mr Lewis supposes, for I am going to quarrel with Mr Lewis's interpretation of Elegy XVI largely by appealing to the reader's ear. He admits that he 'may be deceived' when he finds here 'a sickened male contempt for the whole female world of nurses and "midnight startings" '. Most certainly he is deceived, and the varied rhythms of that poem are an important index of the extent of that deception. One of the most remarkable things about the poem is the contrast between the solemn, tender music of the verse whenever Donne addresses the woman, and the boisterous staccato in which he describes the foreign lands to whose dangers she will be exposed if she insists upon following him abroad. I must beg leave to quote at sufficient length to illustrate the nature and extent of this difference.

> By our first strange and fatall interview,
> By all desires which thereof did ensue,
> By our long starving hopes, by that remorse
> Which my words masculine perswasive force
> Begot in thee, and by the memory
> Of hurts, which spies and rivals threatned me,
> I calmly beg : But by thy fathers wrath,
> By all paines, which want and divorcement hath,
> I conjure thee, and all the oathes which I
> And thou have sworne to seale joynt constancy,
> Here I unsweare, and overswear them thus,
> Thou shalt not love by wayes so dangerous.
> Temper, ô faire Love, loves impetuous rage,
> Be my true Mistris still, not my faign'd Page.

It is tempting to quote even more of this melodious pleading, but this is enough to illustrate the liturgical music of his address to this beloved of whom Mr Lewis can think Donne is contemptuous. When, in the same poem, he wants to express contempt, his music is very different :

> Men of France, changeable Camelions,
> Spittles of diseases, shops of fashions,
> Loves fuellers, and the rightest company
> Of Players, which upon the worlds stage be,
> Will quickly know thee, and no lesse, alas !
> Th'indifferent Italian, as we passe
> His warme land, well content to thinke thee Page,
> Will hunt thee with such lust, and hideous rage,
> As *Lots* faire guests were vext.

And now, in case the point is not yet proven, let us hear how he speaks of her 'midnight startings', and how the rhythm changes once again as she comes back into the picture :

> When I am gone, dreame me some hapinesse,
> Nor let thy lookes our long hid love confesse,
> Nor praise, nor dispraise me, nor blesse nor curse
> Openly loves force, nor in bed fright thy Nurse
> With midnights startings, crying out, oh, oh
> Nurse, ô my love is slaine, I saw him goe
> O'r the white Alpes alone; I saw him I,
> Assail'd, fight, taken, stabb'd, bleed, fall, and die.
> Augure me better chance, except dread *Jove*
> Thinke it enough for me to'have had thy love.

I said I would argue my case 'almost' solely on the grounds of rhythm, but in case Mr Lewis is right in thinking modern readers are for the most part impervious to the music of verse, they will, I trust, be convinced that the mere prose sense of the last line is incompatible with contempt for the woman.

No one will deny that at one period of his life Donne wrote of women with contempt. At this time he despised them equally for yielding to his lust or for denying themselves to him. There is nothing to choose between his contempt for the woman whom he

addresses as 'Nature's lay Idiot' in Elegy VII and his contempt for
the woman who has refused him, and to whom he addresses that
brilliant piece of vituperation 'The Apparition'. (Whether either
situation had its exact counterpart in real life is beside the point,
the contempt in the poems is real enough.) At this time he treats
with equal scorn the whore, both

> Her whom abundance melts and her whom want betraies,

and the 'fain'd vestall', and the woman who

> will bee
> False e'er I come, to two or three.

But the measure of his contempt for easy virtue, coyness, and faithlessness is the measure of his admiration when he finds a woman
to whom he can say

> So thy love may be my love's sphere.

But to Mr Lewis that, too, sounds contemptuous; and as 'Aire and
Angels' has been variously understood, it is worth while to pause
and examine the sentence in its context. The poem is an account
of Donne's search for, and final discovery of, the true object of
love. It begins with much the same idea as he expresses in the first
stanza of 'The good-morrow' :

> If ever any beauty I did see,
> Which I desir'd, and got, t'was but a dreame of thee.

In 'Aire and Angels' :

> Twice or thrice had I loved thee,
>   Before I knew thy face or name,
> So in a voice, so in a shapelesse flame,
> Angells affect us oft, and worship'd bee;
>   Still when, to where thou wert, I came,
> Some lovely glorious nothing I did see.

And here, as so often elsewhere in the *Songs and Sonets,* Donne
asserts his belief that 'pure lovers soules' must 'descend t'affections,
and to faculties' :

> But since my soule, whose child love is,
> Takes limmes of flesh, and else could nothing doe,
> More subtile than the parent is,
> Love must not be, but take a body too.

And at first he imagines that the physical beauty of the loved woman is the object of his search :

> And therefore what thou wert, and who,
> I bid Love aske, and now
> That it assume thy body, I allow,
> And fixe it selfe in thy lip, eye, and brow.

So far the progress is one to which we are accustomed, both in the literature of love and in experience; from a general reaching out after beauty to a particular worship of one person who sums up and overreaches all that had seemed fair in others. So Romeo catches sight of Juliet and forgets Rosalind :

> Did my heart love till now? forswear it, sight!
> For I ne'er saw true beauty till this night.

But Donne is not satisfied. There is no rest for his love in the bewildering beauty of his mistress :

> Whilst thus to ballast love, I thought,
> And so more steddily to have gone,
> With wares which would sinke admiration,
> I saw, I had loves pinnace overfraught,
>   Ev'ry thy haire for love to worke upon
>   Is much too much, some fitter must be sought;
>   For, nor in nothing, nor in things
> Extreme, and scatt'ring bright, can love inhere.

The search is not yet over. But it is to end in a discovery surely more pleasing to any woman in love than would be the mere worship of her beauty. Beauty is transient, but love can last if it be for something which, though expressed in the body, is yet not the body :

> Then as an Angell, face and wings
> Of aire, not pure as it, yet pure doth weare,
> So thy love may be my loves spheare.

The doctrine of St Thomas Aquinas, about the Angels assuming a body of air, provided Donne with the analogy he wanted :

> Et sic Angeli assumunt corpora ex aere, condensando ipsum vir-tute divina, quantam necesse est ad corporis assumendi formationem.

So much is necessary; the point of the image for Donne is that the air-body of the Angels is neither nothing, nor too much, but just sufficient to confine a spirit on earth. So the woman's love for him is a resting-place for his spirit. It is, of course, that final couplet of the poem that has led to mis-understanding. Dr Leavis, in *Revaluations*,[4] speaks of 'the blandly insolent matter-of-factness of the close' of 'Aire and Angels'; and, isolated from its context, that is how it sounds :

> Just such disparitie
> As is twixt Aire and Angells puritie,
> 'Twixt womens love, and mens will ever bee.

There are two possible ways of reading this. The way which I am combating supposes that Donne, reversing the sentiment of the rest of the poem, throws out a contemptuous generalization about the impurity of woman's love in comparison with man's. My own view is that Donne, satisfied with the logical aptness of his image, is, characteristically, indifferent to the associations of the word 'purity', whose meaning is, to his mind, made sufficiently clear by the context. The air-body is only less pure than a man's in so far as it can exist on earth and so enable a spirit to appear to men. A woman's love is only less pure than a man's in so far as it is focused upon a single object and does not continually reach out towards 'some lovely glorious nothing'. I would support this view by referring the reader to other instances in which Donne shows a similar indifference to the irrelevant associations his words may suggest. The use of the word 'pure' in 'Loves growth' is similarly circumscribed by its context :

> I scarce beleeve my love to be so pure
> As I had thought it was,
> Because it doth endure
> Vicissitude, and season, as the grasse.

The sense in which it is not so pure is explained in the next stanza :

> Love's not so pure, and abstract, as they use
> To say, which have no Mistresse but their Muse,
> But as all else, being elemented too,
> Love sometimes would contemplate, sometimes do.

Donne is not saying that love is unclean, or less clean than he had supposed; we have already seen that he does not think of the flesh as impure in that sense, but that, like everything else on earth, it is composed of diverse elements. He is arguing that the quickening of love in the springtime is not an increase, since his love was complete before,

> And yet no greater, but more eminent,
> Love by the spring is growne;
> As, in the firmament,
> Starres by the Sunne are not inlarg'd, but showne;

and, to make his meaning clear, Donne adds three more images or illustrations :

> Gentle love deeds, as blossomes on a bough,
> From love awakened root do bud out now.

> If, as in water stir'd more circles bee
> Produc'd by one, love such additions take,
> Those like so many spheares, but one heaven make,
> For, they are all concentrique unto thee.

And finally, the 'blandly matter-of-fact' image :

> As princes doe in times of action get
> New taxes, but remit them not in peace.

Here, however, the last line of the poem,

No winter shall abate the springs encrease,

prevents the reader from supposing that the prosaic image implies
a reversal of the emotional tone of the poem. The point relevant
to my argument about 'Aire and Angels' is that Donne always
trusts the reader to ignore irrelevant associations. The political
image here is logically apt, and that is a sufficient reason for him
to use it. In a sermon on *The Nativity* he develops at some length
an image in which the Saviour is likened to a good coin with which
man's debt to God is paid :

First he must pay it in such money as was lent; in the nature and
flesh of man; for man had sinned and man must pay. And then it was
lent in such money as was coined even with the image of God; man
was made according to his image : that image being defaced, in a new
mint, in the womb of the blessed Virgin, there was new money coined;
the image of the invisible God, the second person in the Trinity, was
imprinted into the human nature. And then, that there might be all
fulness, as God, for the payment of this debt, sent down in bullion,
and the stamp, that is, God to be conceived in man, and as he provided the mint, the womb of the blessed Virgin, so hath he provided
an exchequer, where this money is issued; that is his church, where
his merits should be applied to the discharge of particular consciences.

No one, I suppose, will imagine that because Donne uses this mun-
dane imagery he is speaking irreverently of God, of the Virgin
Mary, of Christ, and of the Church. He chooses the image, here
as elsewhere, because it provides him with an apt analogy.

I hope I may have persuaded some readers that Donne did not
think sex sinful, and that contempt for women is not a general
characteristic of his love poetry. But Mr Lewis brings yet one more
accusation against him : 'He is perpetually excited and therefore
perpetually cut off from the deeper and more permanent springs
of his own excitement'. Now one way of answering this would be
to say that love is an exciting experience, and that great love poetry
is therefore bound to communicate excitement. But with this I am
not quite content. Love is exciting, but it is also restful. Unrecipro-
cated love is a torment of the spirit, but reciprocated love is peace
and happiness. In the astonishment and uncertainty of the early
stages of love there is excitement and there is also fear, but there

comes a time when there is confidence and a sense of profound security. Donne is a great love poet because his poetry records and communicates these diverse experiences. He would be less great if it were true that he is 'perpetually excited'. The truth is that, just as his early contempt for women is the measure of his later reverence for one woman, so his vivid experience of the torment of insecure love has made him the more keenly relish the peace of a love

> inter-assured of the mind.

He tells in 'The good-morrow' of lovers who

> watch not one another out of feare;

and in 'The Anniversarie' the final glory of a well-spent year is the sense of safety with which it has endowed the lovers :

> Who is so safe as wee? where none can doe
> Treason to us, except one of us two.

In 'The Canonization' he tells us that future lovers will address him and his mistress as

> You, to whom love was peace, that now is rage.

And in 'The Dissolution' we read of a love so secure that the 'elements' of love, 'fire of Passion, sighs of ayre, water of teares and earthly sad despaire' were 'ne'ere worne out by loves securitie'. There are two alternative readings of this line; it may be 'ne'ere worne out' (never) or 'neere worne out' (nearly). The former seems to me the more probable reading, since Donne is arguing that he is now overburdened with elements, which he is more likely to be if they had not been spent. Moreover, in 'loves securitie', 'fire of Passion, sighs of ayre, water of teares and earthly sad despaire' are not 'worne out' (such love does not call for the expense of spirit); 'never' fits the sense better than 'nearly', but, for my present argument, it is not of vital importance which reading we choose, the significant word is 'securitie'. Nor does Donne merely tell us of the fearlessness, safety, peace, and security that love may give; the serenity of which he speaks is reflected in the movement of his verse, the quiet speaking voice is heard in the rhythm of 'The

good-morrow', and in 'A Valediction : forbidding mourning', and
quiet pleading in the last stanza of 'A Valediction : of weeping' :

> O more then Moone,
> Draw not up seas to drowne me in thy spheare,
> Weepe me not dead, in thine armes, but forbeare
> To teach the sea, what it may doe too soone;
> Let not the winde
> Example finde,
> To doe me more harme, then it purposeth;
> Since thou and I sigh one anothers breath,
> Who e'r sighes most, is cruellest, and hasts the others death;

and in that gracious lyric, 'Sweetest love I do not goe'.

Since writing the above I have read Professor Crofts's article on
John Donne in *Essays and Studies,* vol. xxii, in which he presents
much the same case against the love poetry as Mr Lewis. Their
hostility to Donne springs from the same causes. Both are unable
to believe that a poet so brilliantly cynical is to be taken seriously
when he is reverent or tender. Yet this very diversity of experience
and feeling is among Donne's singular merits. Professor Crofts
complains (p. 131) that for Donne 'Love when it comes is not an
experience which . . . wipes away the trivial, fond records of youthful apostasy'. And that is true; the memory of trivial and bitter
moments was clear enough for him to draw upon them for
analogies even in the *Holy Sonnets*; whether this is regrettable or
no is a matter of taste. There is no doubt, however, that Donne's
habit of drawing upon all and any of his past experience bewilders
some readers; it is not customary. Equally unusual is the absence
of description which vexes both Mr Lewis and Professor Crofts.
'He cannot see her – does not apparently want to see her; for it is
not of her that he writes but of his relation to her.' That also is
perfectly true; the only question is whether good love poetry need
be descriptive.

But, in addition to these matters of taste and opinion, Professor
Crofts adduces two matters of fact in opposition to the view that
Donne's conception of love was altered by his relations with Anne
More. The first is Ben Jonson's remark in the *Conversations with
Drummond* that 'all his best pieces were written ere he was twenty
five years of age'. But we neither know which poems Jonson had

read when he made this remark, nor which he thought were the best. The second fact is that the *Metempsychosis* was dated by Donne himself Aug. 1601, four months before his marriage, and it contains cynical generalizations about women. As it is a fragment of a bitter satire against Queen Elizabeth, prompted by the sacrifice of Essex, that is not surprising. Moreover, is it so strange to be contemptuous of many, or even of most women and to love and reverence a few? The love and friendships which Donne enjoyed did not expunge his former experiences, but they enlarged his understanding so that the body of his poetry has a completeness which it could not otherwise have had. He had felt almost everything a man can feel about a woman, scorn, self-contempt, anguish, sensual delight, and the peace and security of mutual love. And he shapes such poems out of all this that we are, as Professor Crofts says, 'aware of the man speaking in a manner and to a degree hardly to be paralleled in our reading of lyric poetry. Every word is resonant with his voice, every line seems to bear the stamp of his peculiar personality.' Is this not enough to set him among the great love poets?

SOURCE: *Seventeenth Century Studies Presented to Sir Herbert Grierson* (1938).

NOTES

1. *The Faerie Queene*, I ix 51.
2. On p. 14.
3. *Paradise Lost*, Bk VIII, 622 9.
4. p. 12.

Arnold Stein

'THE GOOD-MORROW'

I take this poem as one of several for which Donne deserves Jonson's praise as 'the first poet in the world in some things'. It is a poem that immediately engages the reader; he is drawn into its action at once, but soon discovers that he must make his own exertions or fall behind. Perhaps it will be helpful first to quote the poem in full.

> I Wonder by my troth, what thou, and I
> Did, till we lov'd? were we not wean'd till then?
> But suck'd on countrey pleasures, childishly?
> Or snorted we in the seaven sleepers den?
> T'was so; But this, all pleasures fancies bee.
> If ever any beauty I did see,
> Which I desir'd, and got, t'was but a dreame of thee.
>
> And now good morrow to our waking soules,
> Which watch not one another out of feare;
> For love, all love of other sights controules,
> And makes one little roome, an every where.
> Let sea-discoverers to new worlds have gone,
> Let Maps to other, worlds on worlds have showne,
> Let us possesse one world, each hath one, and is one.
>
> My face in thine eye, thine in mine appeares,
> And true plain hearts doe in the faces rest,
> Where can we finde two better hemisphEares
> Without sharpe North, without declining West?
> What ever dyes, was not mixt equally;
> If our two loves be one, or, thou and I
> Love so alike, that none doe slacken, none can die.

A major initial problem, as in many of Donne's poems, is that we have no given tone, no stable attitude or defined position from which we can follow a clear development. Things appear to be in violent motion from the very beginning, and when the explosive dissonances of the first stanza come to an end, the sustained intensity and the dazzling nimbleness of effects will have imposed an impression on us that cannot end as abruptly as the stanza. The aesthetic question, which asks itself, is: will this return, or are we really done with it? To shift, as we must, to an imaginative world of peace in a cozy little room of love is a wrench that we also experience as a kind of violence, even though the subject presented is the peaceful satisfaction of love. And then, though we shall have studied the traditional basis from the metaphysical argument of the final three lines and found the argument 'correct' – still, how are we to take it? Not literally? And yet, have we acquired in motion enough sense of the tone of the poem to be able to gauge the degree of the literal in that argument? There may seem to be a kind of intellectual violence in the sudden introduction of an abstruse argument out of nowhere, and perhaps we may feel plunged back into the beginning of the poem, even if on a different plane.

Where tone is a problem, we may be helped by looking for stable elements of structure on which the poem is built. The three stanzas, we may notice at once, correspond to three stages. For instance, in terms of time we have a progression from past to present to future. At least that is the rough division; when we look more closely we can see a finer organization in the basic progression. But the fact of progression is definite, though the stages themselves are not limited only to their correspondence with time. We may also mark a movement from the first world of flesh to that of mind and thence to a world of spirit. The movement also corresponds to a turning from disparate multiplicity to a singleness of identity, with the middle term a kind of unified twoness. Parallel to this, there is a motion from restless change to conscious peace and rest, and thence to an idea of eternal motionlessness. All of these parallel movements refer to a single metaphysical concept expressed by the traditional argument which leads upward from sense and particular experience to a unifying transcendence. But the movements of the arguments are not without some enigma and reserve.

The apparent violence of the first stanza is due only in part to the explosive opening and to the startling rhetoric of physical reference. There is also a strenuous intellectual surprise, a play between

time-honored idealizing concepts of love and a sensuality which,
though dismissed, is given an overemphasis that may seem to dominate imaginatively, by vivid detail and rhythmical energy, the
ideal before which it ostensibly makes way. One aspect of the ideal
is a common one, a fact in experience and a convention in art :
that compelling contrast between the life before and the life after
the awakening of love. In retrospect all previous experience is fused
into a single, dull dimension of existence, and the awakened lover
sees with new eyes that all the objects passionately pursued were
unreal phantoms – at worst figures of evil distraction, at best
cloudy misrepresentations of the true object he now sees. If his
memory is keen, and the false objects can still be imagined with
sensuous immediacy, he is likely to disparage the authority of the
senses. The experience is common to lovers, but it may occur whenever there is an awakening in religion, or in philosophy, or in any
department of knowledge that aspires to some claim on reality.
Donne has united this familiar experience of the lover with its
philosophical counterpart, the Platonic contrast between the illusion of sensuous appearances and the truth of the ideal reality. And
something of the Platonic movement of love is also incorporated,
that turning from the sensuous multiplicity of the individual to a
purged love of universal beauty.

But Donne refuses to make the contrast absolute, and there is
mischief in his Platonizing. We do not emerge from the cave of the
senses, from the sucking and snorting and weaning, with no more
of a look backward than is necessary to dismiss the past. That is the
apparent effect of the 'T'was so' – a summary and a dismissal before the triumphant announcement of the new, exclusive definition
of reality. It starts properly enough, by equating pleasures and fancies : 'But this, all pleasures fancies bee'. However, the verbal form,
'be', is a little ambiguous; we have no ordinary statement of fact.
Nor is it clear, logically or syntactically, that the marvelous new
'this' is excluded from the definition of pleasures. If we are being
awakened to a higher form of pleasure, then we cannot apply the
apparent Platonic formula in its usual way. Some of the same
embarrassment attends that higher vision of beauty. The earthly
examples may have been only anticipations of the true ideal, part
of the fancy and the dream from which the lover now awakes; but
those muddy particles of beauty intrude themselves with such low,

concrete immediacy that they thrust themselves into the very presence of the ideal. Confession and rejection, if wholehearted and single-minded, should have come earlier. One does not re-create, with such imaginative authority, the whole process or cycle of the mistaken past – not as the last step before celebrating the entrance into the new life. And these intimations of the true beauty are not polite, self-rejecting harbingers, as properly they should be; nor are they suffering servants, whose most important service, after adequate self-reproach, is to disappear absolutely, with no afterimpression. Instead, these have been seen, desired, and got – as individual 'beauties'.

So an intellectual structure of the violence may be discerned in the imaginative disproportion between the immediate prominence of the rejected life and the formal dominance of the heralded ideal. The sensual past advertises itself up to the doorsill of the ideal present. If we solemnly expect a literal use of the Platonic distinctions, then we may be justified in thinking Donne mischievous. But we are not required to take the philosophical part as both central and seriously literal. The structure we feel suggests itself to us, intellectually, as building upon an imaginative disproportion. But this may in part be due to our trained expectations that the ideal will triumph absolutely and erase the past at once. Let us take another view. Is it not possible that we have less an imaginative disproportion, of the sort I have been describing, than strenuous tension of interests maintained to the end of the stanza – perhaps beyond? The poem is a witty poem, but the wit, I suggest, does not lie in any intellectual mischief or shocking outrageousness of details; it lies in the sustained imaginative power and imaginative consciousness we experience in the poem. The kind of structure we might expect from such a poem ought not depend too heavily on mere disproportions between elements put into simple contrasting relationship.

We have not tried to *hear* any of the structure yet, for we have been too busy trying to get other matters in their right place. As a matter of fact, the kinds of ambiguities we have been noticing are present whenever we try to read the first stanza aloud. Let us notice a distinguishable voice of some importance which may easily go unremarked.

The opening of the poem is ordinarily felt and described as

explosive. Is it? The first question is abrupt, but it differs from the
three questions that then fellow. These offer three strikingly individual images of physical activity, but they all serve the purpose of
presenting possible answers to the first question :

> I Wonder by my troth, what thou, and I
> Did, till we lov'd?

The tone of an oath is difficult to judge. If the speaker is aiming
only at the reader's shock over the weaning, sucking, snorting, then
we should minimize the difference between the first question and
the three that follow. But suppose the oath is not just a casual
mouth-filler, but tends toward the serious and swears by a newly
discovered faith in love. Suppose the speaker's wonder may be that
of genuine personal surprise, not to be translated into anything
quite like 'what the hell', 'who'd have thought'.

The chief justification for these remarks, and the first hint, is
what must happen when we read the most emphatic word until the
last line of the stanza – 'Did'. 'Did' and 'dreame' are the two most
important words in the stanza; between them they control the imaginative structure and so create an emphasis and resonance which
oppose the force generated by the more physically immediate, but
more nearly local, images. The noncommittal indefiniteness of
'Did', elevated by rhythmical position, and held up for a long
moment of contemplation, creates the possibility of a real wonder,
a surprised recognition of something not understood.

The 'Did' is indefinite and abstract, even though it surely includes the connotations of sexual *doing*. It is an immature abstraction, the summary of a youthful imagination, often bored, incapable of seeing the woods for the trees. What shall we do – what did
we ever do with the time? The doing is a summary blank; its
abstraction is an unindividualized version of immediate experience.
It precedes the account of rejected concrete experience, and then
another version of that concrete experience reappears in the more
sophisticated abstraction, the philosophical summary of the
'dreame of thee'. The wonder occurs in the present and looks backward; it produces the insulting items of a sleeping, a preconscious,
dream, the 'Did' of an *id,* infantile sexuality. But the 'dreame of
thee' is a waking dream of consciousness; it also occurs in the

present. When it looks backward to the past it does not do so with full immediacy; it does not immerse the imagination in the action of the past. Nevertheless, the items produced also impose their pressure upon the ideal state of the waking dream. The items from the past may be thought insulting, and they are not rejected with passionate contempt, as they were earlier. The chief point is that Donne has created a kind of progression familiar in musical structure, and when the items from the past reappear in their second version, they have been imaginatively modified. The first version expressed the full passion of utter rejection. That feeling then can make way for the recognition that the past led to the present, in ways that do not need to be liked but do not need to be hated – once the hate has been expressed, and once a kind of substantial meaning and purpose has been won from the progress. In a sense the development, the form of the progression, is its own justification. It leaves the speaker, as the first question did not, firmly in control of his wonder. The past has been brought into a significant, and subordinate, relationship to the present. The achievement may not be so clean – and the unpublished statistics on the varieties of human temptation might suggest that it is not so generally desired – as a complete and absolute break with the past. But there are compensations too. The honesty is its own reward; and in a poem celebrating the awakening of consciousness in love, imaginative deceptions become progressively harder to conceal.

And so the past is made to serve the present, even if some of the clear and triumphant independence of the present, its pure and underived uniqueness, may be diminished. Instead of uncertainty and reserve concerning Donne's concept of a unifying transcendence, we have a working demonstration of a movement upward that does not cut itself off from the past but imaginatively assimilates the fully recognized crudities of the past into the pattern of progression.

'And now good morrow to our waking soules.' The line hails and celebrates an arrival. Its most impressive effect is its newness; for the whole first stanza acts as contrasting background – as if, for the moment, this were the realized purpose, negative and defining, of the first stanza. The imaginative qualities of the line are those of openness and confident approval. In the speaker's voice we seem to hear an unreserved intellectual identification with what he says.

We are being invited to believe that this is what he has been moving toward, the unifying idea in the present toward which all the previous images have been progressing.

The first stanza, as first stage, brought the memory of the unconscious past of flesh toward a conscious relationship with the mind of the present. The second stanza makes declarations concerning that present; it prepares for the next stage but also looks back. Fear as a motivation for the lovers' watching each other, however lightly touched, however denied, is an intellectual equivalent of the misdirected activity which characterized the past history of sensual love. So too are those gay injunctions to the explorers, the sea-lovers and map-lovers – let them *have done* what they like to do! Their activities are dismissed from the present, not because they are contemptible or a passionate threat, but because they are inconsequential. In the third stanza the external world enters again, as another intellectual recollection of the past. In a way the reference is even further remote and abstract. The two hemispheres are those of a merely objective world, with which there can be no significant human relationship – that is, subjective interrelationship – except at the one point of contact, the idea of time and change. The 'sharpe North' and the 'declining West' – these belong to the world of passion and death from which the lovers have awakened. That world, like their preconscious past, has not been annihilated by the poetic imagination; it has been transformed by the lovers' consciousness of purpose; it defines by its cold externality the warm centre of a living present.

In the recurring modulations of the poem, its pattern of related and progressive movement, we may see and hear and feel the imaginative form of the poem. The movement itself leads us from a world of misdirected activities toward a lessened sense of their immediacy and relevance. This imaginative form seems to develop from a single principle, but it is a poetic insight and hard to isolate or name. And it was not given at once, or early, for it could reveal itself only in motion as part of the developing form. Let us call that principle a refusal to annihilate the past and the external. But we still must see what this means, this determination to imagine a mastery of present and future while transforming but not annihilating the elements which are excluded from the center of the experience.

'What ever dyes, was not mixt equally.' This is the applied conclusion of an abstract argument Donne learned from scholastic philosophy. It introduces the idea of death, not imaginatively immediate or threatening, but not quite abstract either; for it sums up all the rejected images from the external world of change, sums them up as a gentle reminder that they have been defeated and that the triumph of the warm present has been won in spite of them. The end of the poem turns, as the end of each preceding stanza has turned, to a summing up that consolidates the stage attained and looks forward to the next. It is this fact, more than the unexpected introduction of an abstract argument, which accounts for the strange tone at the end. That tone is not triumphant; it is not the tone of an enthusiastic voice proclaiming transcendence. Instead it is quiet, even modest. The argument does not undertake to prove, by any pride in the strength and edge of its logic, the infallible safety of the lovers' final arrival. It restates in other terms what has already been learned by the process of their experience, and it points that wisdom toward the future. It points with the modest tentativeness of *two* possible propositions, both based upon an *if*:

> If our two loves be one, or, thou and I
> Love so alike, that none doe slacken, none can die.

Again we must observe that what seemed violent or disproportionate is rather a tension of interests that carries through to the end, and points beyond the end, of the poem. Not that the poem is unresolved. Its problems are defined and true relationships are established. But its triumph is modest and human; it is a triumph of imaginative consciousness and not of intellectual or spiritual invulnerability. The kind of transcendence toward which the poem develops is not a goal which, once achieved, permits consciousness to surrender itself. That is why the poem both ends and seems to go on, pointing beyond itself. The effect is not a trick of wit; it is rather a proof of the imaginative fidelity of the poem to the nature and form of the experience created by it. That the effect is deeply characteristic of Donne, I may simply note without further comment.

Let me try to demonstrate the reliability of these conclusions by turning to matters I have slighted while following one line of the poem's development. The height of the triumph, at least as declaration, is the most ringing musical statement of the poem : 'And now good morrow to our waking soules.' But that arresting line does not proceed directly to further assertion. Instead we have the recapitulated items of the external world, lightly but firmly present to give definition to the imaginative scene in which love realizes its inner world. That inner world has a kind of grandeur in its imaginative extent as it moves out to become 'an every where'. But it is not single and simple either in its materials or in its imaginative reference. For the imagining is a conscious act, and something of the consciousness and the act remain in the effect.

What we have is a metaphor, in which the act and the process of imagining are not completely assimilated into a singleness of identification. It is an imaginative translation that knows it is imagining; the validity lies *both* in the translation (its balanced qualities of precision and fictive power to illuminate and open up just relationships) *and* in the discreet consciousness of the act. The validity lies in both. Although there is a kind of stability in the metaphor itself, which is due to the fact that we recognize the enclosed world of love as having an established form in the human imagination and in human experience, nevertheless it is not a form which is incontrovertible. It is not one of the great and stable symbols presented as lying outside the human mind, and presented so that the mind can merge itself into the symbol without further argument, and with a minimum of consciousness in the act. Let me quote Donne's lines and italicize two words :

> For love, all love of other sights controules,
> And *makes* one little roome, an *every where*.

The everywhere is important to Donne, and not only in this poem. The world of love as it takes shape in the poem defines its pure center both by exclusions and by inclusions. The preconscious dream of sensuality is excluded, but the conscious dream is assimilated into the higher 'dreame of thee'. The distractions of the external world are rejected; they are disunified and an argument for change and death. Yet here the little world of love does not exclude or quite assimilate the external, but it varies the movement by exhibiting its own imaginative power to move out into the world without suffering the consequences of change. It can enjoy the splendor and variety of the world at home, in the possession of its essential unity.

The unity of love is a unity of having and being. It is not single or mystic. It is not an inner world of inviolable subjectivity. It is a world of twoness united. Its stability depends upon a knowledge of its derivation and present condition. For it is a lyric moment precarious in a world of fact. In order to project its truth of feeling into the future, and its present sense of having escaped from the time-ridden to the timeless, the lovers must know what they feel and feel what they know. But the knowing, it is plain, never achieves a fixed and positive clarity like that of the lyric moment. The knowing is expressed in movement, by the tact and balance of the unfolding form, by the exclusions and inclusions of consciousness, by the intelligence that permeates the whole poem.

The most positive expressions of knowing are those which hail the lovers' waking souls and declare the transforming power of the 'one little roome'. But the salutation to their waking souls is less positive than it sounds; it creates the feeling of a state of intellectual clarity, but it does nothing to define, to objectify, to demonstrate – nothing, that is, by itself, removed from the demonstration of the form. Of course, it is not removed, except by our analysis. But our power to do this makes possible a negative distinction : that is, we cannot by analysis remove the positive states of feeling. They are defined, objectified, demonstrated, and they exist in positive moments. For instance, the love that 'makes one little roome, an every where' expresses a positive and demonstrated state of intellectual clarity, by which love declares its transforming power. The inner reality of love dares project itself into external reality without the usual dangers or consequences elaborately worked out in the philosophy books. But we have a positive intellectual state only because we have an imaginative state based upon a positive truth of the feelings. That truth is not only inaccessible to the arguments of the intellect; it has the sanction of universal psychological experience; furthermore, it is presented as an imaginative metaphor; furthermore, it does not pretend to universal validity, but makes its bold assertion from its private certainty within the moment created by the unity of love.

The distinction I am trying to make is that the *feeling* is pro-

jected with a kind of clarity, and positive simplicity, but that the
knowing is not so projected. To make the distinction is, I suppose,
to make a kind of judgment, but it is not one that the poem allows
us to press literally. The *knowing* and the *feeling* do not go their
separate ways; they are complementary and related; the unity of
love depends on their twoness being one, even though they also
maintain a tension of interests in the developing form of the poem.

Finally, let us consider these lines :

> My face in thine eye, thine in mine appeares,
> And true plain hearts doe in the faces rest.

The proof of the lovers' identification is in the having and being, in
the objective recognition of self in another and the feeling of
another in self. In that experience, where the lover sees his own
reflected face directly, while he sees directly the other face, but only
feels its image reflected in his own eyes, there exists the most delicate point of contact between the subjective and the objective.
The two lovers *are* one in the image, and so fulfill for the moment
those propositions that hang over the future. They are one, and
they do love alike. They have been mixed equally, and present an
ancient proof of human integration, the transparency of the heart
in the countenance. It is an ancient proof, mildly modernized and
individualized in the context by the play on 'plain' and by the special relevance of 'rest', which opposes the world of change. But
the familiar idea, and the emphasis of the utterance – its 'true
plain' rhythm, quite lacking in the individuality of the first line –
these express a directness of feeling that approaches the trite and
the obvious. Out of the context the triteness and obviousness would
be unmistakable. In the context they are a remarkable testimony
to a kind of simplicity of feeling not usually associated with Donne.
It is worth noting and remembering.

The consciousness of metaphor still is present, but it is less emphatic than in the imaginative transformation of the little room.
Here the image, as the scene, is more nearly simple and direct, and
the quality of the feeling is different. We have moved from the
ringing announcement of the good-morrow, to the demonstration
of power in the little room, to the climactic warmth of an actual
human relationship. Imaginative consciousness, *inside* the little

room, is only *outside* the present scene, as part of the form. The scene is completely itself, modest and actual, not needing to define or demonstrate, but doing so in the directness of the statement. In the line 'My face in thine eye, thine in mine appeares', the rhetorical emphasis, the meter, and the emphasis of feeling coincide almost exactly. The stress on 'thine . . . thine . . . mine', the reinforcement of that single sound by the 'my . . . eye' – these draw together in a singleness of effect which is deeply moving here, though the stylistic formula in the abstract sounds unpromising. Only 'face' and 'appeares', at the beginning and end of the line, express vowels and consonants different from the central interweaving of the *i-m-n-th*. May we think that this pattern of speech helps project a sense of unity between subject and object, between internal and external world? The line gives us our fullest single expression of the integrity of feelings and action. It is the highest point of feeling in the poem. And when we consider the two previous high points, 'And now good morrow to our waking soules . . . And makes one little roome, an every where', we must recognize that the highest point is also simplest.

Let us look back to bring some of these observations together. In a world of subjects and objects, the imaginative form of the poem refuses to annihilate the past or the external. Though the poem follows a pattern of transcendence, it does not do so by acts of simple exclusion. It is free of all the familiar assertions of intellectual or spiritual pride, and the fruits of a powerful honesty of consciousness are those of tact and grace. The lovers' unity requires intellectual subtlety and imaginative consciousness; they must be fully awake in order to solve the relationships between past and present, present and future, and between inner and outer reality. The imaginative consciousness never flags; it never forgets relationship. Even at the end of the poem there is no claim for immortality through love; the argument is no literal application of stiff metaphysics, but instead a modest proposal. What is literal, and surprisingly so, is the application of the metaphysical lesson to the real world of love : the alternative to the unity of love is the death of love.

And so the subtlety of the poem ends in intellectual modesty and awakened simplicity. In the partnership between knowing and feeling, the knowing is more obviously active in the poem, though less fixed and positive; but there is a partnership, and the progress is toward simplicity. The wit may lie in imaginative consciousness, but it is not what is usually meant by intellectual wit. In fact, if I have interpreted the movement of the poem correctly, one might prefer an opposing coinage and speak of Donne's emotional wit or the wit of simplicity.

Source: *John Donne's Lyrics: the Eloquence of Action* (1962).

Louis Martz

JOHN DONNE: LOVE'S
PHILOSOPHY (1969)

. . . Donne's love-poems take for their basic theme the problem of
the place of human love in a physical world dominated by change
and death. The problem is broached in dozens of different ways,
sometimes implicitly, sometimes explicitly, sometimes by asserting the immortality of love, sometimes by declaring the futility of
love. Thus the *Songs and Sonets* hold within themselves every conceivable attitude toward love threatened by change. At the one
extreme lie the cynical, cavalier songs, the famous 'Goe, and catche
a falling starre', or 'The Indifferent', spoken by one who can 'love
any, so she be not true'. Even beyond this, we have the extreme of
bitter disillusionment in that somber poem 'Farewell to Love',
where the poet asks whether love is no more than a gingerbread
King discarded after a fair :

> But, from late faire
> His highnesse sitting in a golden Chaire,
> Is not lesse cared for after three dayes
> By children, then the thing which lovers so
> Blindly admire, and with such worship wooe;
> Being had, enjoying it decayes :
> And thence,
> What before pleas'd them all, takes but one sense,
> And that so lamely, as it leaves behinde
> A kinde of sorrowing dulnesse to the minde.

At the other extreme, perhaps only a poem or two after some poem
of cynicism, we will find such a poem as 'The Undertaking', where
Donne moves to the opposite extreme of pure platonic love, challenging the reader with these words :

> But he who lovelinesse within
> Hath found, all outward loathes,

> For he who colour loves, and skinne,
>   Loves but their oldest clothes.
>
> If, as I have, you also doe
>   Vertue'attir'd in woman see,
> And dare love that, and say so too,
>   And forget the Hee and Shee;
>
> And if this love, though placed so,
>   From prophane men you hide,
> Which will no faith on this bestow,
>   Or, if they doe, deride :
>
> Then you'have done a braver thing
>   Then all the *Worthies* did,
> And a braver thence will spring,
>   Which is, to keepe that hid.

It is clear that the libertine poems are the obverse, the counterpart, the necessary context, for the poems on constancy. The libertine poems express the fatigue, the cynicism, the flippancy, and the bitterness of the disappointed seeker after the One and True, as Donne very clearly says in his poem 'Loves Alchymie', which appropriately comes quite precisely in the middle of the *Songs and Sonets,* just after the great poem of true love 'A Valediction : of Weeping' :

> Some that have deeper digg'd loves Myne then I,
>   Say, where his centrique happiness doth lie :
>   I have lov'd, and got, and told,

('told' in the sense of 'have counted up the results')

> But should I love, get, tell, till I were old,
>   I should not finde that hidden mysterie;
>   Oh, 'tis imposture all :

Clearly the 'centrique happiness' that is here renounced represents an abstraction that lies beyond the physical. Such a poem as this represents a violent revulsion against the lover who has in such a poem as 'Aire and Angels' sought for an ideal beauty and loved an ideal beauty in his imagination :

Twice or thrice had I lov'd thee,
    Before I knew thy face or name;
So in a voice, so in a shapeless flame,
Angells affect us oft, and worship'd bee;
    Still when, to where thou wert, I came,
Some lovely glorious nothing I did see.
    But since my soule, whose child love is,
Take limmes of flesh, and else could nothing doe,
    More subtile than the parent is,
Love must not be, but take a body too,
    And therefore what thou wert, and who,
        I bid Love aske, and now
That it assume thy body, I allow,
And fixe it selfe in thy lip, eye, and brow.

But he discovers that her physical beauty is too dazzling for love to work upon and that some other abode for his love must be sought, and so he concludes, referring to the medieval doctrine that angels appeared to men in forms of mist or vapor :

Then as an Angell, face, and wings
Of aire, not pure as it, yet pure doth weare,
    So thy love may be my loves spheare;
        Just such disparitie
As is twixt Aire and Angells puritie,
'Twixt womens love, and mens will ever bee.

It may seem at first that the last two lines, with this emphasis upon the superior 'purity' of men's love to women's love, are not exactly complimentary to a being of such angelic nature; and yet, when we think of it closely, it is in fact a version of an old Petrarchan compliment. What he is saying is this : if she will extend her love toward him, if she will come down from her angelic status and deign to love a man, then his love for her may move like a planet within her love for him. But why is her love for him less pure than his love for her? Is it not because of the *direction* of their two loves : hers downward toward him, and his upward toward a creature of angelic purity? Donne appears to be combining here the Platonizing love philosophy of the Renaissance[1] with an older tradition, the tradition of the courtly lover inherited by Petrarch, in which the lady is a superior being of angelic purity and beauty, as is the lady of Spenser's sonnets. Donne is here, surprisingly enough, standing by the old Petrarchan tradition in his own winding way.

So it is with Donne's pursuit of love. It has many temporary conclusions, some cynical, some ennobling, but all only 'for a moment final', as Wallace Stevens might say. Behind all these varied posturings lies the overwhelming question : what is the nature of love, what is the ultimate ground of love's being? His best poems are not those which move toward either extreme in his answer, but they are rather those in which the physical and the spiritual are made to work together, through the curiously shifting and winding manner that marks Donne's movements toward Truth. One can sense that movement at its best in the poem known as 'Loves Growth' (though entitled 'Spring' in many of the manuscripts). It opens with the characteristic brooding over the problem of change :

> I scarce beleeve my love to be so pure
> As I had thought it was,
> Because it doth endure
> Vicissitude, and season, as the grasse;

With such an opening one might expect that the lover is about to lament the fact that his love has decayed; but, on the contrary, what worries him, what proves the instability of his love, is the fact that it seems to be increasing :

> Me thinkes I lyed all winter, when I swore,
> My love was infinite, if spring make'it more.

What then is the nature of love, he asks?

> But if this medicine, love, which cures all sorrow
> With more, not onely bee no quintessence,
> But mixt of all stuffes, paining soule, or sense,
> And of the Sunne his working vigour borrow,
> Love's not so pure, and abstract, as they use
> To say, which have no Mistresse but their Muse,
> But as all else, being elemented too,
> Love sometimes would contemplate, sometimes do.

Having decided then that the nature of love involves the total physical and spiritual being of man, Donne seems to drop the problem entirely in the second half of the poem, shifts his stance completely, and decides that in fact the problem of vicissitude and season does not really exist for this particular love of his :

> And yet not greater, but more eminent,
>   Love by the spring is growne;
>   As, in the firmament,
> Starres by the Sunne are not inlarg'd, but showne.

The scientific sound of the image has a satisfying effect, until one tries to decide exactly what it means, and then, as so often with Donne's conceits, the apparent assurance becomes considerably less sure. 'Eminent' is certainly used in the sense of 'prominent' but from here on the best commentators disagree. Grierson interprets the lines as meaning 'The stars at sunrise are not really made larger, but they are made to seem larger'. Miss Gardner, however, takes 'by the Sunne' to mean 'near the sun', thus : 'Love has risen higher in the heavens by spring and shines the more brilliantly as do stars when near to the sun'.[2] The latter meaning is almost certainly right, since Donne is not talking about sunrise, but about the rising of the spring. But we are not to examine the image closely; we are simply to gain its positive effect of security in love, as the remaining images continue to assure us with their varied action :

> Gentle love deeds, as blossomes on a bough,
> From loves awaken'd root do bud out now.
> If, as in water stir'd more circles bee
>   Produc'd by one, love such additions take,
>   Those like so many spheares, but one heaven make,
> For, they are all concentrique unto thee;
> And though each spring doe adde to love new heate,
> As princes doe in times of action get
> New taxes, and remit them not in peace,
> No winter shall abate the springs encrease.

But the last word 'encrease' would appear to contradict the beginning of this stanza. If there has been 'encrease' then love must have grown greater and love must not then be so pure as he had thought it was. And indeed, if we look closely at the last stanza we see that it does not basically deal with the assurance affirmed in the first four lines of that stanza, but rather carries on from the last line of the first stanza, 'Love sometimes would contemplate, sometimes do'. It soon appears that the speaker is talking about 'love-deeds' and that it is love in action that he wishes to see develop : these are the additions that love will take, like circles stirred in water, or like 'spheares' about one center. New heat is not a quality of a pure substance, in the scientific sense that Donne is broaching in the poem's first line. Love deeds, the buds of spring, circles in the water, the new heat of the season – all these are part of a transient and fluctuating physical universe. And indeed the surprising image

> As princes doe in times of action get
> New taxes, and remit them not in peace,

brings us vividly into the realistic world. Thus the assertion at the end, 'No winter shall abate the springs encrease' stands as a defiance against all the imagery of vicissitude that dominates the poem. We may believe the assertion, or we may believe the whole poem. In the end, I think, the poem is bound to win.

One can never be sure, then, where Donne's probing of the problem of mutability will lead. This is especially clear in the two poems where Donne uses, in different ways, his image 'A bracelet of bright haire about the bone'. In 'The Funerall' the poem begins by creating a symbol of constancy and immortality out of the 'wreath of haire', as the speaker imagines himself dead :

> Who ever comes to shroud me, do not harme
>   Nor question much
> That subtile wreath of haire, which crowns mine arme;
> The mystery, the signe you must not touch,
>   For 'tis my outward Soule,
> Viceroy to that, which then to heaven being gone,
>   Will leave this to controule,
> And keepe these limbes, her Provinces, from dissolution.

But, as with many of Donne's most resounding affirmations, the more the speaker broods about this and attempts to prove its truth, the more it tends to disintegrate. Here, in paralleling the mistress's hair with the nerves that run throughout his body, he is led toward a glimpse of his Lady herself :

> These haires which upward grew, and strength and art
> Have from a better braine . . .

This memory of the Lady in her actual life suggests to him another and more cruel possibility in keeping with her nature :

> Except she meant that I
> By this should know my pain,
> As prisoners then are manacled, when they'are condemn'd to die.

He does not know what she could mean by such a gift and in despair he swaggers with his 'bravery', uttering at the end what amounts to a rude innuendo :

> What ere shee meant by'it, bury it with me,
> For since I am
> Loves martyr, it might breed idolatrie,
> If into others hands these Reliques came;
> As 'twas humility
> To'afford to it all that a Soule can doe,
> So, 'tis some bravery,
> That since you would save none of mee, I bury some of you.

In 'The Relique' the direction of thought is reversed. Whereas 'The Funerall' had moved from thoughts of fidelity to cynicism, 'The Relique' moves from cynical thoughts about love to an affirmation of a miraculous purity in human love. Thus the poem opens with some of Donne's most satirical innuendoes :

> When my grave is broke up againe
> Some second ghest to entertaine,
> (For graves have learn'd that woman-head
> To be to more then one a Bed)
> And he that digs it, spies
> A bracelet of bright haire about the bone,
> Will he not let'us alone,

> And thinke that there a loving couple lies,
> Who thought that this device might be some way
> To make their soules, at the last busie day,
> Meet at this grave, and make a little stay?

Donne accepts the fact that even graves are not sacred, and suggests in the last few lines above that perhaps someone would think that this erotic symbol would indicate that some 'loving couple' have arranged for a last carnal assignation even while the Judge is busy with his work of salvation and damnation. But, as it turns out, this is not at all what these two lovers had in mind. She is not a Mary Magdalene, that is to say, a reformed prostitute, and he is nothing of the kind either. It is only the continuous misunderstanding of man, whether in the field of religion or in the field of love, that makes it certain that people will misinterpret the nature of this symbol.

> If this fall in a time, or land,
> Where mis-devotion doth command,
> Then, he that digges us up, will bring
> Us, to the Bishop, and the King,
>   To make us Reliques; then
> Thou shalt be'a Mary Magdalen, and I
>   A something else thereby;
> All women shall adore us, and some men;
> And since at such times, miracles are sought,
> I would that age were by this paper taught
> What miracles wee harmlesse lovers wrought.

> First, we lov'd well and faithfully,
> Yet knew not what wee lov'd, nor why,
> Difference of sex no more wee knew,
> Then our Guardian Angells doe;
>   Comming and going, wee
> Perchance might kisse, but not between those meales;
>   Our hands ne'r toucht the seales,
> Which nature, injur'd by late law, sets free :
> These miracles wee did; but now alas,
> All measure, and all language, I should passe,
> Should I tell what a miracle shee was.

It is, no doubt, a pure love, as the speaker declares. And yet there is something in the last six lines which doth protest too much. Why

should he regard their rare kisses as 'meales?' Why should he regard the seals of chastity as a restriction placed upon nature by
'late law' which thus injures the freedom of nature itself? And
why should, at the end, his feelings falter ('alas') into such a
desperate compliment? Perhaps the symbol of eroticism is not so
wide of the mark as the speaker declares. In both poems the meaning of that macabre symbol appears to be essentially the same :
it suggests the agonized reluctance of Donne to allow any severance
between the physical and the spiritual.

In a more obvious way, this reluctance to sever physical and
spiritual is shown in the short poem entitled 'The Anniversarie',
which opens with Donne's most splendid affirmation of the immortality of true love :

> All Kings, and all their favorites,
> All glory'of honors, beauties, wits,
> The Sun it selfe, which makes times, as they passe,
> Is elder by a yeare, now, then it was
> When thou and I first one another saw :
> All other things, to their destruction draw,
> Only our love hath no decay;
> This, no to morrow hath, nor yesterday,
> Running it never runs from us away,
> But truly keepes his first, last, everlasting day.

The plurality of the word *times* sums up the evanescence of worldly glories, and stresses, by contrast with the great doxology of the
last line, the eternity of this true love. But then in the second stanza
he remembers that in fact they must part, in some measure :

> Two graves must hide thine and my coarse,
> If one might, death were no divorce.
> Alas, as well as other Princes, wee,
> (Who Prince enough in one another bee,)
> Must leave at last in death, these eyes, and eares,
> Oft fed with true oathes, and with sweet salt teares;
> But soules where nothing dwells but love
> (All other thoughts being inmates) then shall prove
> This, or a love increased there above,
> When bodies to their graves, soules from their graves
>   remove.

We feel the strong clinging to the physical; but of course it is a consolation to remember that the souls will be united in heaven – and yet another thought comes upon the speaker as he remembers that in heaven they will lose the unique, distinctive nature of their love because there everyone will be thoroughly blessed – 'but wee no more, then all the rest'. His mind turns back to earth where their monarchy is unique :

> Here upon earth, we'are Kings, and none but wee
> Can be such Kings, nor of such subjects bee;
> Who is so safe as wee? where none can doe
> Treason to us, except one of us two.
>   True and false feares let us refraine,
> Let us love nobly, and live, and adde againe
> Yeares and yeares unto yeares, till we attaine
> To write threescore : this is the second of our raigne.

We notice how in the last four lines the poet tacitly concedes that this perfect love is not immortal, but is subject to the rule of times. They will celebrate the beginning of the second year of their reign, which will last until they are threescore. He speaks of holding back 'True and false feares'. The false fear is fear that they will ever be untrue to one another, but the true fear is that their mortal love is indeed subject to mortality.

The same problem gives its deep poignancy to the famous 'Valediction : forbidding Mourning', where the affirmation of a spiritual love, presumably between man and wife,[3] has the effect of emphasizing the anguish of being forced to a temporary physical separation. Everyone has admired the delicate opening of the poem in which the separation of lovers is represented as a kind of deathbed scene :

> As virtuous men passe mildly away,
>   And whisper to their soules, to goe,
> Whilst some of their sad friends doe say,
>   The breath goes now, and some say, no :
>
> So let us melt, and make no noise,
>   No teare-floods, nor sigh-tempests move,
> T'were prophanation of our joyes
>   To tell the layetie our love.

What Donne is representing here is the essence of many an airport, or station, or dock-side scene, where true lovers may attempt to repress their tears, not wishing to show the laity their love. And then the poem goes on to say

> Dull sublunary lovers love
>   (Whose soule is sense) cannot admit
> Absense, because it doth remove
>   Those things which elemented it.
>
> But we by a love, so much refin'd,
>   That our selves know not what it is,
> Inter-assured of the mind,
>   Care lesse, eyes, lips, and hands to misse.

'Care lesse', but is it so? The very rigor and intricacy of the famous image of the compass at the end may be taken to suggest a rather desperate dialectical effort to control by logic and reason a situation almost beyond rational control.

The whole problem of the relationship between the soul and body in love is brought to a crisis of ambiguity in the frequently-discussed poem, 'The Exstasie'. This contains a curious and enigmatic combination of traditions in Renaissance poetry and thought. First of all, it grows from the poetical tradition represented by Sidney's Eighth Song in *Astrophil and Stella*,[4] a song in which the lover attempts to persuade the lady in a pastoral setting to give way to the lover's wishes. Donne's prologue in his poem is exactly the same length as Sidney's prologue: seven quatrains. But Donne's interest in nature is so little that it appears as though the flower-bed consists of just a single violet: Donne is not interested in pastoral but in other implications.

> Where, like a pillow on a bed,
>   A Pregnant banke swel'd up, to rest
> The violets reclining head,
>   Sat we two, one anothers best;
>
> Our hands were firmely cimented
>   With a fast balme, which thence did spring,
> Our eye-beames twisted, and did thred
>   Our eyes, upon one double string;

> So to'entergraft our hands, as yet
>   Was all our meanes to make us one,
> And pictures on our eyes to get
>   Was all our propagation.

The physical suggestions of the poem here have led some readers to feel that the following philosophical discourse is simply a smoke-screen, as in 'The Flea', for a libertine design. On the other hand, a very strong tradition in Renaissance thought that lies behind the discussion in the rest of the poem has suggested to other readers that it really does present a true debate over love's philosophy.[5] From this standpoint the poem may be seen as an assertion of the purity of human love in all its aspects. The title then is quite ironi-cal. We are not going to witness here an ecstasy of physical passion (as in Carew's 'A Rapture'). On the other hand, although we do hear the souls of the lovers speak in a Neoplatonic state of ecstasis, in which the souls go forth from the body to discover the True and the One – nevertheless the Truth that they discover is in fact the Truth of Aristotle and the synthesis of St Thomas Aquinas : that the soul must work through the body; such is the natural state of man. The last lines prove the purity of their love. If there is small change when the souls are to bodies gone, then spiritual love has succeeded in controlling passion. From this standpoint Donne is misleading us with false expectations by the physical imagery of the opening part. These lovers will probably go off and get properly married in good Spenserian fashion. And indeed the deep self-con-trol of these lovers is perhaps implied by the strictness of the three-part structure that the poem displays, being (more precisely than usual with Donne) divided into setting, analysis, and resolution. The total effect of the poem suggests a philosophical mode of rational control superimposed upon a libertine situation. The libertine suggestions are finally dominated and transcended by a richer, more inclusive, more spiritual view of love.

And yet each poem within the *Songs and Sonets* can be no more than a temporary house of harmony, where Creative Mind, in Yeats's phrase, brings peace out of rage and creates the lovers' stasis and order, for a moment only. Thus, in the traditional order, the affirmation of the perfect 'patterne' of love in 'The Canoniza-tion' is followed at once by the semi-recantation, 'The Triple Foole'.

> I am two fooles, I know,
>   For loving, and for saying so
>   In whining Poëtry;
> But where's that wiseman, that would not be I,
>   If she would not deny?

And then this half-despairing, half-cynical poem is followed at once by the slow, sad, quiet measures of the beautiful poem entitled 'Loves' [or 'Lovers'] infinitenesse where the word 'all' rings throughout as the dirge of an unattainable Ideal :

> If yet I have not all thy love,
>   Deare, I shall never have it all;
> I cannot breath one other sigh, to move,
>   Nor can intreat one other teare to fall.
> All my treasure, which should purchase thee,
>   Sighs, teares, and oathes, and letters I have spent,
> Yet no more can be due to mee,
>   Then at the bargaine made was ment.
> If then thy gift of love were partiall,
> That some to mee, some should to others fall,
>   Deare, I shall never have Thee All.

In the fifth line above we should note the excellent reading of Miss Gardner's text, taken from the manuscripts : 'All my treasure', in place of the weaker traditional reading 'And all my treasure'; for this manuscript reading throws a proper emphasis upon the thematic word 'all', binding it with the last word of the stanza and with the end rhymes that reinforce the dirge-like repetitions. But then, in Donne's characteristically winding way, the poem shifts its posture and runs over the same ground from a different point of view, pondering a new possibility which at the close is discarded for yet another point of view :

> Or if then thou gav'st mee all,
>   All was but All, which thou hadst then,
> But if in thy heart, since, there be or shall,
>   New love created bee, by other men,
> Which have their stocks intire, and can in teares,
>   In sighs, in oaths, and letters outbid mee,

> This new love may beget new feares,
>   For, this love was not vowed by thee.
> And yet it was, thy gift being generall,
>   The ground, thy heart is mine, what ever shall
>   Grow there, deare, I should have it all.

But as the third and final stanza opens we find the speaker discarding all these previous possibilities and turning toward a point of view which reaches a temporary conclusion in the powerful echo of one of the most famous of religious paradoxes (Mark 8 :35) :

> Yet I would not have all yet,
>   Hee that hath all can have no more,
> And since my love doth every day admit
>   New growth, thou shouldst have new rewards in store;
> Thou canst not every day give me thy heart,
>   If thou canst give it, then thou never gav'st it :
> Loves riddles are, that though thy heart depart,
>   It stayes at home, and thou with losing sav'st it :

But these lovers move beyond the Gospel paradox and have, this lover hopes, an even richer future :

> But wee will have a way more liberall,
>   Then changing hearts, to joyne them, so wee shall
>   Be one, and one anothers All.

Despite that splendid final affirmation of Oneness, the whole poem creates, through its shifts and oscillations, a sense of the painful unlikelihood that this All will ever really be found. This great poem represents in itself the effect that one feels throughout the *Songs and Sonets* – the poignant fragility of human love. It is the state of lovers summed up for us in 'A Lecture upon the Shadow'. Here the lover and his Lady have been walking about in the morning, for three hours, in a situation representing the restless, yearning state of lovers seeking what T. S. Eliot calls the 'still moment, repose of noon'. Now the moment of declaration has come, the moment of 'brave clearenesse' – 'brave' in the old Elizabethan sense of 'splendid', 'superb', as well as 'brave' in our modern sense. They must now declare their loves and try to maintain them against the world of time. Appropriately, the poem opens by creating the impression that the speaker is attempting, by a deliberate act of will, to force a pause in the flow of time.

> Stand still, and I will read to thee
> A Lecture, Love, in loves philosophy.
>   These three houres that we have spent,
>   Walking here, two shadowes went
> Along with us, which we our selves produc'd;
> But, now the Sunne is just above our head,
>   We doe those shadowes tread;
> And to brave clearenesse all things are reduc'd.
>   So whilst our infant loves did grow,
>   Disguises did, and shadowes, flow
> From us, and our care; but, now 'tis not so.
>
> That love hath not attain'd the high'st degree,
> Which is still diligent lest others see.

Up to this point in time the lovers have been disguising the growth of their love from other people : thus their love has been accompanied by shadows in two senses, by disguises and by the worries that come from fear of revealing their love to other people. But now another danger arises, as the rest of the poem explains. Unless they can maintain their love at this high point they will begin to deceive each other and thus new shadows of a sadder kind will fall upon their love.

> Except our loves at this noone stay,
> We shall new shadowes make the other way.
>   As the first were made to blinde
>   Others; these which come behinde
> Will worke upon our selves, and blind our eyes.
> If our loves faint, and westwardly decline;
>   To me thou, falsly, thine,
> And I to thee mine actions shall disguise.
>   The morning shadowes weare away,
>   But these grow longer all the day,
> But oh, loves day is short, if love decay.
>
> Love is a growing, or full constant light;
> And his first minute, after noone, is night.

There is no comfort in this poem, only the presentation of a precarious dilemma. Love's philosophy, it seems, begins with the recognition of the shadow of decay.

SOURCE : *The Wit of Love* (1969).

NOTES

1. See the interesting analysis of this poem by Helen Gardner, *The Business of Criticism* (Oxford, Clarendon Press, 1959) pp. 62–74.

2. *Poems of John Donne*, ed. Herbert J. C. Grierson, 2 vols (Oxford, Clarendon Press, 1912) II 31. *Elegies and Songs and Sonnets*, ed. Gardner, p. 207.

3. Izaak Walton says the poem was given by Donne to his wife when he went abroad with Sir Robert Drury, i.e. in 1611 (*Lives*, p. 42). The point is not essential, though the situation seems plausible to me. But see Miss Gardner's contrary arguments in her edition of the *Elegies and Songs and Sonnets*, p. xxix.

4. See George Williamson, 'The Convention of *The Extasie*', in his *Seventeenth Century Contexts* (University of Chicago Press, 1961) pp. 63–77.

5. See the illuminating account of the poem's relation to the *Dialoghi* of Leone Ebreo by Helen Gardner, 'The Argument about "The Ecstasy" ', in *Elizabethan and Jacobean Studies Presented by Frank Percy Wilson* (Oxford, Clarendon Press, 1959) pp. 279–306; also the study of the poem in relation to a number of Renaissance philosophers of love in Italy, by A. J. Smith, 'The Metaphysic of Love', *Review of English Studies*, n.s. IX (1958) pp. 362–75.

A. E. Dyson and Julian Lovelock

CONTRACTED THUS: 'THE SUNNE RISING' (1973)

I

The poem explodes into fiercely rhetorical argument, pursued through three stanzas of sustained exaltation. First the sun is rebuked as a kind of elderly voyeur; then sent about his business; then accused of vanity; then dispatched (unsuccessfully) to look for 'both the'India's'. Finally contempt gives way to patronage, and the sun is invited to perform his duties with the inertia more fitted to age, standing still.

Clearly, such an argument is provocative and, given the sun's normal role as king of the Heavenly bodies and divine emblem, even blasphemous; like Shakespeare's famous sonnet 130, 'My Mistres eyes are nothing like the Sunne', only more outrageously, it reverses the tradition of hundreds of Petrarchan and Elizabethan love poems in which the sun is a touchstone of ecstatic tribute. As an emotional attitude to the sun it verges on derangement, or at least on that excess of fancy divorced from normal perception and judgement which helped to make metaphysical poetry so generally uncongenial to the eighteenth century, and which to Dr Johnson's tormented mind bore a fearful resemblance to insanity.

On a fairly simple level the exaggeration of language mimes the assurance of love, when time becomes 'rags' and change, decay, diminution all recede. But we see at once that the poem works not directly but obliquely, by indirections finding directions out. The sun is not its true subject; contempt and patronage for the sun are not its true emotional charge. Its true subject is the lady; its true emotion love. Every insult to the sun is a compliment to the mistress, every assertion of the sun's weakness attests her power. This is in no simple manner a split between thought and feeling, since both are involved, in the equation, on either side. The literal argument is, in fact, a pseudo-argument (the term is I. A. Richards's) : it uses an apparent subject and emotional attitude which relates to the real subject and emotional attitude by systematic inversion. The pseudo-argument generates an apparent logic (the sun's antics) and an appropriate emotion (contempt for the sun). The true argument is also logical, with the familiar and simple logic of love, and generates love's appropriate emotion, ecstatic homage.

It is precisely here, however, that we encounter the poem's central complexity and chief strategy. The literal argument is often more (though it is never less) than a pseudo-argument, and circles back even in the first stanza to make a kind of sense in its own right. If men are indeed exalted by love beyond the temporal, are they not entitled to 'look down' on the sun and on its 'spheare'?

> Busie old foole, unruly Sunne,
>   Why dost thou thus,
> Through windowes, and through curtaines call on us?
> Must to thy motions lovers seasons run?
>   Sawcy pedantique wretch, goe chide
>   Late schoole boyes, and sowre prentices,
>   Goe tell Court-huntsmen, that the King will ride,
>   Call countrey ants to harvest offices;
> Love, all alike, no season knowes, nor clyme,
> Nor houres, dayes, moneths, which are the rags of time.

Any potentially comic effect is undercut by a note of seriousness, or perhaps overplayed by a note of exhilaration. Donne's imagery, though bizarre and exaggerated as pseudo-argument, asserts what every Platonist and Christian really believes. At certain moments, any man might be wrapt beyond mortality, in the eternal intimations of spiritual love. Statements like

> Love, all alike, no season knowes, nor clyme,
> Nor houres, dayes, moneths, which are the rags of time . . .

and (in the third stanza)

> She'is all States, and all Princes, I,
> Nothing else is . . .

ride triumphantly over their assumed contempt for the sun, attesting that the world fittingly symbolised in the 'schoole boyes, and sowre prentices', the 'Court-huntsmen' and 'country ants' is indeed tinged with illusion, and at one remove from the truth. In calling the material world (in normal speech, the 'real' world) unreal, the poem is saying, with Plato, that even the world's princes and potentates are mere shadows, an imitation in time of the timeless ideals. Such lines as

> Princes doe but play us; compar'd to this,
> All honor's mimique; All wealth alchimie
> (stanza 3)

are not, on this showing, even paradoxical: Donne is a true Platonist, and perhaps unusually daring only in so far as he risks extending to earthly princes (indeed to James I himself, whose love of hunting is unflatteringly alluded to) the reminder that they, too, are shadows all.

In a similar manner the poem's questions are arranged, with dazzling sleight-of-hand, to confound any normal reading response. In the context of pseudo-logic, 'Must to thy motions lovers seasons run,' looks like a rhetorical question expecting the answer 'no'; but can it be less than a real and tragic question for men in time? Lovers who ignore external pressures and realities must surely be conquered by them : such is the theme of the great romantic tragedies; such is the underlying cause of the sterility of so-called 'free-love'. Yet the poem's strange power is to cancel, or transcend, or mock the obvious – it is hard to say which – perhaps through its suggestions that the sun and the lovers have actually exchanged roles (the 'seasons' are controlled by the lovers, while the sun is linked with the 'motions' of physical love).

Such complexities continue through the second stanza :

> Thy beames, so reverend, and strong
> Why shouldst thou thinke?
> I could eclipse and cloud them with a winke,
> But that I would not lose her sight so long :
> If her eyes have not blinded thine,
> Looke, and to morrow late, tell mee,
> Whether both the'India's of spice and Myne

> Be where thou leftst them, or lie here with mee.
> Aske for those Kings whom thou saw'st yesterday,
> And thou shalt heare, All here in one bed lay.

The sun is accused of hollow boasts, but for dubious reasons; the poet could only 'eclipse and cloud' his 'beames' at a cost. If he closed his eyes, would a greater sun really light him, or would he merely be locked in a dream? Perhaps his love itself would disappear, along with all other values, as the uneasy excuse 'But that I would not lose her sight so long' more than half suggests. Once more, the poem's power pushes aside such doubts without wholly excluding them; the sun and the lovers again change roles, with the mistress for an instant becoming the sun, and her 'eye-beames' (cf. 'The Extasie', line 7) blinding the usurped lord of light.

The stanza ends with the claim that the countries and kings of the world have joined together in the lovers' bed. But, as the poem approaches its climax of supreme confidence, giddy with the richness of 'spice and Myne', it takes a further turn which is ultimately to undermine the warranty of that confidence. If love is indeed to be lifted up to the eternal world it must transcend the temporal; and such apotheosis requires something very different from the heavy sexual imagery of ruler and ruled and the basic language of the bedroom ('lie here with mee'; 'All here in one bed lay'.). The crowning irony, to which Donne would hardly have been oblivious, is that hierarchies sufficiently valid in spiritual contexts (cf. Book IV of *Paradise Lost*) become profoundly tainted when turned only to sexual ends.

In the third stanza, the ideas hover explicitly between the exaggerated rhetoric of love, lost in lies or illusions, and the splendid platonic intimations of ultimate truth :

> She'is all States, and all Princes, I,
>   Nothing else is.
> Princes doe but play us; compar'd to this,
> All honor's mimique; All wealth alchimie.
>   Thou sunne art halfe as happy'as wee,
>   In that the world's contracted thus;
>   Thine age askes ease, and since thy duties bee
>   To warme the world, that's done in warming us.
> Shine here to us, and thou art every where;
> This bed thy center is, these walls, thy sphaere.

As we have suggested, the poet's declarations in the first four lines ring with the conviction of paradox apprehended as truth. But a taint of sexuality remains in the imagery, more dross to the poem (if another Donne image can be inverted) than allay. Such conviction could indeed be justified in some contexts, but not when love's 'contract' is 'contracted' along with the poem's world. If love is in truth to outlast 'seasons' it must be released from the shrinking and sexual connotations of 'contracted thus'; it requires a 'center' not in the bed, but in the soul.

II

Drawing together the complexities of 'The Sunne Rising', we immediately recognize their interdependence as they support, contradict and parallel each other, dictating in these tensions the poem's tone. Our sense that the poem allics love's psychology to the one metaphysic which ultimately validates it is strengthened by the fact that the mistress is always complimented, as it were, at one remove. There is no physical description of her beauty of the kind familiar in most Elizabethan love lyrics; the compliment exists wholly in what the poet feels. It is because she moves him to this dramatic urgency that we know her influence; in a manner wholly characteristic of Donne, it is the intensity of worship which guarantees worth. *Her* value is *his* veneration : and in as much as this does not leave her unbearably vulnerable to fickleness (a theme which Donne pursues in other, more cynical poems) we have to accept the superior truth of the spiritual world. Love is not a mere reflection of the lover's needs, subjective and transient; it is homage to beauty revealed and revered. Its habitat is a world where homage can be appropriate, and loyalty enduring; a world not yet caught in the egocentric snare. One could argue indeed that the outrageousness of the images goes hand in hand with their truth, even at the most literal level : if 'truth' is in their extreme of feeling, their exaggeration, this precisely attests the illusiveness and unimportance of the merely material world, and so of the sun, and of the great globe itself.

But the contempt for the sun which characterizes the literal argument must undeniably affect our response to the poem in its own right (at least partially), and not simply as a signpost to the

intensities of love. If so, it hints perhaps at a degree of unease sur-
rounding the certainty, a residual anger as the poet makes statements which he feels should be true and even are true, but which
must necessarily be dubious when made by mortal man. For so
tormented a temperament, there must be a nagging fear that the
sun might indeed shine on to mock lovers, as their intentions soil
and their professions fade. And this poem is not in its essence
serene and timeless; it is nothing like (say) Henry Vaughan's 'The
Retreate' or T. S. Eliot's 'Little Gidding'. Rather it is violent, even
in its unquestionable beauty, sweeping along moment by moment
on currents of change.

It is at this point, no doubt, that we should take account of the
poet's habitual cast of mind, which colours nearly everything he
writes. Does the emotional charge of the poem relate after all more
to the pseudo-argument, the rhetorical shadow-boxing, than to
the still centre where the sun at last comes to rest? Donne is a
poet who rushes into articulation, creating as he defines, initiating
the reader into experience at its white heat. His soul seemingly
knows itself in linguistic intensity – in this poem, in an extended
conceit which is at once an elaborate game and an exploration, a
supreme dramatization of the whole man. On this aspect of
Donne's poetry, T. S. Eliot's essay 'The Metaphysical Poets' is
of course seminal; and remains valid as a definition of one poet's
peculiar sensibility, even if we reject its extension to quasi-
historical theorizing, as we surely must.

The effect in 'The Sunne Rising' is that statements and questions come alive with alternative meanings, none of which can be
wholly suppressed. The poem thrives on extremes and quintes-
sences, on paradoxes which look at one moment like intellectual
scaffolding round simple emotions, at the next like internal complexities threatening the emotions themselves. We have to return
in conclusion to the question of whether the ideas put forward in
the poem are finally acceptable : or rather, to the question of what
'final acceptability', in such an instance, can be. If the poem's articulation is inseparable from the poet's experience, it must in an
obvious sense be valid; yet the verbal construct remains, by any
standards, bizarre. Few people would address the sun in this way
seriously, or even fancifully; few would argue that human love
can, in the manner asserted, defy time.

The problem turns on the relationship between erotic love and spiritual love; the poem yokes these two together, and apparently unites them, but are they fused, or confused, in the end? Human love naturally links with passionate needs for loyalty, which point, for a religious believer, to truths beyond time. The eternity demanded by love need not be mythic; the thoughts which dominate this poem can be directly and profoundly presented as truth :

Thou, Lord, in the beginning hast laid the foundation of the earth : and the heavens are the work of thy hands.
They shall perish, but thou shalt endure : they all shall wax old as doth a garment;
And as a vesture shalt thou change them, and they shall be changed : but thou art the same, and thy years shall not fail.
                    (Psalm 102, 25–7 : Coverdale translation)

When Donne wrote later in the religious poetry and sermons of his love for God, the extraordinary intensity and deviousness of his conceits remained, but they linked there with the more normal and inescapable paradoxes of Christian faith. The sonnet 'Death be not proud' expresses one of those grand Christian doctrines which separate believer from unbeliever irrevocably, in worlds too disparate for any bridges to link :

> Death be not proud, though some have called thee
> Mighty and dreadfull, for, thou art not soe,
> For, those, whom thou think'st, thou dost overthrow,
> Die not, poore death, nor yet canst thou kill mee.
> From rest and sleepe, which but thy pictures bee,
> Much pleasure, then from thee, much more must flow,
> And soonest our best men with thee doe goe,
> Rest of their bones, and soules deliverie.

For the Christian, death has lost all power to hurt, except for the deep and grievous, but temporary, anguish of bereavement. Such a triumph can scarcely be portrayed without extravagance or be seen as less than aggressive in its hope. In the most serious sense it is shocking : St Paul rightly associates it with the 'scandal' of the Cross, and celebrates it with famous verbal audacities of his own.

But such triumphs must belong, by their nature, to religion, and to hopes which transcend, if they do not exclude, the flesh. When

Donne projects religious assurance into merely sensual experience, he sets up tensions hard to resolve. Love's triumph over time is convincingly asserted by Christian or Platonist only when certain other factors intervene. It is the promise beyond 'till death do us part' in the Christian marriage vows, the sacramental bond only half anchored to the body and to the world of time. But it must reach out beyond the bedroom if it is to carry conviction, to clearer loyalties, stronger renunciations of erotic possessiveness, than this poem affords.

It is because 'The Sunne Rising' celebrates Eros as a true Immortal that it has a real, as well as a rhetorical, nonsense at the heart.

S O U R C E :   First publication from a work in progress.

J. B. Leishman

LOGICAL STRUCTURE IN THE
SONGS AND SONETS (1951)

... There is scarcely one of Donne's poems of which a clear prose
analysis could not be given; in almost every one of them there is
some kind of argument, an argument which is sometimes con-
ducted in almost rigidly syllogistic form. These arguments ... are
sometimes deliberately outrageous and paradoxical, sometimes
playful, sometimes mainly or wholly serious. And these different
kinds of argument are combined in all manner of ways with different kinds and gradations of feeling, the feeling being mainly
perceptible in and through the rhythms and inflections of the
verse, in the interaction between these and the logical structure.
We may, if we like, thinking of the medieval Schoolmen with
whose writings and methods he was so familiar, call this logical
argumentation the medieval element in Donne's poetry, and we
may also, if we like, call the intensely individual defiances and
floutings, experiences and sensations, to which he applies this logic,
the Renaissance element. We must remember, though, that such
neat antitheses often appear to tell us a great deal more than they
really do. Although it is probably true to say that Donne's best
poems are ultimately concerned with sensations rather than with
thoughts, it is equally true that, although these poems cannot be
properly understood until they have been felt, they cannot be
properly felt until they have been understood. Many readers to-day
prefer a poetry which they can never completely understand, feeling, as they do, that what can be completely understood has been,
as it were, exhausted; and it was partly for this reason, and partly
as a reaction against rhetoric and clichés and what Yeats called
the world of the newspapers, that Mallarmé and the Symbolists
rejected logic and meaning and argument as impurities, and tried
to make poetry approximate to the condition of music. In Donne's
best poetry there is always a balance of elements : an intellectual

or logical structure which could be clearly and completely conveyed by a prose analysis, and a content or substance of experience, passion, feeling, sensibility, or whatever you prefer to call it, which could not be so conveyed, and which is perceptible only in and through rhythm and cadence. Perhaps between Mallarmé or some other Symbolist at his most meaningless, or most speechless, and Donne at his most merely ingenious there may not be much to choose. But what of the difference between 'The Anniversarie', or, 'A nocturnall upon S. Lucies day', or 'A Valediction : forbidding mourning', or 'The Extasie' and, let us say, Mallarmé's 'L'Après-midi d'un Faune', or Valéry's 'La Jeune Parque', poems of which almost no two interpretations agree and several have almost nothing in common? Is the intelligibility of Donne's poems an advantage or a disadvantage? Is their argumentative logic, their analysability into prose, an impurity and a defect? Has their undeniable shapeliness and continuity been too dearly bought? Do we prefer the fleeting and tantalizing glimpses afforded by what has been called 'pure poetry'? How much poetry is compatible with logic, or how much logic is compatible with the highest poetical pleasure? These, like that of the importance or unimportance of visual imagery, are some of the many interesting questions about poetry in general which are raised by a careful and comparative study of Donne's. Leaving the reader to answer them for himself, I will proceed to an examination of . . . the more formal elements of the *Songs and Sonets*.

Let us, to begin with, turn . . . to 'The Dreame' :

> Deare love, for nothing lesse then thee
> Would I have broke this happy dreame,
>   It was a theame
> For reason, much too strong for phantasie,
> Therefore thou wakd'st me wisely; yet
> My Dreame thou brok'st not, but continued'st it,
> Thou art so truth, that thoughts of thee suffice,
> To make dreames truths; and fables histories;
> Enter these armes, for since thou thoughtst it best,
> Not to dreame all my dreame, let's act the rest.
>
> As lightning, or a Tapers light,
> Thine eyes, and not thy noise wak'd mee;
>   Yet I thought thee

(For thou lovest truth) an Angell, at first sight,
But when I saw thou sawest my heart,
And knew'st my thoughts, beyond an Angels art,
When thou knew'st what I dreamt, when thou knew'st when
Excesse of joy would wake me, and cam'st then,
I must confesse, it could not chuse but bee
Prophane, to thinke thee any thing but thee.

Comming and staying show'd thee, thee,
But rising makes me doubt, that now,
        Thou art not thou.
That love is weake, where feare's as strong as hee;
'Tis not all spirit, pure, and brave,
If mixture it of *Feare, Shame, Honor,* have.
Perchance as torches which must ready bee,
Men light and put out, so thou deal'st with mee,
Thou cam'st to kindle, goest to come; Then I
Will dreame that hope againe, but else would die.

In a sense, this is a very abstract and intellectual poem, and yet I
think it will be agreed that the *effect* of it is anything but abstract
in the pejorative sense. It is an absolutely consecutive and continuous piece of argument from the first line to the last, and each
simile, whether phenomenal (lightning, taper, torches) or intellectual (angels, simple and compound substances) is almost inseparable from the thought it illustrates and expresses. The pictorial
element, if present at all, is at a minimum : what is described is
not a sight, but (to borrow those depreciating words of Dr Johnson's about Cowley's *Davideis,* which ... contain such an admir-
ably though unconsciously accurate account of Donne's poetry at
its best) such thoughts, and, one must add, such feelings, as the
sight might be supposed to have suggested. The diction is precise
and almost scientific, and the words are completely uncharged
with associations not strictly relevant. In comparison with the
typical Elizabethan or the typical Romantic lyric the poem might
be called abstract and intellectual, but, as I have said, its effect
is anything but abstract in the pejorative sense. There is as much
of drama, imagination, feeling, sensation, experience (whether
actual or imaginary is no matter) as of intellect and logic, and this
sensational or experiential element is conveyed, not by a choice
of words rich in association, but by speech-rhythm, inflection,

cadence. Every line, in fact, is intensely alive. Observe how, in the following passage, there is not one superfluous word, how every word demands precisely the right emphasis, and how even such words as 'beyond', 'what', 'when', 'then', contribute an almost measurable quantity of energy towards the total effect :

> But when I saw thou sawest my heart,
> And knew'st my thoughts, *beyond* an Angels art,
> When thou knew'st *what* I dreamt, when thou knew'st *when*
> Excesse of joy would wake me, and cam'st *then,*
> I must confesse, it could not chuse but bee
> Prophane, to thinke thee *any* thing but thee.

We are confined, though, to the particular experience, the particular bit of personal drama, which Donne is describing; we do not feel that it is in any way symbolic of something else, or that it melts and merges into something else, as we so often do when reading Romantic poetry, or, for that matter, Shakespeare's Sonnets. . . . Donne's love-poetry . . . [has] a certain enclosedness and inclusiveness, as one of its most remarkable characteristics : this, though, is no less characteristic of its manner than of its matter, the two things being indeed, as in all good poetry, ultimately inseparable. It is also one of the most remarkable characteristics of the best poetry of other so-called metaphysical poets : not only is the language strictly denotative, the subject, the experience, is also precise, defined and delimited. The difference between Donne's religious poetry and Herbert's, as the expressions of two different kinds of religious experience, has often been insisted upon, and is, indeed, very obvious, but the resemblances between Donne's serious love-poetry and Herbert's religious poetry, as what may be called dialectical expressions of personal drama, have too often been overlooked . . . Let us now, with an eye to more detailed resemblances, compare Donne's 'The Dreame' with Herbert's 'Dialogue' :

> Sweetest Saviour, if my soul
>   Were but worth the having,
> Quickly should I then controll
>   Any thought of waving.

But when all my care and pains
Cannot give the name of gains
To thy wretch so full of stains,
What delight or hope remains?

What, Child, is the ballance thine,
*   Thine the poise and measure?*
If I say, Thou shalt be mine;
*   Finger not my treasure.*
What the gains in having thee
Do amount to, onely he,
Who for man was sold, can see;
That transferr'd th'accounts to me.

But as I can see no merit,
        Leading to this favour :
So the way to fit me for it
        Is beyond my savour.
As the reason then is thine;
So the way is none of mine :
I disclaim the whole designe :
Sinne disclaims and I resigne.

That is all, if that I could
*   Get without repining;*
And my clay, my creature, would
*   Follow my resigning:*
That as I did freely part
With my glorie and desert,
Left all joyes to feel all smart — —
        Ah ! no more : thou break'st my heart.

The resemblances between this poem of Herbert's and Donne's
'The Dreame', in style and expression though not in substance, are
very striking. First, like Donne's poem, Herbert's is a continuous
argument, or argument and counter-argument, from the first line
to the last, although Herbert's arguments are not ingenious and
scholastic like Donne's, and are not illustrated and supported by
ingenious analogies. Secondly, as in Donne's poem, the language is
precise, strictly denotative, uncharged with romantic associations,
and the subject, the experience, is strictly delimited and particular.

Thirdly, Herbert's poem is, in a sense, even more abstract than
Donne's : not only is there no decoration or ornament, there is not
a single visual image, and the only metaphors, very subordinate
ones, are those of the balance and the transferred accounts in the
second stanza. Finally, in spite of so much plainness, in spite of the
rejection of so many of what had been and have been regarded as
indispensable constituents of poetry, in spite of this limitation to
what one might almost call bare argument, the effect of Herbert's
poem, as of Donne's, is anything but bare or bleak or abstract. It
is, on the contrary, intensely dramatic, and this excitingly dramatic
effect is produced, as in Donne's poem, by an exquisite interaction
between logical structure and speech-rhythm, every word receiving
precisely the right emphasis and performing the maximum amount
of work, every word being, as Herbert himself said of the true
country parson's sermon, 'heart-deep'. In such poetry 'all the
charm of all the Muses' can flower in the humblest monosyllables :

> What, Child, is the ballance *thine,*
> > *Thine* the poise and measure?
> If I say, Thou *shalt* be mine;
> > Finger not my treasure.

> *What* the gains in having *thee*
> Do amount to, onely *he,*
> Who for man was sold, can see;
> That transferr'd th'accounts to me.

How very similar, as a poetic method, as a way of saying something in metre, how very similar this is – if one may say so without
irreverence – to Donne's method and manner in 'The Dreame' :

> But when I saw thou sawest my heart,
> And knew'st my thoughts, *beyond* an Angels art,
> When thou knew'st *what* I dreamt, when thou knew'st *when*
> Excesse of joy would wake me, and cam'st *then,*
> I must confesse, it could not chuse but bee
> Prophane, to thinke thee *any* thing but thee.

It is in this dialectical expression of personal drama that Herbert,
like Donne, excels; and, in trying to describe and analyse what

seems to me most characteristic in these two poems, I have also
described what seem to me the most important stylistic qualities
which Donne, Herbert and some other seventeenth-century poets
have in common, which distinguish them from the poets of the
School of Jonson, and which justify us, to some extent, at any rate,
in speaking of a School of Donne or of a Dialectical School.

The strictly delimited subject and the strictly denotative style
of such a poem as 'The Dreame' differs entirely from the substance
and style of Shakespeare's Sonnets, where the language is deeply
coloured and charged with all manner of associations, so that it sets
up infinite vibrations, 'awakening all the cells where memory
slept'.

> O how shall summers hunny breath hold out
> Against the wrackfull siedge of battering dayes,
> When rocks impregnable are not so stoute,
> Nor gates of steele so strong but time decayes?

This, like so much else in Shakespeare's Sonnets, is not really pictorial, although here as elsewhere there is a suggestion of some
vast allegory, some unsubstantial pageant, unrolling itself on this
huge stage on which the stars in secret influence comment. But
although Shakespeare's language is not predominantly pictorial,
it is much less precisely denotative, much more highly charged with
complex associations, than Donne's, and Shakespeare's Sonnets
are much less self-enclosed than Donne's Songs. And I should not
be disposed to quarrel with anyone who should insist that they are
much more inexhaustible. You can classify Shakespeare's Sonnets
to some extent, but it would be rather absurd to attempt detailed
prose analyses of them. In a sense, they are really all variations on
the same great theme, that of Mutability and Time, destroyers of
youth and beauty and glory, and of everything except, perhaps,
of love. That same unsubstantial pageant is for ever fading and re-
forming; Beauty is pleading with action no stronger than a flower,
or stealing away as imperceptibly as a dial-hand from its figure;
Time is transfixing the flourish set on youth, the once-foiled
famous victor is being razed from the book of honour, captive
Good is attending Captain Ill. *Ibant obscuri.* What we have are
not so much points and arguments and demonstrations as brood-

ings and meditations, *suspiria de profundis, lacrymae rerum*. But Donne's poems are nearly always argumentative rather than meditative, and he confines himself to the development and illustration of some very definite point, however tender or impassioned or excited his argument may be.

This does not mean that we always or chiefly remember Donne's poems as arguments; neither, although the logical structure is always there, is it always equally apparent, or, as it were, obtrusive. The logical structure of 'The Anniversarie' might be briefly exhibited as follows :

(1) Everything passes and decays except our love.
(2) Even after death it will be increased rather than diminished.
(3) But whereas then we shall be no more blest than the other spirits, here on earth we are kings.

When one tries to recall this poem one tends, as with some other of the *Songs and Sonets,* to forget the argument, the logical structure, and to remember only the superb dramatic expression :

> All other things, to their destruction draw,
>   Only our love hath no decay;
> This, no to morrow hath, nor yesterday,
> Running it never runs from us away,
> But truly keepes his first, last, everlasting day.

In this poem the argumentative structure, the logical skeleton, is comparatively unobtrusive. On the other hand, in 'A Valediction : forbidding mourning' the argument is closer and less general and far more essentially and inseparably blended with the substance of the poem. The poem is also a good example of one of Donne's favourite methods or formulaes – that of a proposition supported by arguments from analogy. In the first three stanzas the proposition, let our parting be peaceful, is stated, and amplified by two similes or analogies : let it be as peaceful as the deaths of virtuous men and as inconspicuous as the supposed trepidation, or oscillation, of the crystalline sphere. Then an argument is advanced in support of this proposition : our love is independent of the senses, and cannot therefore be affected by absence; and this argument is illustrated by two analogies : our two-fold soul will not be broken by absence, but merely expanded by it, like gold beaten into leaf; or, if we have two souls, they are like the two legs of a compass.

As virtuous men passe mildly away,
    And whisper to their soules, to goe,
Whilst some of their sad friends doe say,
    The breath goes now, and some say, no :

So let us melt, and make no noise,
    No tear-floods, nor sigh-tempests move,
T'were prophanation of our joyes
    To tell the layetie our love.

Moving[1] of th'earth brings harmes and feares,
    Men reckon what it did and meant,
But trepidation of the spheares,[2]
    Though greater farre, is innocent.

Dull sublunary lovers love
    (Whose soule is sense) cannot admit
Absence, because it doth remove
    Those things which elemented it.

But we by a love, so much refin'd,
    That our selves know not what it is,
Inter-assured of the mind,
    Care lesse, eyes, lips, and hands to misse.

Our two soules therefore, which are one,
    Though I must goe, endure not yet
A breach, but an expansion,
    Like gold to ayery thinnesse beate.

If they be two, they are two so
    As stiffe twin compasses are two,
Thy soule the fixt foot, makes no show
    To move, but doth, if th'other doe.

And though it in the center sit,
    Yet when the other far doth rome,
It leanes, and hearkens after it,
    And grows erect, as that comes home.

Such wilt thou be to mee, who must
    Like th'other foot, obliquely runne;
Thy firmnes makes my circle just,
    And makes me end, where I begunne.

The poem, in fact, is both a close and continuous argument, and, at the same time, continuously poetical; and although, by means of a prose analysis, you can separate the argument from the poetry, you cannot separate the poetry from the argument, as you can, to some extent, in 'The Anniversarie'. In a sense, it is an abstract poem about abstract ideas. The only visual image is that of the compass, which is really a geometrical image, and although, as it were, accidentally visual, as essentially conceptual as the famous one in Marvell's 'Definition of Love' :

> As Lines so Loves *oblique* may well
> Themselves in every Angle greet :
> But our so truly *Paralel,*
> Though infinite can never meet.

That compass image, as Professor Wilson has recently pointed out, had already been used by Joseph Hall in his *Epistles,* which were printed three years before Donne wrote his poem, and it would not have appeared to their contemporaries either so striking or so ingenious as it does to us.[3] Nevertheless, in spite of the closeness of the argument, the abstractness of the ideas, the absence of visual imagery, and the strictly denotative use of words, the effect of the poem is no more abstract in the pejorative sense than that of 'The Dreame'.

In 'A Valediction : forbidding mourning' argument, logical structure, and what we may roughly call substance are really inseparable. But while, on the one hand, in such a poem as 'The Anniversarie', the substance is to some extent independent of the logical structure, or at least, rememberable apart from it, there are several points, more witty than impassioned, where structure and pattern are almost everything, and where the experiental or emotive content is almost negligible. One of the most elaborate of such poems is 'The Will', where the logical pattern of each stanza is as rigidly prescribed in advance as the verse-pattern itself. Each stanza, in fact, is a compressed syllogism, the conclusion and the minor premiss being combined or telescoped and stated first, and the major premiss being reserved, as a kind of surprise, until the end.

> Before I sigh my last gaspe, let me breath,
> Great love, some Legacies; Here I bequeath
> Mine eyes to *Argus,* if mine eyes can see,
> If they be blinde, then Love, I give them thee;
> My tongue to Fame; to'Embassadours mine eares;
>   To women or the sea, my teares.
> Thou, Love, hast taught mee heretofore
> By making mee serve her who'had twenty more,
> That I should give to none , but such, as had too much before.

If the argument here were reduced to strict syllogistic form, it would run as follows :

Major Premiss : Gifts should be given only to those who have too much of the gift already.
Minor Premiss : Argus has too many eyes.
Conclusion :   Therefore I give my eyes to Argus.

Donne continues :

> My constancie I to the planets give;
> My truth to them, who at the Court doe live;
> Mine ingenuity and opennesse,
> To Jesuites; to Buffones my pensivenesse;
> My silence to'any, who abroad hath beene;
>   My mony to a Capuchin.
> Thou Love taught'st me, by appointing mee
> To love there, where no love receiv'd can be,
> Onely to give to such as have an incapacitie.

> My faith I give to Roman Catholiques;
> All my good works unto the Schismaticks
> Of Amsterdam; my best civility
> And Courtship, to an Universitie;
> My modesty I give to souldiers bare;
>   My patience let gamesters share.
> Thou Love taughtst mee, by making mee
> Love her that holds my love disparity,
> Onely to give to those that count my gifts indignity.

I give my reputation to those
Which were my friends; Mine industrie to foes;
To Schoolemen I bequeath my doubtfulnesse;
My sicknesse to Physitians, or excesse;
To Nature, all that I in Ryme have writ;
    And to my company my wit.
Thou Love, by making mee adore
Her, who begot this love in mee before,
,Taughtst me to make, as though I gave, when I did but restore.

To him for whom the passing bell next tolls,
I give my physick bookes; my writen rowles
Of Morall counsels, I to Bedlam give;
My brazen medals, unto them which live
In want of bread; To them which passe among
    All forrainers, mine English tongue.
Thou, Love, by making mee love one
Who thinkes her friendship a fit portion
For yonger lovers, dost my gifts thus disproportion.

Therefore I'll give no more; But I'll undoe
The world by dying; because love lies too.
Then all your beauties will bee no more worth
Then gold in Mines, where none doth draw it forth;
And all your graces no more use shall have
    Then a Sun dyall in a grave.
Thou Love taught'st mee, by making mee
Love her, who doth neglect both mee and thee,
To'invent, and practise this one way, to'annihilate all three.

This, although formally very characteristic, and an astonishing
example of that prodigious wit which Donne's contemporaries so
admired, is not, I need scarcely insist, a very serious poem, or even
a very important one. There is here little or nothing of that interaction between logical structure and experiential or emotional
content, between intellect and feeling, argument and passion or
tenderness, which we have noticed in 'The Dreame' and in 'A
Valediction : forbidding mourning'. This, though, is not to say that
the poem is merely mechanical, that the metre is merely (in Wordsworth's phrase) 'superadded', or that it in any way resembles those
many versified anecdotes in which that occasionally very great poet
Thomas Hardy amused himself by working out the possible per-

mutations and combinations produced in the relations of A, B and C by the operations of X, the Blind Will. Even here – although it would perhaps require a really gifted reader or reciter to reveal it – Donne's exploitation of the resources of metre and rhythm is scarcely less remarkable than his ingenuity and wit. Consider, for example, the ironical self-depreciation, the Chaucerian swiftness (too swift for dull or inattentive readers) of

> To Nature, all that I in Ryme have writ;
> And to my company my wit,

and the superb and unexpected change of pattern and, as it were, of key in the last stanza.

I remarked that the logical pattern of each stanza was as rigidly prescribed in advance as the verse-pattern itself. Over and over again in the *Songs and Sonets* we find Donne not merely choosing but *inventing* the appropriate stanza-form for the poem he wants to write. Professor Pierre Legouis has calculated that of the forty-nine poems which are in stanzas no less than forty-four are in stanza forms which are not exactly repeated. In respect of this extreme metrical originality, the only other seventeenth-century poet who can be compared with Donne is George Herbert, in whose *Temple,* out of 164 poems, 116 are in metrical forms which are not repeated. Professor Pierre Legouis entitled his short study of Donne's poetry *Donne the Craftsman* : here, indeed, is yet one more paradox in a paradoxical career – the fact that Donne, who did not write for publication, and who never regarded his poetry as the serious business of his life, evidently bestowed more care and pains upon his poems than many poets for whom poetry has been a wholetime occupation. Perhaps one may say of him what Rilke made his Malte Laurids Brigge say of Félix Arvers : *Er war ein Dichter und hasste das Ungefähre* ('He was a poet and hated the more-or-less').

S O U R C E : *The Monarch of Wit* (1951).

NOTES

1. Quaking.
2. The notion of a trepidation, or oscillation, of the ninth, the crystalline, spheare was introduced by an Arab into the Ptolemaic

astronomy in order to account for certain phenomena really due to the motion of the earth's axis.

3. *Elizabeth and Jacobean*, p. 30. Mario Praz (*Secentismo e Marinismo in Inghilterra*, 1925, 109, note) had already noticed that the same image had been used by Guarini in one of his madrigals (No. xcvi, *Rime*, Venice, 1598), a departing lover's reply to the preceding madrigal, in which his mistress had expressed the fear that during his travels he might forsake her : 'I am ever with you, moved about but fixed; and if I steal from you the lesser I leave you the greater. I am like the compass in that I fix one foot in you as in my centre, while the other suffers all the turns of fortune, but cannot do other than turn around yourself.' Since the contexts are identical, it is difficult not to suppose that Donne had Guarini's madrigal in mind. For other, less ingenious and striking, examples of the compass image in Donne, see an article by Josef Lederer, 'John Donne and the Emblematic Practice', *Review of English Studies* (July 1946) pp. 198–9.

Michael F. Moloney

DONNE'S METRICAL PRACTICE
(1950)

Of commentaries upon Donne's prosody there would seem to be no
end and of final agreement upon the details of his metrics there
would seem to be no hope. Nevertheless, in still another attempt to
probe Donne's technical mystery, it may be useful to recall the
rather large area of agreement in principle which can now be
assumed as undebatable. As opposed to Dryden's implication of a
lack of metrical skill the modern student may be certain with
Gosse that 'what there was to know about prosody was ... perfectly
known to Donne'. Most careful readers, too, will accept the essential rightness of Saintsbury's generalization that Donne's poetic
manner is not of one piece. Fletcher Melton's thesisarsis variation
principle remains significantly valid despite the injudicious lengths
to which it was pushed. Mario Praz has stressed the contrast between the 'traditionally poetical and the normally prosaic' in
Donne's poetry, and Sir Herbert Grierson has pointed out that his-
torically the 'poetic rhetoric' of Donne was continued with characteristic originality by Dryden. Arnold Stein, the most recent con-
tributor to the literature of Donnean prosody, has written with
graphic illumination of Donne's use of stress-shift and of his match-
ing of feminine with masculine rime.[1] Concerning elision in
Donne's poetry Stein has commented at some length :

we cannot in a poet like Donne ignore the problem of elision; for
from his practice we may conclude that some elidable [*sic*] combinations are very lightly articulated – these we may leave to the analyst
of rhythm – whereas some receive enough stress to be considered extra
syllables. Because of the admitted difficulty in scanning many of
Donne's lines, it is imperative to distinguish between the elisions that
must be taken account of in the prosodic scheme, and those which
may be left to the individual reader as part of the rhythmical subtleties which he must ultimately experience for himself.

But, finally, he rejects elision as a major element in Donne's art :

But actually, the problem of possible exceptions to elision is not very important so far as the *Satires* are concerned. [Stein bases his study of Donne's prosody primarily in the *Satyres* – 'Donne's Prosody', p. 376, n. 16.] In almost every case the extra syllables are not combinations subject to elision. And in this respect the *Satires* furnish useful evidence that Donne did not intend that extra syllables should be elided, no matter what the damage to rhythm or emphasis.[2]

Contrary to Stein's view, this paper will attempt to show that elision is one of the most important elements in Donne's prosody and that it cannot be disregarded without serious damage to a rightful technical understanding of his poetry. Ultimately the approach here taken has its inception in Robert Bridges's *Milton's Prosody,* and more immediately in Appendix A of Pierre Legouis's *Donne the Craftsman.* But behind the theories of Bridges and Legouis lie those curiously challenging pronouncements of Ben Jonson, Samuel Johnson, and Thomas Gray which must give the student of Donne's prosody pause. Why should Jonson have said that Donne, 'for not keeping of accent, deserved hanging'? If the commonly accepted scansion of Donne's poetry is correct, was not the dogmatic Ben straining at the wrenched accent and swallowing, without demurrer, the violated numbers? Why should Samuel Johnson have observed that the metaphysical poets 'only wrote verses, and very often such verses as stood the trial of the finger better than of the ear' when clearly in the commonly accepted scansion they do not stand the 'trial of the finger', that is, they are not regularly syllabic? And why should Gray have noted that '. . . Dr Donne (in his satires) observes no regularity in the pause, or in the feet of his verse, only the number of syllables is equal throughout'?

Obviously, it is not necessary to prove here the Elizabethan and Jacobean awareness of elision. The heavy weighting of public school and university curricula with classical studies inevitably brought Englishmen of the sixteenth and seventeenth centuries an intimate knowledge of Greek and Roman theory and practice. Apart from the classroom there was the formal justification of Campion's *Observations in the Art of English Poesie* and Gabriel Harvey's *Fourth Letter* as well as Gascoigne's earlier comment on the wide ranging of 'poeticall licence.'[3] But perhaps even more important for Donne, who had been 'a great frequenter of plays' in his youth, was the example of the popular playwrights, notably Shakespeare. All in all, the use of elision in English poetry was an ancient thing in Donne's time; it had come in with Chaucer.[4] The problem, then, is to set forth Donne's specific practice and whatever variations may exist within that practice.[5]

Close analysis would seem to force the student of Donne's metrics to one of two conclusions. Either he must view Donne as a poet who, accepting the basic metrical practice of his age, sought within its framework to achieve a characteristic freedom and spontaneity; or he must frankly judge him to have been an uncompromising revolutionary who, rejecting the conventions of his time, boldly sought to create a new system designed to outrage contemporary sensibilities. Aside from the fact that thoroughgoing revolutions are much more likely to be led by a Whitman who stood on the cultural periphery of his epoch than by a Donne who, from his earliest youth, was established in the center of Elizabethan learning, there is convincing evidence that Donne's innovations derive from the first attitude rather than the second. Whether or not he agree completely with Legouis, the careful reader of the *Songs and Sonets* will soon be convinced that what seems like anarchy on first reading, particularly when approached from the vantage point of Elizabethan song, is not anarchy at all but an effect consciously planned. The reader is jolted to attention by an artful rudeness, the most important element of which is stress-shift in the opening lines of a poem or of a stanza :

> I wonder by my troth, what thou, and I . . .
> Now thou hast lov'd me one whole day . . .
> Blasted with sighs, and surrounded with teares . . .

Yet nearly allied to stress-shift in a rightful understanding of Donne's versification, and contributing largely to the exhilarating shock of stress-shift is, I am convinced, elision. For the effect of stress-shift would be dissipated quickly and certainly were the line length not controlled. And on the other hand, if the line were too mechanically measured, artificiality would result. This is not to say that stress-shift and elision necessarily occur in the same line. Very often they do not. But just as stress-shift breaks up the un-

varied beat of the strict iambic line, so elision protests against, while
still observing, the unvaried line length of the fixed stanzaic pattern.
Both are movements toward freedom, but freedom that is still
governed by law.

If the interpretation of Donne's metrics set forth here be correct,
Donne not only used elision but he used it variously in different
poems, the elisions in the *Songs and Sonets* being quite different in
number and character from those in the decasyllabic couplets. It
must be insisted that to stress the importance of elision in Donne's
prosody is not to reduce the movement of his lines to the 'piston-
like rise and fall' which Stein fears.[6] Donne's prosody, no more
than Milton's, determined the reading of his line.[7] It is an elaborate
fiction which gave the poet wide freedom while preventing his
verses from falling into chaos. 'The prosody is only the means for
the great rhythmical effects and is not exposed but rather disguised
in the reading.'[8]

My scansion of the 1,616 lines of the *Songs and Sonets* identifies
159 unquestionable elisions or 1 to every 10.2 lines. These elisions
are distributed as follows:

'The good-morrow', 3; 'Song', 1; 'The undertaking', 2; 'The
Sunne Rising', 3; 'The Indifferent', 1; 'Loves Usury', 3; 'The
Canonization', 4; 'The triple Foole', 1; 'Lovers infinitenesse', 2;
'Song', 2; 'The Legacie', 3; 'A Feaver', 3; 'Aire and Angels', 2;
'Breake of day', 2; 'The Anniversarie', 3; 'A Valediction : of my
name, in the window', 8; 'Twicknam garden', 2; 'A Valediction :
of the booke', 6; 'Loves growth', 4; 'Loves exchange', 7; 'Confined
Love', 1; 'A Valediction : of weeping', 1; 'Loves Alchymie', 4;
'The Curse', 5; 'A nocturnall upon S. Lucies day', 4; 'The Baite',
5; 'The Apparition', 3; 'A Valediction : forbidding mourning',
6; 'The Extasie', 10; 'Loves Deitie', 3; 'Loves diet', 4; 'The Will',
6; 'The Funerall', 7; 'The Blossome', 9; 'The Primrose, being at
Mountgomery Castle', 8; 'The Relique', 2; 'The Dampe', 2; 'The
Dissolution', 2; 'A Jeat Ring sent', 2; 'Negative love', 2; 'The Prohibition', 2; 'The Expiration', 2; 'The Computation', 3; 'Farewell
to love', 3; 'Sonnet. The Token', 1.

But in addition to elisions there are 124 speech contractions. Although some of these are true elisions, I have thought it advisable
to consider them separately. They are, for the most part, verbal

contractions ('twas, I'am, we'are, thou'art), contractions of the solemn forms occurring frequently (thought'st, lovest, savest, knew'st, goest). (Donne never, I believe, gives syllabic quantity to the solemn endings, although there is no consistency in his spelling, the vowel sometimes being supplied, perhaps more often omitted.) The effect of the speech contractions is very nearly that of the elisions. They contribute as do true elisions to the shattering of the metronomic line beat, but with this important distinction. Whereas the true elisions actually violate the metrical norm, which can then be saved only by an elaborate and often laborious effort on the part of the reader, the speech contractions, for the most part, add weight to the line and impede its facile flow without actually destroying its character. The overall effect is to rescue Donne's lyric, even when it is most Elizabethan, from the artificial atmosphere of courtly song, and to give it the less rarified music of speech.

The conclusion which I reach after a systematic application to the *Songs and Sonets* of the rules of elision, known and applied by Donne's contemporaries in various degrees and unquestionably practised by Donne himself to some extent, as the text of his poems indicates, is that the number of metrically irregular lines is actually somewhat fewer than twenty.[9] Surely then the explanation for the characteristic effect of Donne's verse must be sought elsewhere than in a supposed deliberate disregard for metrical law.

The system of elisions utilized in the *Songs and Sonets* was put to even more daring use in the decasyllabic couplets. The following table shows the frequency of occurrence of elisions and speech contractions in the *Satyres*.

	Lines	Elisions	Contractions
Satyre I	112	24	4
Satyre II	112	36	5
Satyre III	110	25	3
Satyre IV	244	55	5
Satyre V	91	27	8
	669	167	25

By comparison with the *Songs and Sonets* several interesting facts emerge. In the *Songs and Sonets* the ratio of elisions to total number of lines was 1 to 10·2; of elisions plus contractions to total number of lines, 1 to 5·73. In the *Satyres* the ratio of elisions to total lines is 1 to 4·00; of elisions plus contractions, 1 to 3·48. Thus Donne uses proportionately two and one-half times as many elisions in the *Satyres*. Although he uses far fewer speech contractions, the number of lines whose metrical regularity is disturbed remains significantly greater in the *Satyres*. But that is not all. The relatively large number of contractions in the *Songs and Sonets* would seem to indicate that Donne in them was rejecting the facility of Elizabethan song but in a manner which would not too greatly perturb his cultivated readers. Even the true elisions in the *Songs and Sonets* are frequently justified by contemporary speech practice : *seaven, heaven, dangerous, being, reverend, business, etc.* Trying elisions such as that in line 17 of 'The Primrose' are very rare. But in the *Satyres* Donne's practice approaches licence. The multiple and sometimes strained elisions of lines 28, 33, 140, and 144 of 'Satyre IV' rob the decasyllabic line of all but a faint and shadowy reality.

From the evidence here set forth, the following conclusions seem justifiable :

1. That elision is a major and continuous practice in Donne's versification.

2. That it is employed in *Songs and Sonets* deliberately to weight the lines with extra syllables which, being technically elidible, succeed in ballasting the rhythm without destroying it. The elisions of the *Songs and Sonets* are re-enforced by closely allied speech contractions. This device enables Donne to maintain the fiction of regular line length, which is essential to his complicated stanzaic patterns, with surprising success.

3. That the elision practised in the *Satyres* is an accentuation of that utilized in the *Songs and Sonets*. The elisions of the *Satyres* are used more frequently and more daringly. Double and triple elisions in the same line, plus fantastically far-fetched elisions, frequently leave regularity of line length fictional indeed.

4. That Donne indicated the fictional nature of his metrical regularity in the *Satyres* by deliberately violating the decasyllabic norm on frequent occasions.[10] Such frequent violation was possible in the *Satyres,* where the couplet pattern could not escape the

reader's ear, to an extent which would have resulted only in chaos in the multiple stanzaic patterns of the *Songs and Sonets*. Here, too, Donne had the example of Juvenal and Persius, or at least of the renaissance conception of the versification of Juvenal and Persius.

Yet it must be frankly admitted that elision is not the answer to all the problems of Donne's metrical practice. No careful reader can fail to see that some of Donne's most characteristic rhythmic effects are obtained in lines where he does not employ elisions at all. In addition to the lines already quoted consider the following :

> Twice or thrice had I loved thee . . .
> *Love,* any devill else but you . . .
> Before I sigh my last gaspe, let me breath . . .
> Some man unworthy to be possessor . . .
> Of old or new love himselfe being false or weake . . .
> Are Sunne, Moone or Starres by law forbidden . . .
> Comforted with these few bookes let me lye . . .
> Bright parcell gilt with forty dead mens pay . . .
> Sir; though (I thanke God for it) I do hate . . .

There is no question here of elision, yet the effect seems curiously parallel to that of elision. What is sought by the poet is greater ease and naturalness, not by disregarding the linear norm through the introduction of extra syllables (real of fictional), but by imposing the clear and sometimes conflicting rhythms of prose meaning upon the conventional rhythms of verse.[11] Donne assuredly knew this device and I have no doubt that dramatic practice had impressed him with its utility.

Here I hazard a provocative suggestion. T. S. Eliot twenty-odd years ago expressed the then startling opinion tht Donne belongs in the main stream of English poetic tradition.[12] Whether at the time he made that acute critical judgment Eliot was aware of a possible critical reconciliation of Donne and Milton I do not know, although his most recent pronouncement on Milton serves to restore the poet to a position of honor he had formerly denied him. But that Donne may have been one of Milton's prosodic mentors, that he may have served as an intermediary between the Elizabethan dramatists and Milton, seem to me highly possible. I know of only one direct echo of Donne in Milton.[13] Nevertheless, despite Milton's contemptuous reference to 'our late fantastics' there is more than a hint of metaphysical imagery in Milton's early poems.[14] But more significant is the 'centroidal grouping'[15] of rhythms which is common to both Donne and Milton. It is obvious that such lines as the following by Donne do not conform to an iambic pattern :

> Some man unworthy to be possessor . . .
> O desperate coward, wilt thou seeme bold and . . .
> Even our Ordinance plac'd for our defence . . .
> T'have written than, when you writ seem'd to mee . . .
> All whom warre, dearth, age, agues, tyrannies
> Despaire, law, chance, hath slaine, and you whose eyes . . .
> Thou art slave to Fate, Chance, kings and desperate men . . .
> Father, part of his double interest . . .

The rhythmic effect of these lines is very bold, yet granting, when necessary, the fiction of elision (for elision is frequently an inescapable factor in the 'centroidal grouping'), the lines all submit to the decasyllabic limitation. Still the abruptnes here achieved is scarcely more emphatic than that familiar in Milton. For example, from *Paradise Lost* :

> Thick swarm'd, both on the ground and in the air, [I 767]
> Powers and Dominions, Deities of Heav'n, [II 11]
> Alone th' Antagonist of Heav'n, nor less [II 509]
> Days, months, and years, towards his all-chearing Lamp [III 581]
> Your military obedience, to dissolve [IV 955]
> Accompani'd then with his own compleat [V 352]
> This our high place, our Sanctuarie, our Hill [V 732]
> Burnt after them to the bottomless pit. [VI 866]
> Imbu'd, bring to thir sweetness no satietie [VIII 216]
> Sin opening, who thus now to Death began [X 234]

The characteristic effect of the lines of both poets may be assigned to stress-shift. But the origins of stress-shift in the cases of both Donne and Milton may not be too far to seek. Early in the English Renaissance Gascoigne had lamented that 'our Poemes may justly be called Rithmes, and cannot by any right challenge the name of a Verse',[16] very likely basing his regret upon Quintilian's distinction between *metrum* and *numerus*. And certain it is that English poetry, from its beginning, with all of its borrowings and indebtedness to other literatures, classical and vernacular, displayed a sturdy independence in matters of form. The August eclogue of the *Shepherd's Calendar*, as Legouis has noted, was a significant foreshadowing. It was inevitable by the nature of the medium in which they worked that the dramatists should take the lead in accommodating poetry to the rhythms of speech, and the progress of dramatic blank verse from the stiff sonority of Marlowe's early plays through the superb flexibility of Shakespeare's late period to the anarchy of Fletcher is a commonplace. Donne, too, was concerned with the same problem, and much that is puzzling in his rhythms is best understood when approached from the vantage-point of contemporary drama. The metrical practice in the lines of Donne (and of Milton) which we have been considering is not basically different from that of such lines as these of the early Shakespeare :

> Lord of the wide world and wild watery seas [*C. of E.*, II I 21]
> And little mouse, every unworthy thing. [*R. & J.*, III III 31]
> That shall she, marry; I remember it well. [*R. & J.*, I III 22]
> One half of me is yours, the other half yours, [*M. of V.*, III II 16]
> His tedious measures with the unbated fire, [*M. of V.*, II VI 11]

Donne did not follow Shakespeare into the late hypermetrical vagaries which, magnificently as Shakespeare marshalled them, point to rhythmic dissolution. The innovations to be found in his poetry are doubtless there by deliberate intention, but the revolution was achieved by most unrevolutionary means. The most significant technical features of Donne's verse are the consistent employment of elision and the consistent rejection of a fixed iambic rhythm through the utilization of stress-shift. With regard to the first he was no more revolutionary than Milton, if the greatest critic of Miltonic prosody be correct. With regard to the second, he had ample lyric and dramatic precedent. Indeed, unless Shakespeare and Milton are revolutionary, Donne was of the centre not eccentric.

S O U R C E : *PMLA,* LXV (1950).

NOTES

1. *Discourse concerning the Original and Progress of Satire* (1693), in W. P. Ker, *Essays of John Dryden* (Oxford, 1926) II 19; Gosse, *Life and Letters of John Donne* (New York, 1899) II 334; Saintsbury, *A History of Prosody* (London, 1908) II 159 and 161; Melton, *The Rhetoric of John Donne's Verse* (Baltimore, 1906) p. 148; Praz, *Secentismo e Marinismo in Inghilterra* (Firenze, 1925) pp. 97-8 (cited by Pierre Legouis, *Donne the Craftsman* (Paris, 1928), p. 45); Grierson, *Metaphysical Lyrics and Poems of the Seventeenth Century* : *Donne to Butler* (Oxford, 1921) p. xxv; Stein, 'Donne's Prosody', *PMLA*, LIX (1944) 373–97; 'Donne and the Couplet', *PMLA*, LVII (1942) 676–96.

2. 'Donne's Prosody', pp. 389, 392–3.

3. G. Gregory Smith, *Elizabethan Critical Essays* (Oxford, 1904) II 352; I 119–20, 53–4.

4. Robert Bridges, *Milton's Prosody* (Oxford, 1921) pp. 15 ff.

5. The rules for elision which I believe Donne followed, with perhaps certain liberties, are essentially those set forth by Bridges, pp. 19–37. Donne's principal variation is a rather consistent tendency to elide unstressed internal *i*, e.g., the *i* in *medicine* ('Love's Growth', l. 7); in *medicinall* ('Love's Alchymie, l. 10); the initial *i* in *examining* ('Satyre IV, l. 28).

6. 'Donne's Prosody', p. 390.

7. Cf. Bridges, pp. 34–6.

8. Ibid., p. 36.

9. Initial truncation and feminine endings as such are not here considered metrical irregularities in the *Songs and Sonets*. The effect of initial truncation in stanzaic patterns where it is recurrent is quite different from that of its occasional use in rimed couplets. In the latter it thwarts the expected rhythmic pattern, in the former it is a part of the pattern. Lines whose metrical difficulties I am unable to resolve occur in these poems : 'The Indifferent'; 'Song ("Sweetest love, I do not goe")'; 'Aire and Angels'; 'Loves exchange'; 'Confined love'; 'Witchcraft by a picture; 'The Primrose'; 'Farewell to love'; 'Sonnet. The Token'; 'Selfe Love'.

10. In Satyre IV alone I find very nearly as many lines irreconcilable with the decasyllabic pattern as I find resisting the established metrical norms in all the *Songs and Sonets*.

11. Cf. John Crowe Ransom, *The New Criticism* (New Directions, 1941) pp. 268–325.

12. 'The Metaphysical Poets', *Selected Essays: 1917–1932* (New York, 1932) p. 250.

13. The resemblance between lines 1–2 of Sonnet IX of the *Holy Sonnets* and the opening lines of *Paradise Lost* would seem scarcely accidental.

14. Cf. 'At a Vacation Exercise', ll. 19–20, 5–6, 23–6; 'On Shakespeare', ll. 14–15; 'Another on the same', l. 5.

15. Cf. James Craig La Drière, 'Prosody', *Dictionary of World Literature*, ed. Joseph T. Shipley (New York, 1943).

16. Smith, *Elizabethan Critical Essays*, I 50.

Helen Gardner

THE ARGUMENT ABOUT
'THE ECSTASY' (1959)

Whenever opinion is sharply divided on a question it is worth asking what the opponents are agreed upon. This will usually show
what are the genuine grounds of disagreement and narrow the dispute to particular points. But sometimes such an inquiry has a
more interesting result. It may show that the opponents are arguing from a common position which is itself false; and correction
of this common basic misconception may make it possible to put
forward a new view which can take into account elements in the
opposing views which had appeared irreconcilable. The dispute
over the significance of 'The Ecstasy' is, I think, a case in point.
There is no short poem of comparable merit over which such completely divergent views have been expressed, and no lover of
Donne's poetry can be happy to leave the question in its present
state of deadlock. For it is obvious that those who assert that the
poem is the supreme expression of Donne's 'philosophy of love'
and those who declare that it is a quasi-dramatic piece of special
pleading have now no hope of converting each other. The one
side merely adduces fresh parallels from various Italian Neo-
Platonists and from Donne's own works; the other continues to
insist on the sexual overtones of the imagery and to point out
sophistries in the argument. Neither side will recognize that there
are elements in the poem which contradict its interpretation.

To Coleridge 'The Ecstasy' was the quintessential 'metaphysical
poem': 'I should never find fault with metaphysical poems', he
wrote, 'were they all like this, or but half as excellent'.[1] And to a
poet-critic of our own day, Ezra Pound, it is equally, beyond question, a great 'metaphysical poem' in the truest sense. After printing
the poem in his *ABC of Reading*, he commented: 'Platonism believed. The decadence of trying to make pretty speeches and of
hunting for something to say temporarily checked. Absolute belief

in the existence of an extra-corporal soul, and of its incarnation, Donne stating a thesis in precise and even technical terms'.[2] But among scholars there has been flat disagreement over the genuineness of the poem's 'Platonism'; and, even among those who regard it as seriously intended, there has been a recurrent note of reserve in their praise of the poem. Thus Sir Herbert Grierson, in his chapter on Donne in the *Cambridge History of English Literature*, declared that 'The Ecstasy' 'blends and strives to reconcile the material and the spiritual elements of his realistic and Platonic strains'; but added the comment, 'Subtle and highly wrought as that poem is, its reconciliation is more metaphysical than satisfying'. Three years later, in his introduction to his edition of Donne's poems, he expanded this view in a passage which may be taken as the classic statement of the orthodox view of the poem :

The justification of natural love as fullness of joy and life is the deepest thought in Donne's love-poems, far deeper and sincerer than the Platonic conceptions of the affinity and identity of souls with which he plays in some of the verses addressed to Mrs Herbert. The nearest approach that he makes to anything like a reasoned statement of the thought latent rather than expressed in 'The Anniversarie' is in 'The Extasie' a poem which, like the 'Nocturnall', only Donne could have written. Here, with the same intensity of feeling, and in the same abstract, dialectical, erudite strain he emphasizes the interdependence of soul and body.

But, after quoting some lines, he added :

It may be that Donne has not entirely succeeded in what he here attempts. There hangs about the poem just a suspicion of the conventional and unreal Platonism of the seventeenth century. In attempting to state and vindicate the relation of soul and body he falls perhaps inevitably into the appearance, at any rate, of the dualism which he is trying to transcend. He places them over against each other as separate entities and the lower bulks unduly.[3]

Against Ezra Pound's 'Platonism believed' we have to set Grierson's 'Platonism modified and transcended, and yet perhaps not fully believed'.

A wholly different view was put forward by Professor Pierre Legouis in *Donne the Craftsman* in 1928. He denied that the poem

had any philosophic intention and declared that it was, within a
narrative framework, quasi-dramatic, the representation of a very
skilful piece of seduction. He regarded the Platonism as a trans-
parently cynical device by which a clever young man, pretending
that their minds are wholly at one, is persuading a bemused young
woman that there can be nothing wrong in her yielding to him.
After a detailed examination of the poem, Professor Legouis sum-
marized his view of it by saying :

Donne does not set out to solve once for all the difficult problem of
the relations of the soul and body in love. He considers the particular
case of a couple who have been playing at Platonic love, sincerely
enough on the woman's part, and imagines how they would pass from
it to carnal enjoyment; whether he thinks this *in abstracto* a natural
consummation or a sad falling-off matters little; the chief interest of
the piece is physchological, and, character being represented here in
action, dramatic. The heroine remains indeed for the reader to shape,
but the hero stands before us, self-revealed in his hypocritical game.[4]

M. Legouis's interpretation was strongly contested by many
scholars, notably by Professor Merritt Hughes and by the late Professor G. R. Potter.[5] Professor Hughes contested it by referring to
Italian and French Neo-Platonists. He showed that the argument
for the body's rights in love was a common topic in writers such
as Benedetto Varchi, and declared that Donne's poem clearly
descended from the casuistry of the Italian Neo-Platonists. Professor Potter supported Grierson's interpretation by a mass of quotations from Donne's poetry and prose to prove that Donne did
indeed hold the views which Grierson said that the poem put forward. Neither of these writers, nor, as far as I am aware, any other
opponent of M. Legouis, attempted to refute in detail his close
analysis of the poem and his criticism of the sophistries of its supposed argument.

The controversy flared up in a slightly different form when
Professor C. S. Lewis and Mrs Joan Bennett skirmished over 'The
Ecstasy' in the course of a general battle over Donne's merits as a
love-poet.[6] Professor Lewis, classing the poem with 'poems of
ostentatiously virtuous love', declared that it was 'nasty'. If the
idea of 'pure' passion has any meaning, he said, 'it is not like that';
and he concluded by exclaiming, 'What any sensible woman would

make of such a wooing it is difficult to imagine'. Mrs Bennett took
up the challenge and reaffirmed Grierson's view of the poem's
philosophy. The debate had rather shifted its ground here to the
value of the philosophic views put forward, or assumed to be put
forward, by the poem; but Professor Lewis appeared to take for
granted that we may disregard, as M. Legouis does, the poem's
statement that the man and the woman thought as one and take it
that the poem, in fact, presents a 'wooing'. Later, Professor Lewis,
while 'still unable to agree with those who find a valuable "philosophy" of love in "The Ecstasy" ', confessed that he had 'erred
equally in the past by criticizing the supposed "philosophy" '.
Asserting that ideas in Donne's poetry 'have no value or even
existence except as they articulate and render more fully self-
conscious the passion' of a particular moment, he declared that the
real question was 'how that particular progression of thoughts
works to make apprehensible the mood of that particular poem'.[7]

In spite of all the parallels from Italian Neo-Platonists and all
the references to Donne's views on the relation of soul and body
which have been brought against him, M. Legouis has not retract-
ed. On the contrary he has more than once reaffirmed his view. He
must have been encouraged in this obstinacy by the accession of a
notable recruit in Professor Frank Kermode, who, in his British
Council pamphlet on Donne, informs the general public, as if the
case did not need arguing, that 'The Ecstasy' may be classed with
'The Flea' as an example of Donne's 'original way of wooing by
false syllogisms'. He says of 'The Ecstasy' : 'The argument, a
tissue of fallacies, sounds solemnly convincing and consecutive,
so that it is surprising to find it ending with an immodest proposal. The highest powers of the mind are put to base uses, but
enchantingly demonstrated in the process.'[8]

Professor Kermode's quip that the whole argument leads to 'an
immodest proposal' finds certain echoes among those who claim
that the poem's Platonism is seriously intended. Thus, Professor
Mario Praz, who spoke of 'The Ecstasy' as 'un compendio della
metafisica d'amore quale la concepiva il Donne', and repeated
Grierson's view that 'Questa poesia tratta della mutua dipendenza
del corpo e dell' anima', confessed to finding disconcerting notes
in the Platonic poetry of Donne and cited, as an example, 'il con-
trasto tra la macchinosa argomentazione metafisica e il pratico

realismo della perorazione' in 'The Ecstasy'. He thought that one would be inclined to think this the invention of a mocking spirit if one did not recall parallel statements from Donne's letters.[9] Even Professor Merrit Hughes, by using such a phrase as 'the casuistic idealism of the Italians', and by calling Donne's poem 'frankly carnal', shows that he believes the poem finds its culmination in a plea, or a 'proposal', that the lovers should turn from the enjoyment of spiritual communion to the pleasures of physical. This is the common ground on which the dispute about the poem's meaning has arisen. Both sides take it for granted that the main point of the poem is a justification of physical love as not incompatible with the highest form of ideal love. The point of disagreement is whether the justification is seriously meant (and, if so, is it to be taken seriously or is it worthless), or whether the whole argument is intentionally sophisticated and the poem shows somebody 'being led up the garden path'.

The whole dispute has arisen, in my opinion, from a misreading of the last section of the poem (ll. 49-76). The only 'proposal' which is made in these lines is the perfectly modest one that the lovers' souls, having enjoyed the rare privilege of union outside the body, should now resume possession of their separate bodies and reanimate these virtual corpses. The phrases

> But O alas, so long, so farre
>   Our bodies why doe wee forbeare?
>
>   To'our bodies turne wee then,

and

>   . . . when we'are to bodies gone,

have as their obvious and main meaning, and this we must establish before we start listening for overtones, or hunting for ambiguities, the sense 'But, O alas, why do we for so long and to such a degree shun the company of our bodies?', 'Let us then return to our bodies', and 'When we are gone back to (our) bodies'. The final and, one must suppose from its position, the conclusive reason for such a return of the separated souls is not that it will in any way benefit the lovers; but that only in the body can they manifest love to 'weake men'.[10] The fact that an ideal lover is invited to

'marke' them when they are 'to bodies gone' surely makes the
notion that the poem culminates in an 'immodest proposal' absolutely impossible.[11] M. Legouis himself thought it particularly
shocking that 'the hypothetical listener of the prelude reappears
and turns spectator at a time when the lovers as well as we could
wish him away'. But the lovers, far from wishing him away, actually invite his presence. They wish to display the mystery of their
love to one of 'love's clergie' as well as to the 'laity', to one who is
'so by love refin'd' that he can understand 'soules language', as well
as to 'weake men', who can only glimpse these mysteries through
the reports of their senses, and who need, therefore, the body for
their book.

My own position combines elements from both views. I regard
the poem as wholly serious in intention. (Whether it is wholly
successful I must leave undiscussed for the moment.) But if the
conclusion really meant what it has been supposed to mean, I
should be on M. Legouis's side, since the arguments put forward,
regarded as arguments leading to the supposed conclusion, are
beneath contempt. None of the analogies work if taken as elements
in an argument designed to justify the body's claims in love. I am
not, on the other hand, wishing to deny that, as a corollary to its
main line of thought, the poem implies the lawfulness and value of
physical love. I should also not deny that separate lines and stanzas
of the poem, if taken in isolation, are susceptible of a fuller and
richer meaning than they have within the limits of the poem, and
that we can legitimately quote them as expressing more than the
lovers in the poem intend. I am only denying that the poem is in
the least concerned to argue to this particular point. In other
poems, as in the passages which have been quoted from his letters
and sermons, Donne does declare that

> as all else, being elemented too,
> Love sometimes would contemplate, sometimes do;

but in this poem he is concerned with something else. As Professor
Lewis justly says, one of Donne's greatest gifts as a lyric poet is the
intensity with which he abandons himself to the exploration of a
particular mood, or experience, or theme. In this poem, as the
title[12] tells us, his subject is ecstasy. He is attempting to imagine
and make intellectually conceivable the Neo-Platonic conception

of ecstasy as the union of the soul with the object of its desire,
attained by the abandonment of the body. Unlike the great
majority of Donne's lyrics 'The Ecstasy' is a narrative, relating an
experience which took place in the past. But by means of the hypothetical listener it turns into a poem in the dramatic present,
Donne's habitual tense, in the long 'speech' of the lovers, which
occupies two-thirds of the poem. Both the unusual narrative form,
with its exceptionally detailed setting and its description of the
lovers' poses, first seated, then prone in ecstasy, and the introduction of the hypothetical listener are made necessary by the nature
of the experience which Donne is trying to render. It is the essence
of ecstasy that while it lasts the normal powers of soul and body are
suspended, including the power of speech, and the soul learns and
communicates itself by other means than the natural. Ecstasy
can only be spoken about in the past tense. Donne has shown
both a characteristic daring and a characteristic ingenuity in
attempting, by means of his ideal listener, to render the illumination of the soul in ecstasy as a present experience. The conception
of such a listener being refined, beyond even his own high stage of
refinement, by his contact with the lovers in their ecstatic union is
in keeping with a recurrent note in those lyrics of Donne which deal
with the mysteries of mutual love : the claim that he and his mistress can give 'rule and example' to other lovers, that they have a
kind of mission. If we take the poem as concerned with ecstasy and
read its arguments as designed to illuminate the conception of love
as a union by which two become one, we can explain the meaning
of passages which have baffled commentators and have been passed over silently by most disputants over the poem's meaning. I
hope to demonstrate that my hypothesis as to the poem's central
intention[13] can, as the older one could not, thus 'save the
phenomena'.

I

Before considering the poem in detail I wish to establish that
Donne derived his conception of 'amorous ecstasy' from a definite
source. Donne actually wrote two poems on the ecstasy of lovers.
Ironically, Gosse, who has been the butt of scholars for his fantastic attempt to treat Donne's love poetry as autobiographical, saw

the connexion between them. There is often much sense in Gosse's nonsense and in a single sentence on 'The Ecstasy' he hit the mark twice. He connected it with the poem which has, since the edition of 1635, been printed as the tenth elegy, under the title 'The Dreame', and he owned to being puzzled by 'the obsession with the word "violet" ', which he thought 'had, unquestionably, at the time of its (the poem's) composition an illuminating meaning which time has completely obscured'.[14] The tenth elegy is not, in fact, an elegy at all, but a lyric. It should be printed in stanza form, and its title, given to it by whoever edited the edition of 1635 and placed it with the *Elegies*, should be altered. I wish it could be called simply 'The Image'; but a wholly new title would be inconvenient. I propose, therefore, to call it 'Image and Dream', which both preserves a link with the older title and serves to connect the poem with, and differentiate it from, the poem called 'The Dreame' which appears among the *Songs and Sonets*. The poem puzzled Grierson, who was misled by the title 'The Picture' which is given to it by one unreliable manuscript. His error in taking the opening words, 'Image of her', to mean 'picture of her', instead of 'intellectual idea of her',[15] led him to dismiss the poem in his commentary as 'somewhat obscure', and it has never received much attention. Since it is not generally familiar. I print it in full.

'Image and Dream'

Image of her whom I love, more then she,
    Whose faire impression in my faithfull heart,
Makes mee her *Medall,* and makes her love mee,
    As Kings do coynes, to which their stamps impart
The value : goe, and take my heart from hence,
    Which now is growne too great and good for me :
Honours oppresse weake spirits, and our sense
Strong objects dull; the more, the lesse wee see.

When you are gone, and *Reason* gone with you,
    Then *Fantasie* is Queen and Soule, and all;
She can present joyes meaner then you do;
    Convenient, and more proportionall.
So, if I dreame I have you, I have you,
    For, all our joyes are but fantasticall.
And so I scape the paine, for paine is true;
    And sleepe which locks up sense, doth lock out all.

> After a such fruition I shall wake,
>   And, but the waking, nothing shall repent;
> And shall to love more thankfull Sonnets make,
>   Then if more *honour, teares,* and *paines* were spent.
> But dearest heart, and dearer image stay;
>   Alas, true joyes at best are *dreame* enough;
> Though you stay here you passe too fast away :
>   For even at first lifes *Taper* is a snuffe.
>
> Fill'd with her love, may I be rather grown
> Mad with much *heart,* then *ideott* with none.

The importance of this poem to my argument is that it can be shown to depend directly upon a source, and the same source lies, I believe, behind 'The Ecstasy'.

I cannot believe that Donne could have written 'Image and Dream' if he had not very recently been reading one of the most famous and beautiful works of the Italian Renaissance, Leone Ebreo's *Dialoghi d'Amore*.[16] Written about 1502 and published in 1535, the *Dialoghi d'Amore,* if we judge by the number of editions, rivalled Ficino's commentary on the *Symposium (De Amore)* and Pico's commentary on some sonnets by Beneviente as a main source of sixteenth-century Neo-Platonism. It was twice translated into Spanish, and twice into French, as well as into Latin and Hebrew. The distinction which 'Image and Dream' turns on, between the 'dulling' of the senses by 'strong objects' and the 'locking up' of the sense in sleep, is handled at length in the third and last of the dialogues in which Philo instructs his mistress Sophia in the mysteries of love.

The dialogue opens with the lover, Philo, being reproached by Sophia for being oblivious of her presence. He excuses himself by saying that his mind was rapt in contemplation of her beauty, whose image 'impressed' upon it has made him dispense with his external senses.[17] Sophia asks how something so effectively impressed on the mind cannot, when present, enter the eyes. Philo acknowledges that it was through the eyes that her radiant beauty pierced into the very midst of his heart and the depth of his mind ('nel centro del cuore e nel cuore de la mente'). Sophia recurs to her point later, when in reply to Philo's saying that if she must complain she should complain against herself, since she has 'locked the door' against herself, she answers, 'Nay, I lament rather that the image of my person has more sway over you than my person itself' : the paradox with which Donne begins his poem. Philo agrees that the image has more power, since an image within the mind is stronger than one from without.[18] This is stock Neo-Platonic doctrine and parallels could be adduced from Ficino, Pico, Bembo, and many others. What makes it certain that Donne read it in Leone Ebreo is that Philo's first defence against Sophia is that she would not have blamed him for being unaware of her presence if she had been asleep. She owns that sleep would have excused him, since its custom is to remove all sense-perception (*che suole i sentimenti levare*). He declares that he has a better excuse than sleep and she asks what can blot out perception more than sleep which is a semi-death (*che è mezza morte*). He retorts that ecstasy brought about by a lover's meditation is more than semi-death. When she protests that thought cannot divorce a man from his senses more than sleep does, which lays him on the ground like a body without life, he answers that sleep restores life rather than destroys it, which is not true of ecstasy.[19] This leads to a long comparison between the physiology of ecstasy and the physiology of sleep. In the one, the mind withdraws, taking with it the greater part of its powers and spirits ('la maggior parte de le sue virtú e spiriti'), leaving only the vital spirit to keep the body just alive. In the other, the spirits are drawn to the lower regions of the body to perform the work of nutrition, the mind is deprived of its reasoning power, and the imagination (*la fantasia*) is disturbed by dreams engendered by vapours arising from the concoction of food.[20] Both sleep and ecstasy, that is to say, discard and inhibit sense and motion; but in the one case the spirits are withdrawn and collected, either in the midst of the head, the seat of all knowledge, or in the centre of the heart, the abode of desire ('in mezzo de la testa, ove è la cogitazione, o al centro del cuore, ove è il desiderio'); in the other they are drawn down to the lower regions of the body. The heart is the link between the head and the belly, and is the seat of the soul, the intermediary between the intellectual and the corporal in man. The vital power of the heart preserves the mind and body from dissolution. But in ardent ecstasy it may happen that the soul will wholly enfranchise itself from the body, or loosened or untied (*resolvendosi i spiriti*), by reason of the force and closeness with which they have been gathered together.[21] This is the blessed death of ecstasy. Philo, whose mistress will not confess that she loves him, declares that her image is acting upon him like poison, which goes straight to the heart and will not leave until it has consumed all the spirits. Her image, which he contemplates in ecstasy, arouses in him insatiable desire, and this desire would destroy the spirits which it has gathered in his heart, if her presence did not save him from death by restoring his spirits and senses to their natural functions. But the return to waking life does not take away the pain of desire which her beauty, contemplated or perceived, arouses.[22]

In his poem Donne has combined the conception of the image in the lover's heart, greater than the beloved in her person, whose contemplation 'shuts out' sense, and which 'oppresses the spirits', with an old familiar poetic theme, deriving from Petrarch : the theme of the sensual love-dream, in which the lover finds in sleep the satisfaction which his mistress denies him waking. The image is 'too great and good', and the lover turns from contemplation which may destroy life to sleep which restores it, bidding farewell to his heart as seat of reason and rational desire and allowing 'fantasy' and sensual appetite to reign. But at the close he decides that of the two ways of being 'out of one's senses', he prefers the madness of ecstasy, born of rational contemplation of her image, to the irrationality of sleep, in which he may enjoy the pleasures of fantasy and escape the pain of truth.

In discussing this poem we can point to a definite passage which provided Donne with his basic idea, the likeness and difference between ecstasy and sleep, as well as with certain phrases. The relation of 'The Ecstasy' to the Italian treatise is less immediately obvious but more interesting. The long discussion of the physiology of ecstasy, culminating in the description of the 'blessed death of ecstasy' and including an analysis of the nature of the soul and of its relation to the spirits, is patently the source of Donne's conception of ecstasy, as will be apparent shortly when I use it to explicate the poem. But Donne found much more than this in the *Dialoghi d'Amore*. The discussion of ecstasy does not arise out of the experience of an ecstatic union of the lovers, but from the lover's experience of an ecstatic union with the idea of the beauty of his beloved. The charm and strangeness of Leone Ebreo's book lies in its combination of metaphysical, theological, and cosmologi-

cal speculation of the most daring kind with a delightful battle of
wits between two persons; for Philo, while instructing Sophia in
the mysteries of love,[23] is also wooing her, and Sophia is both the
very clever pupil, asking leading and often awkward questions,
and also the mistress who denies. The work, as it was printed, is
unfinished. The close of the third and last dialogue looks forward
to a fourth, in which Philo will teach his mistress about the effects
of love.[24] It is clear from the close of the third dialogue that Sophia
is weakening fast and that the whole work was intended to move
towards the blissful moment when Philo and Sophia will be no
longer the one the Lover and the other the Beloved, but both will
be equally Lover and Beloved. This happy consummation is continually looked forward to and anticipated throughout the work
as we have it; but it has not been achieved by the time the book
ends. There is then no single passage describing an ecstatic union
of lovers to which we can point as the source of 'The Ecstasy'. Instead, we find scattered through the whole work ideas and phrases
which have been woven into the substance of the poem.[25]

The first dialogue, which is much the shortest, handles the
fundamental problem of the relation of love to desire. Although
short, it ranges over the whole subject of love, raising the questions
which are to be treated extensively in the subsequent dialogues.
The second dialogue deals with the universality of love and is
concerned with love throughout the cosmos; the third is on the
origin of love, and treats of the love of God. Love between human
beings is left to be treated in the missing fourth dialogue, on the
effects of love. We can form a good idea of what it was to contain,
for the first dialogue contains a brief treatment of love between
human beings, and there are references in the others which relate
human love to Leone Ebreo's definition of love as the desire for
union: 'an affect of the will to enjoy through union the thing
judged good'.[26] Thus in the first dialogue he proceeds from this
general definition to define 'the perfect love of a man for a woman'
as 'the conversion of the lover into the beloved together with a
desire for the conversion of the beloved into the lover'. And he
adds 'when such love is equal on both sides, it is defined as the
conversion of each lover into the other'.[27] this mutual and equal
love is the love which Donne is writing about in 'The Ecstasy'.

What has convinced me that the poem was directly inspired by the reading of the *Dialoghi d'Amore* is that phrases which have puzzled me and other commentators and readers cease to be obscure or doubtful in meaning when we read similar phrases in Leone Ebreo, and that, while it is possible to find illustrative and explanatory parallels for separate ideas referred to in the poem in a wide variety of authors, once an editor can turn to Leone Ebreo the task of annotating 'The Ecstasy' is child's play. Almost all the *idées reçues* to which Donne refers in the poem are referred to or handled at length by Leone Ebreo. Finally, one of the most striking statements of Donne's lovers echoes a fundamental and distinctive idea of Leone Ebreo. This idea, which is directly opposed to the orthodox view as it appears in the writings of such Platonic doctors as Ficino and Pico and such popularizers of Platonism as Bembo, is exactly what is usually referred to as 'Donne's philosophy of love'.

The best example of a difficulty which can be solved by reference to the *Dialoghi d'Amore* is the doubt which most readers in my experience feel as to what Donne's lovers mean by saying that love mixes souls

> And makes both one, each this and that.

In the first dialogue Philo, at Sophia's request, speaks briefly of human friendship, differentiating those lesser friendships which are for the sake of utility or pleasure from true friendship which generates the good and conjoins the virtuous. This is the 'friendship of perfect union':

> Such union and conjunction must be based on the mutual virtue or wisdom of both friends; which wisdom, being spiritual, and so alien to matter and free from corporeal limitations, overrides the distinction of persons and bodily individuality, engendering in such friends a peculiar mental essence, preserved by their joint wisdoms, loves and wills, unmarred by divisions and distinctions, exactly as if this love governed but a single soul and being, embracing, – not divided into, – two persons. In conclusion I would say that noble friendships make of one person – two; of two persons – one.[28]

This notion that in the union of love one becomes two and two become one is recurred to in the third dialogue when Philo repeats that 'two persons who love each other mutually are not really two persons'. Sophia, in her role of Dr Watson, asks how many they are, and receives the answer that they are 'only one or else four', since

Each one being transformed into the other becomes two, at once lover and beloved; and two multiplied by two makes four, so that each of them is twain, and both together are one and four.

'I like this conception of the union and multiplication of the two lovers', comments Sophia.[29] These mystical mathematics also pleased the author of 'The Primrose', who not only rendered them succinctly in the line

> And makes both one, each this and that,

but also remembered that the union of love was a multiplication when he supplied an anology from nature in the violet which, when transplanted, 'redoubles still and multiplies'.

As for passages illustrating the poem, the following topics, given in the order in which they occur in the poem, are handled by Leone Ebreo : that sight is by means of rays emitted from the eye,[30] that although the soul is one and indivisible, it is also 'compounded', that is, it contains 'mixture of things'; that intelligences love the spheres which they animate, a conception which is discussed at great length to explain why the spiritual intelligence of man is united to his body. Reference to the *Dialoghi d'Amore* supports Grierson's adoption of the reading of the manuscripts against that of the editions in line 55, where the plural 'forces' renders 'le virtú' in the recurring phrase 'le virtú e i spiriti', and supports an emendation which I had intended to propose independently in line 67. In discussing the soul's relation to the body, Leone Ebreo uses the metaphor of gold and alloy.

More exciting is the fact that the first thing which is revealed to Donne's lovers in their ecstasy is something which Philo was at great pains to teach Sophia :

> This Extasie doth unperplex
> (Wee said) and tell us what we love,
> Wee see by this, it was not sexe,
> We see, we saw not what did move.

Philo first 'unperplexes' Sophia by teaching her that love and desire are not opposites. In arguing this Leone Ebreo sets himself against orthodox Platonism, as expressed in Ficino's commentary on the *Symposium* or in Bembo's *Asolani,* where the young man who puts forward this view is corrected later by the wise hermit. Sophia, who ably argues for the view that love and desire, or appetite, are clean contrary, is converted by Philo who explains that there are two kinds of love. Imperfect love is engendered by sensual appetite, and since desire, as soon as it is satisfied, dies, this love, which is the effect of desire, dies with its cause. But perfect love 'itself generates desire of the beloved, instead of being generated by that desire or appetite : in fact we first love perfectly, and then the strength of that love makes us desire spiritual and bodily union with the beloved'.[31] Sophia then asks 'If the love you bear me does not spring from appetite, what is its cause'? and Philo replies :

Perfect and true love, such as I feel for you, begets desire, and is born of reason; and true cognitive reason has engendered it in me. For knowing you to possess virtue, intelligence and beauty, no less admirable than wondrously attractive, my will desired your person, which reason rightly judged in every way noble, excellent and worthy of love. And this, my affection and love, has transformed me into you, begetting in me a desire that you may be fused with me, in order that I, your lover, may form but a single person with you, my beloved, and equal love may make of our two souls one, which may likewise vivify and inform our two bodies. The sensual element in this desire excites a longing for physical union, that the union of bodies may correspond to the unity of spirits wholly compenetrating each other.[32]

When the desire which is born of this perfect love is satisfied and ceases, the love which inspired it does not cease, nor is the desire to enjoy the fullest union with the beloved lessened by the temporary satisfaction of physical desire. The first thing which Donne's lovers learn in their ecstasy is that theirs is this 'perfect love', not born of desire or appetite, but of reason.

It may now very well be pointed out that having as I hope proved the close dependence of 'The Ecstasy' on the *Dialoghi d'Amore,* I have ended by producing a passage which makes the same point as it has been assumed that Donne was making in his

poem : that lovers who are united in soul must, in order that their
union should be complete, unite also in body. Here in Leone Ebreo
is what has been called 'Donne's metaphysic of love'. I would
agree; but I would not agree that in this particular poem this conclusion is being argued for, although it is implied. I would say that
'The Ecstasy' originated in Donne's interest in Leone Ebreo's long
description of the semi-death of ecstasy and in the idea that the
force of ecstasy might be so strong that it would break the bond
between soul and body and lead to the death of rapture. This death
in ecstasy his lovers withdraw from, to return to life in the body.
What they are concerned to argue, in the concluding section of the
poem, is that the bond of the 'new soul' will still subsist when their
souls once more inhabit their separate bodies, and that they have a
function to fulfil in the world of men which justifies their retreat
from the blessed death of ecstasy.

II

'The Ecstasy' falls into three parts. The first twenty-eight lines are
a prelude. They set the scene, the 'pregnant banke' which rests 'the
violets reclining head'; they describe the pose of the lovers; they
tell how their souls went out from their bodies; and they introduce
the hypothetical ideal lover who is capable of 'hearing' the word-
less communication of the separated souls. The scene is unusually
detailed for Donne, and M. Legouis has commented on it sarcasti-
cally as showing Donne's incapacity as a poet of nature : 'Even
when for once he lays the scene of his action outdoors, his metaphors take us back to the boudoir or the rake's den. The epithet
"pregnant", though not voluptuous, is also sexual, and the droop-
ing violets suggest languor'. The violet, which puzzled Gosse, is not
here because of any symbolic associations; but it may be as well to
add that, although in classical poetry it has erotic associations, in
Elizabethan literature it is invariably 'modest', 'pure', and the
'virgin of the year'. It is here because it is a flower which is found
in two forms, the single and the double violet, and Donne is going
to refer later to this phenomenon of nature in an analogy which he
did not find in Leone Ebreo. The setting is a natural one. It is
spring, the traditional season for a dialogue of lovers. The bank is

pregnant with new life and the wild, or uncultivated, single violet
grows upon it. The word 'entergraft' which is used to describe the
clasp of the lovers' hands, is taken from horticulture; and 'propa-
gation' has horticultural connotations also. It is to horticulture and
not to boudoirs that we must look for the explanation of the presence of 'the violets reclining head'. The language of the first twelve
lines is 'pregnant' with sexual meanings. The 'balme' which
'ciments' the lovers' hands, as M. Legouis rightly pointed out,
implies that they are young and fit for all the offices of love. I have
no objection at all to his suggestion that the stanza

> So to'entergraft our hands, as yet
> Was all the meanes to make us one,
> And pictures in our eyes to get
> Was all our propagation[33]

implies that, although these are so far the only physical means
which the lovers have employed, they will soon enjoy that union
in the body which perfect love desires. But the main meaning is
that so far their only union is through the corporal sense of touch
and the spiritual sense of sight. It is by these means, particularly
through their gazing into each others' eyes, that soul is being 'conveyed' to soul and such an ardent desire for union is being engendered as will cause the souls of each to abandon their bodies.

This ecstasy, or 'going out' of the souls, is described in the first
of the analogies which Donne found for himself and not in his
source. They have all puzzled commentators. Their difficulty lies
in the precise sense of the connectives 'as' and 'so'. A paraphrase,
'As Fate suspends uncertain victory between two equal armies,
our souls hung between her and me', shows we need to expand
'as'. The parallel is not between Fate's action and the souls hanging in the air. The connexion there is purely verbal – between the
old Homeric metaphor of the scales of battle 'hung out' in the
heavens and the souls being 'suspended' above their bodies. This is
an extra adornment of wit over and above the point of the simile
whose sense is 'Just as when two equal armies are locked in battle
so that neither side is advancing or retreating, so our souls hung
motionless, face to face, in the air'. The point which is being established is the absolute equality of the souls and their immobility.
While the souls thus 'negotiate' or confer, the bodies lie inanimate

on the ground, like statues on a tomb. They are 'her' and 'me'.
This is the only use in the poem of the singular pronouns. Elsewhere there is an almost monotonous insistence on the plural pronouns 'we', 'us', and 'our', repeated, at times within a single line,
and continually given metrical stress.

So far there has been no suggestion of a union of souls. Indeed,
the implications of the souls being like 'two equall Armies', and of
the word 'negotiate', hint at the opposite. The notion that equality
implies identity does not occur until line 25, when it is stated that
this was no parley between opposing sides, but a 'dialogue of one',
as it is called at the close : 'both meant, both spake the same'. In
order that we may know what the souls said, the hypothetical
bystander, another perfect lover, is introduced. He is sufficiently
'refin'd' to understand; but, even so, he will receive a new 'concoction' from his experience, and 'part farre purer then he came'.
This is the language of alchemy. The only other use of the word
'concoction' in Donne's poetry is in 'The first Anniversarie'
(l. 456), where the 'example' and 'virtue' of Elizabeth Drury
works upon her 'creatures' to give them 'their last, and best concoction'. But the idea that gold, the perfect metal, can be refined
into a tincture which will transmute baser, that is less pure or
more mixed, metals to its own perfection is common in his verse.
The soul, as Leone Ebreo, citing Plato, teaches in his discussion
of ecstasy, is of a mixed nature, 'compounded of spiritual intelligence and corporeal mutability'. But it can at times withdraw
from the exercise of its bodily functions and unite itself wholly to
its intellectual nature.[34] It is then, as he says elsewhere, like gold
without alloy.[35] The souls of Donne's lovers, which have thus
withdrawn from their bodies, in order to enjoy 'true intellectual
light', can, like tincture of gold, give a new concoction to the soul
of anyone capable of receiving it, making it 'farre purer'. The
conception of the soul as containing 'mixture of things', which
underlies the use of the alchemical terms 'refin'd' and 'concoction', is referred to explicitly in the next section of the poem
(ll. 29–48), which contains the illumination which the lovers
received in their ecstasy.

The first thing which the lovers learn is 'what they love'. By a
supernatural experience they learn what is hidden from the lovers
of 'The Relique' who 'loved well and faithfully',

> Yet knew not what they lov'd, nor why;

and from the lovers of the 'Valediction : forbidding Mourning', who loved with a love

> so much refin'd,
> That our selves know not what it is.

(It is a Neo-Platonic commonplace that perfect lovers do not know what it is they love.) Donne's lovers here see that it was 'not sexe', the 'difference of sex', what distinguishes man from woman, that each loved in the other. It was something invisible, what they did not see, which drew them to each other, or 'moved' them both. By the mingling of their two souls, the invisible essences which drew them together, there has arisen by the power of love a 'new soule', and this new and 'abler soule' is, unlike all separate and individual souls, gifted with complete self-knowledge. It understands its own essence, or nature. The final ecstatic revelation which the lovers receive is the answer to the question which Lord Herbert of Cherbury's lovers debated in a poem which, as Grierson noted, is plainly inspired by 'The Ecstasy'. They learn that their love 'will continue forever'.

The 'new soul' has come into being through the action of love upon individual souls, which alone or 'separate' contain 'a mixture of things'. 'When the spiritual mind (which is heart of our heart and soul of our soul), through the force of desire, retires within itself to contemplate a beloved and desired object, it draws every part of the soul to itself, gathering it into one indivisible unity.'[36] It is two such 'recollected' or 'reconcocted' souls, 'mixed again' by love or desire for union, which love unites to make of two one and of each one two. This union is indissoluble because it is the union of perfect with perfect, or like with like. It is only those things which are unequally mixed which are subject to decay or mutability. The force of love has united all the diverse parts of each soul wholly to its own intellectual nature, which is its true essence, and the 'new soul' of their union, being wholly intellect, knows itself. The union of the lovers is the union of their intellectual souls, or spiritual minds. In their triumphant certainty the lovers borrow a word from the contrary philosophy of materialism, the Epicurean doctrine that the world came into being and exists through the chance congruence of atoms. It is by 'congruence' that they exist, but the atoms from which they grow are souls, and they have not come together by chance but by the force of love, which is the desire for union. Such a congruence is, according to Leone Ebreo, the secret of the whole universe.

In a parenthesis Donne provides an analogy from the natural world. I take the stanza on the transplanting of violets as parenthetical, pointing to the existence of something in nature which is both one and multiple, and regard the 'so' of the line 'When love, with one another so' as referring back, beyond the parenthesis, to love's making 'both one, each this and that'. Like a modern scientist, trying to explain some scientific mystery to laymen, Donne refers to something rather similar in nature to the union which love effects in souls. The idea, often referred to in this period, that certain flowers, including the violet, will grow double by frequent transplantation is perfectly true: 'It is a curiosity', writes Bacon, 'also to make flowers double, which is effected by often removing them into new earth; as on the contrary part, the double flowers, by neglecting and not removing, prove single.'[37] Marvell gives the right reason, in speaking of the 'double pink': 'the nutriment did change the kind'.[38] The richness of the new soil stimulates the growth of a superabundance of petals. But in Elizabethan writers I have found certain hints that the 'doubling' of single flowers, and the production of parti-coloured flowers, such as Perdita calls 'nature's bastards', was the result of the mingling of seeds in the earth, and that the 'double' flower, or the 'streaked' flower, was actually two flowers in one. Since it was not recognized until late in the seventeenth century that stamens and pistils were sex organs, the phenomenon of hybridization was not understood. The passage in *The Winter's Tale* describes grafting as a means of producing pied flowers and Bacon wonders whether 'inoculating', that is grafting, might not make flowers double.[39] But he also refers to another method of making shoots 'incorporate'; the putting of diverse seeds into a clout and laying it in well-dunged earth.[40] This method of planting seeds together in a bag is referred to by the sixteenth-century botanist, Giambattista Porta, in his *Magia Naturalis*.[41] He appeared to think that by this method particoloured flowers could be produced by 'commixtion of seeds'. And

Puttenham, who distinguishes between 'aiding nature', by enrich-
ing the soil in which plants grow, and 'altering nature and sur-
mounting her skill', gives as an example of the latter the production
of double flowers from single, as if more were involved in this than
mere mulching.[42] I believe that some such notion of 'commixtion'
of seeds in the earth lies behind Donne's reference to the 'single
violet' which, when transplanted, 'redoubles still and multiplies'.
If so, the analogy is a very good one, because the so-called 'double
violet' has far more petals than twice a single violet would produce. Union has produced not 'two violets in one', but something
much nearer the 'one and four' of the lovers' union.

With the revelation that their love is immortal, the ecstasy of the
lovers reaches its climax. Unless they are to enjoy the 'blessed
death' of ecstasy, they must now return to their bodies. The conclusion of the poem (ll. 49–76) justifies this return by reference to
the doctrine of the circle of love. The heart of Leone Ebreo's doctrine is that the world as it exists and was created is such a circle.
The inferior desires to unite itself in love with what is superior;
but equally the superior desires to unite itself in love with what is
inferior. The inferior desires the perfection which it lacks; the
superior desires to bestow its own perfection on what lacks it. The
final cause of love in each is the desire for perfection, for the union
of all the parts of the Universe so that it may perfectly realize the
divine Idea of its being, and be itself united to its perfect Source
and End. The illustration which Philo gives at some length to show
the love which superior bears for inferior is the love of intelligences
for the spheres which they move and govern, and Sophia comments : 'I suppose it is for the same reason that the spiritual intelligence of man unites with a body as frail as the human : to execute
the divine plan for the coherence and unity of the whole
Universe.[43] The same force, love or the desire for union, which has
united the lovers' intellectual souls brings those souls back to their
bodies. 'Love is the condition of existence of the world and all in
it'; and intelligent souls would not 'unite with human bodies to
make them rational, if love did not constrain them thereto'.[44]

The souls of the lovers yearn towards their bodies, which are
'theirs', though not 'they'. They own their debt to them. By the
joining of hands and the gazing of the eyes the desire for union
became so strong that soul was conveyed to soul. (The word 'thus'

in line 53 is meaningless unless we take it that the 'thankes' for the bodies' aid refers to the experience of the poem and not to some remote first meeting.) It was because the bodies yielded up their own faculties, the powers of the senses, and allowed the 'sensible soul' to be wholly united to the intellectual soul, leaving themselves deprived of motion and sense, that the ecstasy came to pass. The lovers turn to their own purpose the metaphor of gold and alloy, to declare that the body is alloy and not dross, and find an analogy to support them in their belief that they need not fear that the descent of their souls from ecstatic union to inhabit their separate bodies will make it impossible for soul to flow into soul. Donne is here referring, I think, to the fundamental Paracelsian doctrine that the influence of the heavenly bodies, whether good or evil, is the 'smell, smoke or sweat' of the stars mixed with the air.[45] It is, like the analogy with violet, an illustrative parallel : 'heavenly bodies cannot act upon man without the material intermediary of air, so we may believe that souls which are in the body can communicate through the body's aid'. The famous lines which follow display the working of the cosmic principle of the circle of love in the microcosm, or little world of man :

> As our blood labours to beget
>   Spirits, as like soules as it can,
> Because such fingers need to knit
>   That subtile knot, which makes us man :
>
> So must pure lovers soules descend
>   T'affections, and to faculties,
> That[46] sense may reach and apprehend,
>   Else a great Prince in prison lies.

The blood strives to become spiritual, to produce the spirits, or powers of the soul, which are necessary to unite the intellectual and corporal in man. Conversely souls must condescend to the affections and faculties of the body in order that man's sense organs may become rational. The mind, as Philo teaches Sophia, 'controls the senses and directs the voluntary movements of men'. 'For this purpose it must issue from within the body to its external parts and to the organs of sense and movement, in order that man may approach the objects of sense in the world around him, and it is then that we are able to think at the same time as we see, hear and speak'.[47] If the soul does not thus inform all the activities of the body, it is abandoning its task which is 'rightly to govern the body'.[48] Its duty is to take 'intellectual life and knowledge and the light of God down from the upper world of eternity to the lower world of decay' and thus realize the unity of the Universe. A soul that does not perform this divinely appointed function is like a prince in a prison. The concordance to Donne's poems shows how fond he is of the metaphor of the soul as prince and the body, with its limbs, as his province. If the soul does not thus animate the body in all its parts, it is imprisoned in a carcass instead of reigning in its kingdom. Donne is contrasting the Platonic view of the soul imprisoned in the flesh with the Aristotelian conception of the union of the soul and body in man. A prince is no prince if he does not rule his kingdom and a kingdom without a prince is a chaos. Prince and kingdom need each other and are indeed inconceivable without each other. In the final lines of the poem the lovers find a further justification for life in this world, in the duty to reveal love to men, and declare that, if one of 'love's Divines' has heard their 'dialogue of one', he will not be aware of much difference between their union when 'out of the body' and their union when they have resumed possession of their kingdoms.

III

It remains to ask how successful 'The Ecstasy' is in what it attempts, and this question is connected with the problem of why it has given rise to such contradictory interpretations. 'The Ecstasy' is remarkable among Donne's lyrics for its length and for its lack of metrical interest and variety. Although it has fine lines and fine passages, it lacks, as a whole, Donne's characteristic *élan,* and at times it descends to what can only be described as a dogged plod. It is also remarkable for an excessive use of connectives, such as 'as' and 'so'. It was this which first suggested to me that it depended on a written source. (Anyone who has ever corrected large numbers of *précis* knows how hard these little words can be worked in summarizing discursive arguments.) The word 'argument', I think, holds the clue both to the slight sense of dissatisfaction which Grierson expressed and also the variety of misinterpretations which the poem has suffered. There is a tone of argument throughout the lovers' speech which is out of keeping with the poem's subject. The essence of any illumination received in ecstasy, if we accept the conception of such illumination being possible, is that it is immediate and not arrived at by the normal processes of ratiocination. In ecstasy the rational faculty is laid aside and in a holy stillness the intellect rests in the contemplation of what is, and in the peace of union. Donne's lovers seem very far from this blissful quiet. Their minds are as active as fleas, hopping from one idea to the next. Although we are told that the two souls speak as one and that we are listening to a 'dialogue of one', the tone is that of an ordinary dialogue in which points are being made and objections met. When Donne was inspired by the *Dialoghi d'Amore* to write a poem showing the achievement of union in love, he caught from his source that tone of persuasion which has misled readers. The poem *sounds* as if someone is persuading someone. The defect of 'The Ecstasy' is that it is not sufficiently ecstatic. It is rather too much of an 'argument about an ecstasy'. It suffers from a surfeit of ideas.

For all that it is a wonderful poem and a poem that only Donne could have written; and it holds the key to Donne's greatest love-poetry. No poet has made greater poetry than Donne has on the theme of mutual love. He has no predecessors here and virtually no successors of any stature. The poems which Donne wrote on the subject of love as the union of equals, such poems as 'The good-morrow', 'The Anniversarie, or 'A Valediction : forbidding mourning' are his most beautiful and original contribution to the poetry of human love; for poets have written very little of love as fullness of joy. I am in no way depriving Donne of his glory when I suggest that it was in Leone Ebreo's book that he found this conception, which he made so wholly his own, of love as not being love 'till I love her that loves me'. I do not believe that Donne was very deeply moved by the conception of ecstasy. He too often in his sermons disparages the idea of ecstatic revelation for me to feel that it had ever had a strong hold on his imagination. He was, on the other hand, profoundly moved by the conception of love as union. 'Image and Dream' and 'The Ecstasy' would seem, from their closeness to their source, to be the first poems which Donne

wrote on this theme. In other poems on the same subject we can
explain ideas and phrases by referring to Leone Ebreo,[49] but we
cannot in the same way speak of the *Dialoghi d'Amore* as a source.
I cannot at present suggest when Donne first read Leone Ebreo,
though I think it may be possible to discover this. But it seems
likely that Donne's love poems, like his divine poems, came in
bursts, a new theme leading to a group of poems, and that we can
legitimately think of his poems on love as 'peace', like his youthful
poems, the Elegies, on love as 'rage', as having been written fairly
close to each other in time. More than one of the poems of mutual
love assumes the presence of a king on the throne, and so must
have been written after 1603. I do not wish to follow Gosse in trying to make Donne's love-poetry autobiographical and deprecate
attempts to connect particular lyrics with Mrs Herbert or with
Lucy, Countess of Bedford. At the same time I cannot believe that
we can divorce a man's intellectual life and the sources of his
creative inspiration from his experience. Certain books, and certain ideas which we meet with in our reading, move us deeply and
become part of our way of thinking because they make us conscious of the meaning of our own experience and reveal us to ourselves. I find it impossible not to connect Donne's mariage with his
discovery of a great new subject for poetry in Leone Ebreo's dis-
courses on love as union.

It is the fashion today in scholarly circles, in reaction against
earlier idolizing of Donne, to exalt his wit at the expense of his
artistic and intellectual integrity, and to deny that ideas had any
value to him as a poet except as counters to be used in an argument. Donne's greatness needs restating. One element in that greatness is that certain ideas mattered to him intensely and that he
made them wholly his own. It is characteristic of his intellectual
stature that his Platonism was derived, not at second-hand from
fashionable poets, but directly, from one of the great books of the
early Renaissance. The *Dialoghi d'Amore* is an ambitious attempt
to bring into a synthesis all the intellectual traditions of Europe. It
attempts to include in its docrine of a living universe, moved and
united by love, the cosmology and physiology of Aristotle, the Platonic doctrine of Ideas, the Neo-Platonic doctrine of the Transcendence of the One and of procession from and conversion to the One
by means of the Emanations, and the Jewish doctrine of Creation.

Anyone who is familiar with Donne's religious writings knows how deeply he meditated the doctrine of Creation. It is the stress on this distinctively Judeo-Christian doctrine – that the High and Holy One Himself loves the world which He made – which distinguishes Leone Ebreo from the other masters of Neo-Platonism, Ficino and Pico, making him give the material universe and the body a greater dignity. We are not depriving Donne of his greatness and originality as a poet of love if we think of him as inspired in part by a book which, in its Hebrew translation, was in the library of Spinoza, and from which, it has been suggested, he took the idea which we most associate with him of 'the intellectual love of God'. In 'The Ecstasy' Donne is too tied to his source. It smells a little of the lamp. In other, more wonderful, poems he was able to tell in his own language and in his own way what he had learned in his experience, as illuminated by the Jewish Platonist, of love's power to 'interinanimate two souls'.[50]

SOURCE : Herbert Davis and Helen Gardner (eds.) *Elizabethan and Jacobean Studies* (1959).

NOTES

1. *Coleridge's Miscellaneous Criticism,* ed. T. M. Raysor (1936) p. 138.
2. *ABC of Reading* (1934) p. 126.
3. *Poems of John Donne* (1912) II, pp. xlvi–xlvii.
4. *Donne the Craftsman* (Paris, 1928) pp. 68–9.
5. Merrit Y. Hughes, 'The Lineage of "The Exstasie" ', *M.L.R.* XXVII (Jan. 1932), and 'Kidnapping Donne', *Essays in Criticism* (Berkeley 1934) pp. 83–9; G. R. Potter, 'Donne's *Extasie*, Contra Legouis', *P.2.* xv (1936).
6. In *Seventeenth-Century Studies presented to Sir Herbert Grierson* (1938) pp. 64–104; see particularly pp. 76 and 96–7.
7. *English Literature in the Sixteenth Century* (1954) p. 549.
8. *John Donne* (Writers and their Work, no. 86) (1957) p. 12.
9. *Secentismo e Marinismo in Inghilterra* (Florence, 1925) pp. 28 and 27.
10. In his 'Platonic' poems Donne constantly, as here, makes distinction between himself and his mistress, who are 'saints of love', worthy of canonization and capable of performing miracles; those

who are capable of understanding these mysteries, Doctors, as it were, of Amorous Theology; and the 'laity', who either need simple instruction, or to whom it would be 'prophanation of our joyes' to speak.

11. It is one thing for a narrative poet to describe two lovers in passionate embrace oblivious of a bystander, as Spenser does at the original ending of Book III of *The Faerie Queen*; it is quite another for lovers themselves to call for an audience at their coupling.

12. 'The Ecstasy' always occurs with a title, and the same title in manuscript. We are, therefore, justified in assuming, as we cannot with most of Donne's poems, that the title is the author's.

13. In declaring that the poem does not conclude with a proposal to 'prove, while we may, the sweets of love', I have been anticipated by one critic, Donaphan Louthan, in *The Poetry of John Donne, an Explication* (New York, 1951). I regret that I cannot agree with the details of his analysis.

14. *Life and Letters of John Donne* (1890) I 75–6.

15. The right interpretation was put forward by E. Glyn Lewis, the only critic who has discussed the poem at length; see *M.L.R.*, XXIX (Oct. 1934).

16. Translated, under the title *The Philosophy of Love,* by F. Friedeberg-Seeley and Jean H. Barnes (1937). Page references are to this translation. Quotations in Italian are from the edition by S. Caramella (Bari, 1929). The translators, in attempting to render the Italian into modern English, are often nearer to Donne's words than a literal translation would be. For a discussion of Leone Ebreo as a philosopher see Heinz Pflaum, *Die Idee von Liebe. Leone Ebreo* (Tübingen, 1926).

17. p. 198: 'La mente mia, ritirata a contemplar, come suole, quella formata in te bellezza, e in lei per immagine impressa e sempre desiderata, m'ha fatto lassare i sensi esteriori' (p. 172).

18. p. 229, *Filone*. 'Si che se lamentar ti vuoi, lamentati pur di te, che a te stessa hai serrate le porte.' *Sofia*. 'Pur mi lamento che possi e vagli in te, piú che mia persona, l'immagine di quella.' *Filone*. 'Può piú, perché giá la rappresentazione di dentro a l'animo precede a quella di fuore' (p. 197).

19. p. 199, *Sofia*. 'Come può la cogitazione astraere piú l'uomo de' sensi che 'l sonno, che getta per terra come corpo senza vita?' *Filone*. 'Il sonno piú presto causa vita, che la toglia: qual no fa l'estasi amorosa' (p. 173).

20. pp. 200–3. See particularly p. 201: 'Ma quando la mente se raccoglie dentro se medesima per contemplare con somma efficacia e unione una cosa amata, fugge da le parti esteriori, e abbandonando

i sensi e movimenti, si ritira con la maggior parte de le sue virtú e spiriti in quella meditazione, senza lassare nel corpo altra virtú che quella senza la quale non potrebbe sustentarsi la vita . . .; questo solamente resta, con qualche poco de la virtú notritiva, perché la maggior parte di quella ne le profonda cogitazione è impedita, e perciò poco cibo longo tempo i contemplatori sostiene. E cosi come nel sonno, facendosi forte con virtú notritiva, arrobba, priva e occupa la retta cogitazione de la mente, perturbando la fantasia per l'ascensione de' vapori al cerebro del cibo che si cuoce, quali cansano le varie e inordinate sonniazioni, cosi l'intima ed efficace cogitazione arrobba e occupa il sonno, nutrimento e digestione del cibo' (p. 174).

21. p. 205 : 'Cosi pungitivo potrebbe essere il desiderio e tanto intima la contemplazione, che del tutto discarcasse e retirasse l'anima dal corpo, resolvendosi i spiriti per la forte e ristretta loro unione in modo che, afferandosi l'anima affettuosamente col desiderato e contemplato oggetto, potria prestamente lassare il corpo esanimato del tutto' (pp. 177-8).

22. pp. 230–1; pp. 198–9 in Italian.

23. In spite of her name, she needs a great deal of instruction; but I suppose that we can take it that she is instructing her lover in Socratic fashion.

24. It is uncertain whether the fourth dialogue, which contemporaries inquired for in vain, was ever written. The last record of Leone Ebreo is in 1520, so that, since he was born about 1460, he had probably been dead for some time when his book was published in 1535.

25. Parallels for most of these can be found separately in other Neo-Platonic writers. It is the collocation of these ideas in Leone Ebreo which is striking.

26. p. 12 : 'affetto volontario di fruire con unione la cosa stimata buona' (p. 13).

27. p. 55 : 'La propria diffinizione del perfetto amore de l'uomo e de la donna è la conversione de l'amante ne l'amato, con desiderio che si converti l'amato ne l'amante. E quando tal amore è eguale in ciascuna de la parti, si diffinisce conversione de l'uno amante ne l'altro' (p. 50).

28. p. 31 : 'E la causa di tale unione e colligazione è la reciproca virtú o sapienzia di tutti due gli amici. La quale, per la sua spiritualitá e alienazione da materia e astrazione de le condizione corporee, remuove la diversitá de le persone a l'individuazione corporale; e genera ne gli amici una propria essenzia mentale, conservata con sapere e con amore e volontá comune a tutti due, cosi privata di

diversitá e discrepanzia come se veramente il suggetto de l'amore fusse una sola anima ed essenzia, conservata in due persone e non multiplicata in quelle. E in ultima dico questo, che l'amicizia onesta fa d'una persona due, e di due una' (p. 30).

29. p. 260 : *Filone*. 'Li due che mutuamente s'amano non son veri due.' *Sofia*. 'Ma quanti?' *Filone*. 'O solamente uno, o ver quattro'. *Sofia*. 'Che li due siano uno intende, perché l'amore unisce tutti due gli amanti e gli fa uno; ma quattro a che modo?' *Filone*. 'Trasform-andosi ognuno di loro nell'altro, ciascuno di loro si fa due, cioè amato e amante insieme : e due volte due fa quattro; si che ciascuno di loro è due, e tutti due sono uno e quattro'. *Sofia*. 'Mi piace l'unione e multiplicazione de li due amanti' (p. 222).

30. p. 215; pp. 175–6 in Italian. Philo explains that the eye sees by the transmission of rays to the object, but that the representation of the object on the pupil is also necessary, and that, further, the eye must direct its ray a second time on to the object to make the form impressed on the pupil tally with the object. This is a highly charac-teristic attempt to combine two theories (sight by extramission and sight by intramission), or to reconcile Plato and Aristotle on vision. It has suggested to Donne two conceits : the twisting of the eye-beams and that the lovers were 'looking babies'.

31. p. 56 : 'Ma l'altro amore è quello che di esso è generato il desiderio de la persona amata, e non del desiderio o appetito; anzi, amando prima perfettamente, la forza de l'amore fa desiderare l'unione spirituale e corporale con la persona amata' (p. 51).

32. p. 57 : 'Il perfetto e vero amore, che è quello che io ti porto, è padre del desiderio e figlio de la ragione; e in me la retta ragione conoscitiva l'ha prodotto. Che, conoscendo essere in te virtú, ingegno e grazia non manco di mirabile attraizione che di ammirazione, la volontá mia desiderando la tua persona, che rettamente è giudicata per la ragione in ogni cosa essere ottima e eccellente e degna di essere amata; questa affezione e amore ha fatto convertirmi in te, generan-domi desiderio che tu in me ti converti, acciò che io amante possa essere una medesima persona con te amata, e in equale amore facci di due animi un solo, li quali simigliantemente due corpi vivificare e ministrare possino. La sensualitá di questo desiderio fa nascere l'appetito d'ogni altra unione corporea, acciò che li corpi possino conseguire in quella la possibile unione de li penetranti animi' (p. 52).

33. We may compare, if we choose, Ficino's description of how Lysias gazed on Phaedrus and Phaedrus on Lysias (*Commentary on the Symposium,* VII 4); and indeed Ficinio's description of the soul and spirits in ecstatic contemplation is much the same as Leone

Ebreo's. But Ficino would hardly allow the lower, corporal sense of touch to play a part. Professor Mario Praz drew attention to a sonnet by Petrarch (Sonnet 63, *in vita*) which may have suggested to Donne the idea of two lovers united by the passionate intensity of their gazing on each other.

34. p. 206 : 'L'anima . . . non è uniforme, anzi per esser mezzo fra il mondo intellettuale e il corporeo . . . bisogna che abbi una natura mista d'intelligenzia spirituale e mutazion corporea, altramente non potrebbe animar i corpi. . . . Pur qualche volta si ritira in sé e torna ne la sua intelligenzia, e si collega e unisce con l'intelletto astratto suo antecessore . . .' (p. 178).

35. p. 396 : 'E cosi come l'oro quando ha la lega e mescolanza de li rozzi metalli e parte terrestre, non può essere bello perfetto né puro, ché la bontá sua consiste in essere purificato d'ogni lega e netto d'ogni rozza mescolanza : cosi l'anima mista de l'amor le bellezza sensuali non può esser bella né pura, né venire in sua beatitudine se non quando sará purificata e netta de l'incitazioni e bellezze sensuali, e allor viene a possedere la sua propria luce intellettiva senza impedimento alcuno, la quale è la felicitá' (p. 333).

36. p. 204 : 'Quando . . . la mente spirituale (che è cuore di nostro cuore e anima di nostra anima) per forza di desiderio si ritira in se stessa a contemplate in uno intimo e desiderato oggetto, raccoglie a sé tutta l'anima, tutta restringendosi in una indivisibile unitá' (p. 177).

37. *Natural History*, Century VI, section 513.

38. 'The Mower against Gardens'.

39. *Natural History*, ibid.

40. *Natural History*, Century V, section 478.

41. Translated as *Natural Magick*, printed for Thomas Young and Samuel Speed, 1658; see p. 70.

42. *The Arte of English Poesie*, ed. G. D. Willcock and A. Walker (1936) pp. 303–4.

43. p. 189 : 'Credo che per questa medesima causa l'anime spirituali intellettive degli uomini si collegano a corpo si fragile come l'umano, per conseguire l'ordine divino nella collegazione e unione di tutto l'universo' (p. 164).

44. p. 191 : 'Siccome niuna cosa non fa unire l'universo con tutte le sue diverse cose se non l'amore, séguita che esso amore è cause de l'essere del mondo e di tutti le sue cose.' Also : 'Né mai l'intelligenzie . . . s'unirebbero con li corpi celesti . . . se non l'amassero; né l'anime intellettive s'uniriano con li corpi umani per farli razionali, se non ve le constringessi l'amore' (p. 165).

45. *Paramirum,* ɪ viii. *Der Bücher und Schrifften* (Basle, 1589–90) ɪ 15.

46. Although I cannot claim support from the manuscripts, I am reading 'That' for 'Which'. 'Which' gives no sense, because 'sense' does not 'reach and apprehend' affections and faculties, but 'reaches and apprehends' objects of sense by means of them. I am assuming that 'which' has been substituted for 'that' under the mistaken notion that 'that' was a relative. Copyists tend to treat the two forms 'which' and 'that' as interchangeable. If we read 'That', as I do above, the action of the souls becomes purposeful, so that it parallels the purposeful action of the blood. I had decided that this emendation was necessary before I came upon the passage quoted below which supports it.

47. p. 201 : 'La mente è quella che governa i sentimenti e ordina i movimenti voluntari degli uomini : onde per far questo offizio bisogna che esca de l'interior del corpo a le parti esteriori, a trovare l'instrumenti per fare tali opere e per approssimarsi agli oggetti de' sensi che stanno di fuora, e allor pensando si può vedere, odire e parlare senza impedimento' (p. 174).

48. See pp. 189–90; p. 164 in Italian. The soul is able to mount to Paradise 'con rettitudine del suo governo nel corpo'. If it fails, 'resta ne l'infimo inferno, sbandita in eterno dalla unione divina e dalla sua propria beatitudine'. Donne's prison may be this 'lowest hell' to which the soul which has not fulfilled its function as a 'great Prince' is banished; but I prefer the interpretation suggested in the text, because of his use of the present and not the future tense.

49. In annotating some of the *Songs and Sonets* I have found the *Dialoghi d'Amore* as useful as I found the Glossed Bible when I was editing the *Divine Poems.*

50. Since this Essay was written I have read with great interest Mr A. J. Smith's discussion of 'The Ecstasy' in 'The Metaphysic of Love', *Review of English Studies* (Nov. 1958). Mr Smith gives an admirable summary of amorous philosophising in sixteenth-century Italy in order to demonstrate how little Donne's 'metaphysic of love' has the right to be called original. Although he makes more use of Leone Ebreo than of any other writer he does not suggest direct dependence, and his interpretation of the last section of Donne's poem differs greatly from mine. I must own that I think he has forced the sense of Donne's words.

SELECT BIBLIOGRAPHY

Serious students of *Songs and Sonets* should consult at least some of the following works, referred to in the Introduction; in particular, they should return to the sources (marked with an asterisk) of extracts reproduced in this volume.

TEXTS

Helen Gardner (ed.), *John Donne : The Elegies and the Songs and Sonnets* (Oxford, 1965).

H. J. C. Grierson (ed.), *The Poems of John Donne* (Oxford, 1912).

H. J. C. Grierson (ed.), *Donne : Poetical Works* (London, 1933).

Theodore Redpath (ed.), *The Songs and Sonets of John Donne* (London, 1956).

CRITICISM, BIOGRAPHY AND BACKGROUND READING

A. Alvarez, *The School of Donne* (London and New York, 1961).

*Anonymous, 'Donne's Poems', in *Retrospective Review,* VIII (1823).

R. C. Bald, *John Donne : A Life* (Oxford, 1970).

J. B. Broadbent, 'Donne', in *Poetic Love* (London, 1964).

Cleanth Brooks, 'The Language of Paradox', in *The Well Wrought Urn*, rev. edn (New York, 1968).

*Samuel Coleridge, 'John Donne', in Roberta Florence Brinkley (ed.), *Coleridge on the Seventeenth Century* (Durham, N.C., 1955).

*John Dryden, 'A Discourse Concerning the Original and Progress of Satire', in, for example, George Watson (ed.), *Of Dramatic Poesy and Other Critical Essays,* II (London, 1962).

*T. S. Eliot, 'Lecture on Milton', in *On Poetry and Poets* (London, 1958).

*T. S. Eliot, 'Donne in our Time', in Theodore Spencer (ed.), *A Garland for John Donne* (Gloucester, Mass., 1958).

*T. S. Eliot, 'The Metaphysical Poets', in *Selected Essays,* 3rd edn (London, 1958).

William Empson, chapter 4 of *Seven Types of Ambiguity*, 3rd edn (London, 1956).

William Empson, 'Donne in the New Edition', in *C.Q.* VIII (1966).

Helen Gardner, 'Interpretation', in *The Business of Criticism* (Oxford, 1959).

Helen Gardner, Introduction to *The Metaphysical Poets*, 2nd edn (Oxford, 1967).

*H. J. C. Grierson, Introduction to *The Poems of John Donne* (Oxford, 1912).

H. J. C. Grierson, Introduction to *Metaphysical Lyrics and Poems of the Seventeenth Century* (Oxford, 1921).

Donald L. Guss, *John Donne, Petrarchist* (Detroit, 1966).

*William Hazlitt, 'Lectures on Comic Writers, III', in, for example, *The Complete Works of William Hazlitt* (Dent, 1931).

*Samuel Johnson, 'Lives of the Poets : Abraham Cowley', in, for example, Mona Wilson (ed.), *Johnson : Prose and Poetry* (London, 1966).

Frank Kermode, 'The Dissociation of Sensibility', in *Kenyon Review,* XIX (1957).

F. R. Leavis, 'The Line of Wit', in *Revaluation* (London, 1936).

Pierre Legouis, *Donne the Craftsman* (Paris, 1928; New York, 1962).

*J. B. Leishman, *The Monarch of Wit*, 7th edn (London, 1965).

C. S. Lewis, *The Discarded Image* (Cambridge and New York, 1964).

*Louis Martz, 'John Donne : Love's Philosophy', in *The Wit of Love* (Notre Dame, Ind., and London, 1969).

Mario Praz, 'Donne's Relation to the Poetry of his Time', in Theodore Spencer (ed.), *A Garland for John Donne* (Gloucester, Mass., 1958).

*George Saintsbury, 'John Donne', preface to E. K. Chambers (ed.), *The Poems of John Donne* (London, 1896).

A. J. Smith, 'The Metaphysic of Love', in *R.E.S.* IX (1958).

*Arnold Stein, *John Donne's Lyrics : The Eloquence of Action* (Minneapolis, Minn., and London, 1962).

Kathleen Tillotson, 'Donne's Poetry in the Nineteenth Century', in Herbert Davis and Helen Gardner (eds), *Elizabethan and Jacobean Studies* (1959).

George Williamson, *The Donne Tradition* (Cambridge, Mass., 1930).

NOTES ON CONTRIBUTORS TO PART THREE

JOAN BENNETT. Life Fellow of Girton College, Cambridge, and formerly Lecturer in English at Cambridge. Her publications include *Virginia Woolf: Her Art as a Novelist* (1945), *George Eliot: Her Mind and Her Art* (1948) and *Five Metaphysical Poets* (1965).

A. E. DYSON. Honorary Fellow, and formerly Reader in English, University of East Anglia. His publications include *The Crazy Fabric: Essays in Irony* (1965), *The Inimitable Dickens* (1970), *Between Two Worlds: Aspects of Literary Form* (1972) and *Yeats, Eliot and R. S. Thomas* (1981).

DAME HELEN GARDNER. Merton Professor of English Literature, the Oxford University, 1966–75. She has edited *The Divine Poems of John Donne* (1952) and *John Donne: The Elegies and the Songs and Sonets* (1965). Her other publications include *The Art of T. S. Eliot* (1949), *The Metaphysical Poets* (1957), *The Business of Criticism* (1959) and *A Reading of 'Paradise Lost'* (1965). In 1972 she chose and edited *The New Oxford Book of English Verse, 1250–1950*.

J. B. LEISHMAN (1902–63). Formerly Senior Lecturer in English, Oxford University. His publications include *The Metaphysical Poets* (1934), *The Monarch of Wit* (1951) and *Themes and Variations in Shakespeare's Sonnets* (1961).

C. S. LEWIS (1898–1963). Late Professor of Medieval and Renaissance Literature, Cambridge University. His many publications included *The Allergory of Love* (1963), *A Preface to 'Paradise Lost'* (1942), *English Literature in the Sixteenth Century*

(1954), *Studies In Words* (1959), *An Experiment In Criticism* (1961), *The Discarded Image* (1964) and a number of religious works, and novels for children.

JULIAN LOVELOCK. Currently Headmaster at Akeley Wood School, Buckingham. His publications include the Casebooks on *'Comus' and 'Samson Agonistes'* and (with A. E. Dyson) *Paradise Lost*, and he is co-author (with A. E. Dyson) of *Masterful Images: English Poetry from Metaphysicals to Romantics*.

LOUIS L. MARTZ. Formerly Professor of English, Yale University. His numerous publications include *The Poetry of Meditation* (1954) and *The Wit of Love* (1969).

MICHAEL F. MOLONEY. His *John Donne: His Flight from Medievalism* was published in New York in 1944.

ARNOLD STEIN. Formerly Professor of English, University of Washington, Seattle. His *John Donne's Lyrics: The Eloquence of Action* was published in Minneapolis in 1962.

INDEX

Figures in bold type denote essays or extracts printed in Part III of this Casebook